The Althouse Press
Faculty of Education, The University of Western Ontario
Barrow, UNDERSTANDING SKILLS: THINKING, FEELING, AND CARING

Other books by Robin Barrow

Happiness (Martin Robertson & St. Martin's Press)
Radical Education (Martin Robertson & John Wiley)
Common Sense and the Curriculum (Allen & Unwin)
Moral Philosophy for Education (Allen & Unwin)
Introduction and Commentary on Plato's Apology (JACT)
Plato, Utilitarianism and Education (Routledge & Kegan Paul)
Plato and Education (Routledge & Kegan Paul)
Language and Thought (The Althouse Press)
The Canadian Curriculum (The Althouse Press)
Sparta (Allen & Unwin)
Greek and Roman Education (Macmillan)
Athenian Democracy (Macmillan)
The Philosophy of Schooling (Wheatsheaf & Halsted Press)
Injustice, Inequality, and Ethics (Harvester & Barnes and Noble)
Giving Teaching Back to Teachers (Wheatsheaf, Barnes and Noble &
The Althouse Press)

(With R. G. Woods) *Introduction to Philosophy of Education*
(Routledge)

(With Geoffrey Milburn) *A Critical Dictionary of Educational Concepts*
(Wheatsheaf & Barnes and Noble)

UNDERSTANDING SKILLS:

Thinking, Feeling, And Caring

Robin Barrow

Professor of Education, Simon Fraser University

THE ALTHOUSE PRESS

First published in Canada in 1990 by
THE ALTHOUSE PRESS
Dean: H.K. Fisher
Director of Publications: G. Milburn
Faculty of Education, The University of Western Ontario
1137 Western Road, London, Ontario, Canada N6G 1G7

Editorial Assistants: K. Butson, W. Borré
Cover Design: Bothwell Graphics

CANADIAN CATALOGUING IN PUBLICATION DATA

Barrow, Robin
    Understanding skills

ISBN 0-920354-26-2

1. Education—Philosophy. 2. Education—Aims and Objectives.
I. Title

LB880.B37 1989   370'.1   C89-095449-6

Printed and bound in Canada by Aylmer Express Limited, 390 Talbot Street East, Aylmer, Ontario, Canada N5H 1J5

For Geoff Madoc-Jones, who gave me the rivers of India, parts of Wales, and much else besides.

CONTENTS

Acknowledgements

I am grateful to Kieran Egan, Tasos Kazepides, Patrick Keeney, Geoffrey Madoc-Jones and Stuart Richmond, each of whom read an earlier draft of this book and made a number of extremely useful comments. It is conventional to attribute many improvements to the diligence of such colleagues and to assure the reader that the remaining faults are "all my own." As to that, I don't know. Perhaps one of them has led me into some dreadful absurdity? But this I am confident of: overall the book has been considerably improved by their combined insight, understanding, and hard work. I am no less grateful to Surjeet Siddoo who handled the typing, editing, and conflating of various manuscripts and typescripts with her customary efficiency, high standards, and good nature.

Foreword

I am indebted to Dr. Don Cochrane of the University of Saskatchewan for the ambiguous title, *Understanding Skills*. It indicates, I hope, that I have something to say about what skills are, and about which so-called skills truly are skills, and also about the importance of understanding in education. By the end of the book, the reader will appreciate that there is a conscious irony in my referring to "understanding skills" in the sense of the "skills of understanding."

The theme of the book is that, while there is a widely shared view that education should involve the development of understanding, critical thinking, imagination, and creativity, our view of these key concepts is confused and inaccurate. The consequence is that what we do in schools to attain our ideal is generally inappropriate.

I argue that our tendency to think in terms of generic skills, the dominance of the scientific paradigm in educational research, and the materialistic and relativistic tenor of our culture, combine to totally distort our understanding of intellectual qualities, such as intelligence and critical thinking, of the imaginative and creative powers, and of interpersonal relations. Other concepts examined include caring, values clarification, brainstorming, and education of the emotions. A chapter on giftedness plays the important role of providing a case study of what happens when educationalists fail to do their conceptual ground-work properly, in addition to illustrating the ways in which an educational issue can become more or less unintelligible when we succumb to a superficial relativism, a too rigid scientism, and what I term "the generic fallacy."

In the following pages, I shall argue for a particular view of teaching and education and shall criticise some of our current assumptions and practices. I have placed emphasis fair and square on reason, suggesting that the question for the reader should be one of the clarity and coherence of the argument as presented. I hope that, for the most part, I write in measured and reasoned tones. However, I make no secret of the fact that I write from passion. Passion for reason, and passion in relation to what I see as a wasted opportunity in education and potentially disastrous social consequences. "A wasted" opportunity, because the opportunity is there. However reluctant governments may be to part with our money, or to support various inspiring initiatives and ideas, the fact remains that, compared with most civilisations in most periods of history, there is today a widespread and large scale commitment, both material and idealistic, to education. I regard it as wasted, not because I think what we do is wholly bad or ineffective, but because I believe that we could do so much more, if we could get a clearer idea of what we want to do.

Many democracies face a crisis of faith. There is plenty of reason to suppose that people fear freedom, even while valuing it. Witness the appeal of religious fundamentalism, of political ideologies, and of herd instincts throughout history, never mind the testimony of those such as Erich Fromm who have specifically attempted to analyse this phenomenon.[1] In their crises of faith—in their lack of conviction and commitment even to their own supposed ideals—individuals, I fear, are increasingly drawn towards alienation or dogmatism. No longer inspired by the values and achievements of their civilisation, they either withdraw from active involvement and face problems of isolation, loneliness, and estrangement, or else they revert to some ready-packaged system of thought that will provide security, brotherhood, and purpose. Both groups represent a real threat to the continuation of our society in anything like its present form, the former by the sin of omission, the latter by the sin of commission.

Connected to this phenomenon is another feature of our times: increased centralisation of government and other institutions such as schooling, and increased bureaucratisation. The self-help philosophy that imbues the economic theory of many contemporary governments rests ill alongside the emergence of the nanny-state that increasingly interferes with individual freedom in social and moral affairs. But it seems reasonable to depict our age as on balance re-asserting society's control over individual lives at many levels. This might matter somewhat less, if one did not have reason to think that many of our leaders (in parliament, on school boards, in schools, etc.) have the intellectual stature of Pygmies. If it were not for the laws of libel, one might cite numerous politicians, university administrators, school district superintendents, directors of education, and school principals, who are clearly ill-equipped to do their job, and do it badly.

First-rate people choose first-rate people, it is said. But, increasingly, positions of authority and power have been occupied by second-rate people, who choose third-rate people. More generally, we are characterised by poor and superficial thinking (often of an ideological kind), parochial interests, narrow-mindedness, simple-minded solutions to extremely complex problems, obsessive involvement with shifting fads and fancies, and a marked ability to confuse patronising with caring, lack of concern with tolerance, and information with understanding.

It is no part of my brief to argue about whether we are worse or better than other civilisations in these respects. It is sufficient for my purposes to suggest that to some extent these are features of our way of life and characteristics of ourselves, and that we could improve the situation. That is where education comes in. Behind the more specific things that I shall have to say in subsequent chapters is the assumption that, if we approached education in a different way, we would make a substantial contribution to ameliorating such problems and deficiencies—we would develop and promote the autonomy of the individual that is so vital to the health of a democratic society.

Chapter 1

The Ideal and the Reality

I: The ideal

In bold and simplified outline my thesis is that there is an ancient and venerable social and educational ideal, particularly but not exclusively associated with the Western democratic tradition, of which we have effectively lost sight. The tendency of much that we say and do in the name of education, while it may sometimes be thought to subserve the ideal, is actually misconceived as being in the tradition of, or conducive to, maintaining and promoting such democratic values as freedom, tolerance, respect for persons, and autonomy. Sometimes our theorising and our practice are positively antithetical to the ideal. Furthermore, I maintain, this matters. What we are doing is to a considerable extent detrimental to an ideal, and that ideal is a glorious and inspiring one towards which we should still be striving and for which we should still be fighting. I do not say this in ignorance of the fact that there are other traditions and ideals that have their champions. Nor do I make the mistake of assuming that because the ideal exists and is part of our tradition it must therefore be sacrosanct and good. I am aware also of the difficulties involved in arguing for the value or superiority of particular ideals. But it is my intention throughout the following pages not only to explicate this ideal and to point to its educational implications, but also to argue for its quality and value.

Essentially, the ideal is of a community that takes active steps to bring up its citizens in such a way that they come to have substantial understanding of a range of important matters. Most of the words used here need to be stressed: "understanding" rather than "knowledge" in the sense of mere "information or know how." "Substantial" understanding rather than "cursory or superficial acquaintance," and understanding across a range of subject matters, rather than highly specialised and narrowly focussed understanding. Above all, understanding of matters that are deemed to be important rather than trivial or peripheral. In particular, people will have understanding of certain distinctive types of reasoning or ways of thinking that are delineated by their logic rather than simply by their subject matter; for, such types of understanding can be shown to be powerful and necessary means for making sense of and controlling our world, and hence have the requisite importance to a considerable degree. For example, understanding the nature and manner of scientific inquiry and the kinds of problem and question to which it is appropriate, is considerably more powerful, useful, and important than being an expert in some subject such as Mexican post-war politics or photography. Similarly, understanding the nature of aesthetic discourse and judgement is more important than being an expert on Rembrandt.[1]

The ideal does not welcome ignorance, but it is less concerned about people who lack information and specific skills than about people who in their reasoning and related activity misconceive or in various other ways make errors. In other words, the emphasis falls on the quality of reasoning rather than the accumulation of facts. We aim, for example, for people who are good historians in the sense of able to examine historical issues well and blessed with an historical awareness, rather than for people who are very well informed about the Tudor kings and queens of England or the development of the American West Coast.[2] Errors of fact may invalidate an argument. But they can be readily corrected. Much more serious, because more ingrained, harder to detect, and harder to rectify, are deep-seated misconceptions and flaws in one's ability to reason.

The ideal values reason highly. But it is not an exclusively rational ideal. In the first place, it wants to develop in people a passionate concern for truth, accuracy, precision, and appropriateness, at least as much as to ensure that they are able to exhibit these qualities. For this reason alone it cannot be said that the ideal is cold, heartless, or purely intellectual. It posits a world in which people can not only reason well, but in which they also care—care about getting it right, rather than scoring points, winning arguments, or getting their way, care about finding the truth, rather than being consistent with some second-hand ideological stand-point, care about understanding the way the world is rather than finding ways to keep it at bay or to escape from reality. In addition there is a host of other values, such as love, honesty, kindness, justice, respect for persons, friendship, beauty, and equality, which those who subscribe to the ideal may be committed to (not to mention those values that are an integral part of the ideal, such as freedom and autonomy). But it is characteristic of this view to argue that, while such passion and such values are of central importance, they should be rationally ordered. This does not mean that passion, emotion, and virtue should be subordinated to reason, let alone crushed by it, but that they should be organised and regulated by it.

More generally, in terms of this ideal, there is a desire to awaken in people a sense of awe at the amazingness, what some would call the mystery, of the world in general and human endeavour and achievement in particular, and a recognition of the complexity of life, even as we seek to understand and master it. Simplistic, partial, and stereotypical explanations and understandings are anathema to the ideal. Individuals will seek to understand by means of developed and sophisticated types of inquiry, as already indicated. They will not confine themselves to one particular all-embracing type of explanation, as, for example, some people see all problems from a sociological perspective only; they will not rest content with a pre-determined system of explanation, as certain ideological or religious believers may do, and they will not attempt to understand particular individuals and situations purely in terms of standardised categories, whether derived from psychology, religion, sociology, or anywhere else. On occasion, indeed, they will see reason to modify, and in extreme cases even abandon, the very forms of inquiry which they have hitherto utilised to increase their understanding of the world. In a word, the ideal calls for autonomy: for individuals who, while they naturally imbibe and develop the wisdom of others, ultimately seek to base their views and conclusions on no other person, school of thought, or motivation than their own reasoning ability. In principle, they test every claim and argument for themselves, acknowledging only the rules of sound reasoning and the evidence that they are satisfied with.

Finally, the ideal is also concerned with cultural and aesthetic qualities. The products of this education will have aesthetic sensibility and cultural aspirations. They will display imagination, creativity, and compassion. But it will be argued that these qualities are not of a wholly different order and entirely distinct from rational qualities. On the contrary, the true display of imagination and creativity, the display of genuine compassion, are partially dependent on a correct understanding of people, situations, and facts. The ultimate goal is thus a community of autonomous, liberal-minded, imaginative, compassionate, rational people, wedded to the idea of pursuing a true understanding of the world and the nature of humanity, both of which they recognise, with due wonder and humility, to be exceedingly complex matters.

Many readers will recognise in the above sketch an ideal that may be said to have originated with the Ancient Greeks—more specifically with the fifth-century B. C. Athenians and, in terms of its explicit elaboration, the fourth-century philosopher Plato. But its origins, and the question of how far what I have written imitates or deviates from Plato, do not concern me here. The ideal, in more or less the same form, has been with us for centuries, sometimes in the ascendant, at any rate amongst scholars and even from time to time rulers, sometimes on the defensive, even in hiding from the barbarities and philistinism of a particular age or setting. But the fact of its longevity, though that may give us pause for thought, and the question of who first expounded it, have no bearing on its quality. The question about this or any other ideal is whether we can make sense of it, judge it to be coherent, and provide reasons for holding on to it. Can we produce an argument to convince ourselves and others that we want the kind of education that will most likely contribute towards attaining in some measure to this ideal or something very like it?

I think we can. But it should be noted at the outset that, whether we choose to draw attention to the fact or not (and often these days we do not, because it has somehow become regarded as "bad form" to overtly assert the superiority of a way of life, a culture, or ideal), this ideal does not fit easily with a number of other widely held positions. It is fundamentally at a variance with the ideals associated with certain dogmatic and fundamentalist forms of religion, as well as with certain political ideologies.[3] Some values and beliefs may be held in common by people with widely different viewpoints, and some individuals who regard themselves as Catholic, Marxist, Islamic, Capitalist, or whatever, may nonetheless subscribe more or less to this ideal. But, if we have an unswerving commitment to Islamic, Catholic, Capitalist, or Marxist doctrine, then we cannot consistently subscribe to this ideal, and vice versa. And it will do us no good in the long run to blink this fact, or to ignore it out of a misplaced sense that it is somehow hitting below the belt to criticise another person's beliefs, or that the tolerance and liberality that are associated with the democratic ideal demand our turning a blind eye to it. Democratic states can and should tolerate Islam, Catholicism, and Marxism, because democracy values freedom of thought and the open pursuit of truth. It must therefore allow the expression of rival opinions. That does not mean that democracy accepts the value of incompatible ideals. And the educational ideal of producing autonomous people of the type described is simply not consistent with the aims of upbringing implicit in thoroughgoing commitment to such ideologies.

No more is it consistent with any system of upbringing that aims in the end to produce conformity and the acceptance of received opinion at the expense of the active inquiring mind, regulated only by the canons of logic and the evidence as it is perceived. There are those who seek to minimise the differences between this ideal and the views of education associated with various ideologies by arguing that the liberal-democratic tradition is itself an ideology; and it may be said that talk of being guided only by the evidence and rules of logic ignores the fact that different people see different evidence and interpret it differently, and have different views of what is logical. But such an argument is confused. Of course, one who purports to be a liberal-democrat may have his prejudices, may regard as relevant evidence something that others would not, may interpret evidence in a particular way because of his proclivities, and may, for example, find it "logical" to countenance abortion where others would not. But the difference in question, the difference that matters, is between those, on the one hand, who deal with particular issues in the light of a framework of received opinions, values, and types of explanation of a substantive kind (an ideology), and those, on the other, who in principle are bound only by formal rules of logic (such as rules of non-contradiction and valid syllogistic reasoning) and the concern to see things as they are, regardless of what the consequences may be for any or all of their current assumptions. It is the difference, so to speak, between the Catholic who is concerned to take a position on abortion in terms of the traditional Catholic view of the world, and the Catholic who is prepared to examine the issue without reference to any peculiarly Catholic doctrine and see whether his conclusion accords with the orthodox Catholic view or not. One (current) Catholic presumption on this issue is that the foetus is human. It is not part of liberal-democratic orthodoxy that the foetus is not human. Rather it is part of the network of formal values enshrined in any ideal that values rationality that the question of whether the foetus constitutes something human is part of what has to be examined *de novo* in any discussion about abortion.

The type of education implied by the ideal in question would be referred to by many as "liberal education." It makes no difference to the overall argument of these pages whether we call it that, or say that anything worthy of the name of education would be a form of liberal education. But it is important to recognise the implications of the above paragraphs: the education or liberal education that we are concerned with is to be contrasted with and distinguished from other commodities such as indoctrination, training, and socialisation.   Any form of upbringing that is primarily concerned to initiate individuals into a set of substantive beliefs about the world in such a way as to ensure unwavering commitment to them constitutes indoctrination, whether the attempt to do this succeeds or not. It is the precise converse of education.   Training, by which is meant the business of bringing people to perform certain specific tasks, is not necessarily opposed to education, and indeed is likely to play a part in schooling both for its own sake and as a means to furthering education, but it is distinct from it.   While, on almost any view, we have to train people to behave in various ways and to perform certain tasks such as writing, counting, and blowing their noses, if we are to educate them we have to do something quite different in addition, namely develop their understanding. Socialisation, by which is meant the business of habituating people to the customs and expectations of their particular society, will likewise be a legitimate part of any society's schooling, but it should not be confused with education.[4]

Education is primarily concerned to liberate the individual, and thereby ultimately the community, from the dead and stultifying hands of ignorance, error, superstition, and fear.   Hence the phrase "liberal education."   And hence its value, both intrinsic and extrinsic, both in itself and as a means to some further good.[5]   It need not be denied that people will sometimes differ in their view of what is erroneous or confused, but for the moment we want only to establish the principle that error and confusion are in themselves to be avoided.   To admit as much is to admit the intrinsic value of this educational ideal.   Its extrinsic value is surely equally self-evident: is it too much to say that at bottom all the miseries and injustices of life throughout history have stemmed from ignorance, superstition, error, and fear of one sort or another?   If it is, it will not be an overstatement to assert that the world will at any rate be a better place for conquering these evils.

One assumption that lies behind this humanistic vision and educational ideal should perhaps be brought into the open, since it is one that is implicitly ignored if not denied by some features of the present intellectual climate.   It is the belief that human beings are an exceedingly special and complex form of life, one that, in particular, cannot be entirely reduced to explanation in mechanistic terms.

In explaining this claim, it is necessary to make a few brief qualifications. First, I do not wish to enter the debate as to whether some other higher forms of animal life may not be more akin to humans than we tend to recognise, maybe in some cases potentially indistinguishable.[6] If, in principle, monkeys could develop all the characteristically human attributes, that would not affect the tenor of an argument about humans and the kind of education that is appropriate to them. It would merely follow that we should extend the argument to cover monkeys as well. Secondly, in using the phrase "exceedingly special," I do not wish to imply anything specific in respect of metaphysical matters. Rather I intend to emphasise that the complexity of the human being includes such things as the capacity to think in terms of souls, gods, love, and justice, which, as far as we know, is not given to other animals. Whatever the truth about such matters, whatever the answer to such questions as what a soul may be, whether we truly have one, whether it makes sense to point to the existence of gods, whether love is a natural phenomenon or a man-made construct, and whether justice has some absolute significance or is merely the name we give to rules that arise by convention, it is an undeniable fact that mankind is remarkable for being able to think in these and such-like terms. One of the single most noteworthy things about human beings is their capacity to conceptualise in abstract terms, and to become aware of or create (as the case may be) a number of ideas that cannot be directly apprehended except by the mind. Thirdly, in denying that humans can be entirely explained in mechanistic terms, I do not wish to deny that there is a great deal about them that can be so explained, and indeed that one of the notable advances of recent years is the extent to which we are beginning to understand the environmental, physical, and physiological bases of some of our behaviour and thought. It seems undeniable that to some extent what we do, how we feel, and what we say can be explained in terms of such things as our chemistry.[7]

But, with these qualifications in mind, it must be said that it is a presumption of this ideal that men are not simply machines of a particularly complex variety. This is implicit in some of the terms that have already been introduced. For example, it does not make sense to refer to machines having a sense of awe or being autonomous. The very concept of mind, as distinct from brain, implies an organism that is qualitatively different from the most sophisticated computer imaginable. Minds are capable of the creative act of conceiving, while computers are capable only of calculating. Of course, this is disputed by those who believe that computers already can, or will shortly be able to, perform all the functions of the human mind. In my view such claims misunderstand the nature of the mind, but, in any case, as with the issue of animals, it makes no difference to my overall argument: if computers can indeed be the equivalent of minds, then the conclusion should hardly be that we should treat humans as computers, but rather that we should start treating computers as humans. (The idea that we might educate computers just as we educate people strikes me as sufficiently absurd to settle the issue.)[8]

It may be noted further that the ideal rests ill alongside contemporary rhetoric to the effect that this is the age of information and information processing. Of course, it is a time when information is spawning to a point at which it is hard to control, one does need access to information, and it is necessary to find suitable means of storing and retrieving it.[9] But these facts should not tempt us to adopt metaphors for education and development of mind based on information processing, or to a substantive view of education centred on information. Let us use our technical wizardry to house information (and therefore let us be capable of developing and using technical wizardry), but let us not lose sight of the fact that we have always to be able to query and test information and to make use of it. Understanding without information may be impossible. But information without understanding is barren. The fundamental conviction of those committed to the ideal is that human beings are distinctive in having consciousness. They are capable of, and need to develop their powers of, systematic inquiry of various types, creative thought, and rational argument. Those are the qualities that should be of central concern to educators.

II: Two approaches to an aspect of the ideal

The ideal that I have outlined had some ascendancy at the time that the classical curriculum held sway in Britain from Tudor times to the end of the last century. Of course, the teaching of classics was not always undertaken in this spirit, and it was not always particularly effective in these terms. There is no need to romanticise an often dispiriting story of rote-learning, boredom, gerund-grinding, and fairly useless information regurgitation, nor to make wild empirical claims about the capability of the classicist. Nonetheless, at least in some places at certain times, the intention was to study the classics in such a way as to develop dispositions towards accuracy, attention to detail and precision, to provide a grasp of the power of language in general and the workings of Latin and Greek in particular, to explore the interrelationships between syntax, style, and content, to develop aesthetic awareness, to develop rational thought, and to imbibe the spirit and culture of the ancient world which, like it or not, has powerfully shaped our own.[10] This was done partly in the belief that a mind so developed was the better for it, and partly in the belief that wise leadership of the self and others (for much of the time this was a curriculum for the ruling elite) arises more out of broad understanding and experience (vicarious and direct) and commitment to certain values, than out of specific knowledge or expertise relating to a particular field, or out of mastery of the sort of generic management skills that are so popular today. (What was once argued in respect of classics may and has been argued with more or less success in respect of other subjects such as English and science.)[11]

The contrast is worth stressing: on the one hand the contemporary view, exhibited in a thousand management courses throughout the world, is that one can and should train people to manage—so that, in theory, they can manage anything from a school to a business with the addition of a minimal familiarity with a particular organisation.[12] Closely bound up with this view is a tendency to treat all organisations, irrespective of their particular function, in terms of models drawn from business and industry; this seems unfortunate to those of us who think that the differing purposes of hospitals, schools, and orchestras necessitate rather different approaches. On the other hand, there is the traditional view that sound management and leadership are the product of a well-educated mind and require no training in management skills as such—a view that perhaps finds its origin and apotheosis in Plato's ideal of the philosopher-king. As I say, this is not the place to make empirical claims about the efficacy of the old-fashioned view, although there are studies that claim it is proven superior.[13] But by the same token it would be rash to make claims about the superiority of the new. Despite the claims, the empirical question of which approach actually produces better leadership cannot be said to have been answered, and this is scarcely surprising since it is very difficult to conceive of how one might satisfactorily conduct research into it. What is going to count as success? Do not the two approaches have different conceptions of success? How does one monitor aspects of success such as employee satisfaction? How does one weigh employee satisfaction against profit? How does one determine to what extent profit should come into the running of, say, a hospital? What constitutes profit in a schooling context? How do you assess it? How do you collect data concerning the past that can be compared with data collected by different means in the present?

It is but one small indication of the extent to which we are dominated by the scientific mode of inquiry, that we so naturally ask first for empirical evidence. Some questions, such as what constitutes success in leadership, are not empirical at all and literally cannot be answered by empirical means. Many other questions that are about contingent matters and should ideally be answered by some empirical means, cannot in fact be settled in this way, as, I am suggesting, the complex question of whether a past tradition produced superior leaders cannot be. It is therefore worth drawing attention to, and metaphorically underlining, the point that there is often another way to establish the conclusion that something is a desirable practice and one that is efficacious in some particular terms, and sometimes this other way is the only feasible way.

This other way involves exploring what is involved in the idea of success in a particular field and what is involved in the practices that are under consideration as a means to success, and establishing that there are certain conceptual and other logical links that show that it is reasonable to suppose that these practices will lead to that success. Thus, given what is involved in the idea of broad understanding, it becomes self-evident that some teaching strategies are more likely to be conducive to developing it than others. One does not need to conduct empirical research to establish whether wide reading of certain types of literature is a desirable practice to encourage in schools as a means to education. For, as I shall argue below, what we mean by being well educated must necessarily be enhanced by wide reading of certain kinds of literature, because of what is involved in the latter and its logical connection with the former. Such a form of justification does not entail the conclusion that the approach cannot fail. Some people who are initiated into literature may not emerge as very well educated people, and some well-educated people may emerge who have not read extensively. For the claim is not that being well educated means having read widely, as being a bachelor means being unmarried. The connection in the former case, though still conceptual and logical, is looser and more indirect. But that will not alter the fact that those who wish to educate (as opposed to train, indoctrinate, etc.,) would be well advised to seek to initiate their students into the business of wide reading of literature.

In the particular case of the classics curriculum, the argument would be that when it was taught with certain objectives in mind it was an entirely appropriate means to the end in view, because the values embodied in the end coincided with values that could well be developed by the means. If your aim was to produce leaders whose qualifications for the role included a sense of their cultural heritage, awareness of the hard path between aspirations and success, awareness of the varieties of human nature and the vagaries of chance, a commitment to the standards of scholarship, facility with language, understanding of a range of intellectual disciplines, and commitment to liberal values, it was sensible enough to subject them to a classical curriculum grounded in belief in those qualities. By the same token, a course in management as generally conceived today would self-evidently be largely irrelevant. The issue, in other words, is not really the empirical one of which approach is more successful, but the conceptual and evaluative one of what kind of leadership you want. For different approaches to the ideal may distort the nature of the ideal.

III: The reality

It is my contention that in general terms the reality we face is the obverse of the ideal.

We are tending to produce school leavers (and in many cases university graduates) who have little sense of awe—or, if they do, have a limited sense of humility in the face of an existence which they are trained to see only in terms of increased technical complexity. But the kind of philosophical awe that Plato saw as the inspiration and foundation of true wisdom, the Socratic sense of one's own and mankind's vast ignorance, not about how to do this or that, or about what this or that action may lead to, but about the meaning of life, the way to live the good life, the question of an after life, and so forth, the awe of the artist, the lover, the mystic, seems to be largely absent.[14] With more confidence, because this is an easier concept to define and to recognise than a sense of awe, I would say that our students lack broad understanding and often find it difficult to disentangle different kinds of question, such as the moral from the prudential, or the empirical from the conceptual, or to pursue any of them in the appropriate kind of way. Such a failure must necessarily inhibit their powers of sound reasoning, but, further than this, many of them prove inadequate at abiding by the basic laws of logic in their reasoning. This may sometimes be a matter of their being, in general, illogical thinkers—failing to recognise implications, failing to see that if all As are B and C is an A it must be a B, and so forth. But, for reasons that will become apparent later, it is more likely to be due either to a failure to recognise particular instances of logical fallacy or to a failure to stand out for standards of logic.[15] That is to say, the problem is not so much that we fail to teach people what the formal rules of logic are or that they matter in reasoning. Few people cannot, when pushed, recognise some forms of argument as valid and others as invalid. Poor argument seems more often to be the result of failing to apply logic, either because what is logical in a particular context is obscured by ignorance of the subject matter, or because something else such as emotion gets in the way of logic.

One particular intellectual capacity, however, does seem to be very poorly developed in most people and that is the ability to analyse concepts. In many cases, people's vocabularies outstrip their thoughts. They can use words and phrases such as "love," "beauty," "education," "justice," "imagination," and "critical thinking," but they do not have very clear ideas of these concepts. They know the sort of thing they are saying when they describe a painting as beautiful (they are commending it, indicating that they like it, revealing that its appearance pleases them), but they cannot explain precisely what they mean or distinguish "beautiful" from "alluring," "charming," "lovely," "graceful," and "attractive." Conceptualisation is itself one of the concepts that is far from clear in many people's minds. The word, admittedly, is ubiquitous, in a way that it certainly was not fifty years ago. People are forever talking about the need to conceptualise, the child's ability to conceptualise, or the importance of the conceptualisation stage in designing empirical research. But usually their idea of conceptualisation is a hazy and general one of forming an idea, without much appreciation of the different kinds of idea or concept that there are, and consequently the different ways in which one has to set about conceptualising different things. More particularly, people are by and large not very practised or proficient in engaging in the kind of conceptual analysis referred to in the previous section of this chapter, and distinguishing it from other kinds of definition and pseudo-definition. Thus, all too often, the "conceptualisation" of a piece of research amounts to a statement of the aims and methodology to be employed, rather than a clear and coherent explication of those aims and a logically appropriate methodology. In general terms, people neither have very clear ideas of various important abstract concepts nor have the wherewithall to set about the task of clarifying them, sometimes by lack of inclination, sometimes by lack of ability, and sometimes by both.[16]

So far as the domain of reasoning goes, then, I am painting a picture of a generation of students who, while they may have a lot of information, while they may be able to do a lot of things, and while they may have extensive vocabularies, are not possessed of a wide range of clear ideas of important things, are not good at clarifying those ideas if called upon to do so, are not good at remaining rational when the issue calls for it, are not good at proceeding logically in a number of important areas, are not good at distinguishing logically distinct kinds of question, and don't have much sense of their shortcomings in these respects. In so far as there is truth in this description, it is small wonder that discussions on such topics as protectionism, abortion, pornography, disarmament, and marriage are hardly worth listening to. For even when people have access to all the necessary information pertaining to such issues, they are in no position to make use of it.

But this is not all. There are not only grave intellectual deficiencies and a lack of passion for the rigorous pursuit of truth and understanding to be noted. There are also illiberality, a materialistic outlook, superstition, and ennui to be combated. To some extent these are connected with the intellectual shortcomings. True liberality, for example, is not simply a function of broad sympathies and is not a purely emotional state; it is also the product of understanding the complexity and open-endedness of much of life. Liberals do not condone homosexuality because they like it or feel warm about it, but because they understand the extraordinary mish-mash of bad argument against it, the historical and cultural explanations of the taboo against it, and the difficulty of establishing in what sense it or any other sexual practice is "unnatural" or "morally unacceptable." They tolerate Marxism, even while it is antithetical to their views, because they understand complicated arguments about the ultimate value of free thought in terms of truth. They want a minimum of state interference in people's lives, because they understand arguments about human freedom, and have understood both the appeal and the consequences of ideology and totalitarianism. Similarly, a materialistic outlook, although it might be opted for in the light of reason, is all that is left for people who have not developed the powers of the intellect and hence are not capable of enjoying the pleasures of the mind or those cultural and aesthetic pursuits that have to be understood to be enjoyed.[17] A retreat to superstition is the natural refuge of those who cannot explain things in any other way, and ennui is the natural concomitant of a life that one cannot do much to control or take advantage of.

Even as I paint this pessimistic picture, I am not presuming that people are without redeeming talent or virtue; millions of young people have manifest talent and ability. Nor am I suggesting that they do not care about anybody or anything. They may not appear—may not even be—particularly intolerant or dogmatic in particular cases. They will help a neighbour in distress. They will live decent lives, if they can. They will not rob, cheat, or steal. But to be truly compassionate they will need to be capable of imaginative understanding. To be truly tolerant they will need to understand people and situations. To be truly moral, as opposed to inclined to abide unquestioningly by rules, they will need to understand the nature of morality. To truly appreciate art, they will need to understand it. And if anyone doubts that our society is less liberal than it might be, then let them consider some fairly obvious empirical evidence: study our television, read our newspapers, witness the growth in fundamentalism and adherence to weird and woolly cults, scrutinise the people we elect and what they say and do, observe the dogmatism and puritanism that abounds. Look at the resurgence of demands for creationist science, look at the insistent attempts to censor children's books, look at the trend towards technical and consumer education, look at the self-righteousness of single-issue fanatics such as the anti-smoking or the anti-abortion lobby, look at the increasingly stringent demands made on teachers in their private lives. Granted there are many commendable features of our society, many clear improvements on the ways of our forefathers, nonetheless it is surely hard to resist the conclusion that the evidence does not support the contention that we are near to realising the ideal.

But, fundamentally, my argument is such that we do not need to cite empirical evidence. It must be so, it must be the case that we are producing many people of the type I depict, because, as I shall argue in detail in subsequent chapters, what we are doing in our schools must tend towards this sort of a product, since there is a logical connection between the sorts of thing we do and this sort of end result. The evidence for my contention is to be found in the kinds of thing we say and do in the name of education, not in attempts to survey society empirically. (If I am right, it must of course be the case that there are such people, and in principle that could be empirically verified. But in fact it would be very hard to establish the point empirically with any more plausibility than impressionistic surveys by those who are on the lookout for such things in an informal way can provide. There are only two serious objections that can be made against making use of this kind of personal impressionistic observation. The first is that the individual who makes the observation cannot be trusted for one or more of a number of possible reasons. But that objection applies equally to more formal and systematic research: all the methodological soundness in the world won't get round the point that the researcher has to know what illiberality is when he meets it. Secondly, it may be suggested that I have encountered a very unrepresentative sample. I probably have, but its unrepresentativeness works in favour of my thesis, since by and large I deal with the presumed successes of our schooling system.)

To summarise this chapter: I have laid out in broad terms a social and educational ideal, predicated heavily on the values of freedom, autonomy, and understanding, but certainly not a purely rationalistic one. Rather it is a humanistic ideal devoted to education in a sense to be contrasted with indoctrination, training, and socialisation, a sense that some would prefer to explicitly label "liberal education" since it is designed to liberate the mind and the person as a whole. A few may explicitly challenge the ideal. Of those few, some will revert to arguments such as that it is clear that the ideal is old-fashioned or advocated by a member of a particular class or background. But since age is not a relevant criterion to establishing truth, and to question the motives of the arguer is to confuse explanation with justification, such arguments can be ignored as irrelevant. Why one is disposed to value this ideal may be of interest, but it has nothing to do with whether one is correct or has good reason to do so. To engage in such *ad hominem* rebuttals is to exhibit one of the kinds of deficiency in reasoning that are at issue. For the rest, those who simply do not value the ideal, I confess that there is not much that can be said. Fortunately, it is surely the case that they are very few and far between.

I have asserted that we are falling short of the ideal by a long way. The assertion is empirically based (a point worth stressing in an age that tends to confuse the *trappings* of various accredited kinds of formal empirical research with the *nature* of such research), but it is not formally or systematically based.[18] I doubt the feasibility of an empirical study that would have much more credence than the conclusions of those who observe informally, because the difficulty here is one of defining and being able to recognise qualities such as autonomy and understanding, rather than one of being able to survey people. But, in any case, the main point is that this book as a whole is concerned to show, by argument, that if we are doing certain things (which I do not think anybody will dispute that we are) then that must tend towards certain kinds of achievement rather than others. What, in so far as we are successful, we must be achieving, I shall argue, for the most part looks superficially as if it is connected with the ideal, but in fact, on closer scrutiny, can be seen not to be. What is required to achieve the ideal and to combat the lack of faith, the fundamentalism, the intolerance, the sheer idiocy of much of our way of life, can likewise be seen to follow from a full understanding of the ideal or the ends to which we are striving. In our end is our beginning. The argument for all of this, in other words, is yet to come.

Chapter 2

Six Erroneous Assumptions

The main reason for concluding that we are not serving a widely shared ideal is that a scrutiny of what we say and do in the name of education reveals that we cannot be. There is a lack of logical fit between the end and our means. In this chapter, I want to indicate, still in general terms, the main aspects of our educational thought and practice which, I shall argue, militate against the ideal.

I am not looking here for psychological or sociological explanations of why we as individuals or groups reject this ideal and strive after others instead, because it is not at all clear to me that in general it is the case that we do. Obviously some people do, valuing conformity or blind allegiance to ideology above autonomy and freedom, or prizing physical and material development above intellectual and cultural development. And there are certainly some values, most notably economic ones, that are widely adhered to but which do not play a prominent part in the ideal. But it is my contention that by and large, and with the exception of the issue of economic well-being and the development of marketable skills, which I shall deal with separately below, the problem is not one of competing ideals so much as that we fail to see what the implications of the ideal are and what we ought to be doing to serve it. In other words, while values such as autonomy, intellectual development, caring, critical ability, and creative skills have fairly widespread support nominally, they are not concepts that are properly understood, and consequently we do the wrong things to achieve the ideal, even while we sincerely claim to be committed to it. The question is not why do we not value these goals, but, why, given that we think we do, we do not take appropriate action. And the answer, in outline, is that we have not thought clearly about the ideal, and therefore fail to see what it involves and hence demands by way of practice.

In broad terms, I shall argue, our failure in education can be traced to certain specific and erroneous assumptions about the nature of human intellect, about the alleged relativity of values and other kinds of truth, and about the appropriate way to inquire after and research into truth in various different domains. Much of what we advocate and do in schools, and by extension in teacher education, is supposed to be done for the sake of intellectual development and to advance the interests of true understanding. But certain features of our thinking about the human mind are fundamentally misconceived, with the result that particular ways in which we approach, say, the development of critical skills do not in fact lead to greater intellectual grasp (and cannot in principle do so). Certain features of our way of thinking about the nature of knowledge in general and values in particular are mistaken, with the consequence that what we do in schools does not in fact lead to a greater grasp on the truth. And certain tendencies in our views about how best to find out the truth, particularly in the area of educational research, are so distorted that much of what we assume has been shown to be the case has not in fact been so, and certain kinds of important question are either examined in a wholly inappropriate way or else not examined at all.

To be more specific, I shall attempt in the following pages to locate and describe six erroneous beliefs that are part and parcel of the way we talk and think about education, that directly or indirectly lead to untenable or false claims about how we should teach and organise school curricula, and that crop up and work their damage in a wide variety of issues. These six fundamental mistakes or misconceptions are:

1) An unheeding commitment to the tenets of faculty psychology.
2) A presumption that mental qualities are skills.
3) A presumption that ideas can be understood divorced from their historical and cultural setting.
4) A presumption in favour of materialistic and technocratic values.
5) A presumption that values are relative.
6) A presumption that the scientific mode is the most developed and best mode of inquiry.

(1) An unheeding commitment to the tenets of faculty psychology

Faculty psychology is a school of thought, prominent in the nineteenth century, which was based on the belief that the mind consists of various specific faculties (such as memory, imagination, and reasoning), each of which can be located as an entity in itself and improved and developed by teaching directed to it. Reasoning, for example, is something that can be tackled directly, and strengthened and improved, in much the same sort of way as muscular strength can be built up by a direct programme of exercising the muscles.

Conventional wisdom has it that faculty psychology has been for the most part long since set aside, if not actually discredited, particularly by the emergence of general theories of intelligence amongst psychologists, which replace the idea of a faculty of reasoning, a faculty of imagination, etc., with the idea of some general factor of intelligence that combines with a variety of more specific competencies. Certainly it is the case that by and large educationalists no longer employ the language of faculty psychology and that formally the view has been widely repudiated.[1] However, the fact is that, while we formally dismiss it, we still proceed as if its basic tenets had some substance. We talk as if, and hence one must presume we believe, individuals are more or less creative, more or less intelligent, more or less critical, or more or less gifted, in general. And we approach teaching as if this were the case too, laying on courses designed to promote creativity or critical thinking in general, devising ways to single out and treat the gifted or the intelligent in general. Our talk and our actions show us to be still wedded to the idea that individuals possess or exhibit giftedness, intelligence, creative, or critical powers, to some extent or another, in some general way across the board.

This, I shall argue, is profoundly mistaken. It makes no sense to conceive of these as generic abilities, meaning abilities that people have and can exhibit, should they choose to do so, in any field. On the contrary, the truth is that people are gifted in some areas and not others, intelligent in some respects only, capable of being creative in some domains but not all. These mental abilities are context specific, rather than generic (which is not to say that they might not be more generally evident in some cases than in others). A further implication of this view is that, whatever the truth about the degree to which things such as intelligence are innate as opposed to acquired through the environment, they can certainly be enhanced and improved, but only in specific contexts. In short, something like intelligence, while it may be displayed to a greater or lesser degree and more narrowly or widely across the range of human activities, and while it may be to some extent limited by the genetic and physiological make up of the individual, is the name that we give to people's capacity to perform certain operations in a particular kind of way. That capacity can be developed, but it has to be developed in relation to particular contexts. We can help somebody to become a more intelligent historian or administrator, but we cannot help somebody to become more intelligent. The latter simply doesn't make sense.

(2) A presumption that these mental qualities are skills

Here again, I take my cue from the way in which we talk and the implications of that manner of talking. We tend to refer to critical thinking, communicative ability, creativity, problem solving, and imagination as "skills." In its usual basic sense a "skill" implies a capacity that is discrete and can be perfected through practice and exercise, as some are skilled jugglers or skilled tight-rope walkers. And these connotations are certainly carried over to the use of the word "skill" to describe various intellectual and interpersonal abilities. For the rationale behind typical critical thinking programmes or courses in communication skills is that one can isolate and practice certain particular behaviours or procedures, and thus develop them. One perfects critical thinking ability by practising critical thinking exercises.

I do not dispute that the ability to communicate or to be critical may involve certain skills, in the strict sense, that can be improved by their exercise. For example, eye-contact may reasonably be called a skill and may be improved simply by the demand that it be exercised. However, what is to be disputed is that this is an adequate way to conceive of critical thinking or communication as a whole. Quite apart from the point that it doesn't make sense to talk of exercising the critical powers except in some context (so that, whereas one can practice dribbling a ball without reference to where or when, one has to practice being critical about some specific kind of problem, and the ability to be so in relation to one problem does not guarantee it in relation to another), there are certain aspects of these mental qualities that have nothing to do with skills as such. For example, to be a good problem solver is not simply a matter of perfecting some general techniques or strategies. One also has to have, at least, a certain disposition or inclination, and some specific understanding.

So long as we think of these abilities as skills, we are bound to think that practising their exercise, perfecting the process, is what crucially matters, and to continue to proceed as we do now, laying on a curriculum that emphasises procedure and strategy, at the expense of understanding and content.

(3) A presumption that ideas can be perfectly well understood divorced from their historical and cultural background and setting

The previous two assumptions already tend to focus our educational provisions on formal abilities at the expense of substantive content. But there seems anyway to be a presumption in favour of the contemporary at the expense of the past. Of course we do teach history, although it is noteworthy the extent to which the emphasis here falls on contemporary and local history, at the expense of a wider perspective. But my concern here is with the wider issue of embedding our knowledge in an understanding of its origins and development through traditions. It does not appear to be felt important to understand a subject such as science partly through its historical development, or to study literature as a long-standing and rich tradition, itself developing in interrelationship with a more general historical social development. Nor when it comes to the study of particular issues and problems, such as abortion, free trade, morality, or peace studies, does there appear to be any strong desire to embed the discussion in some historical understanding. I am not suggesting here that we should adopt the particular, extreme, view that ideas are exclusively the product of particular times and places. But nobody who does have some historical awareness could fail to recognise that intellectual progress and knowledge are affected by and contribute to changed historical and cultural settings. Debates about disarmament may not be settled by a simple appeal to history, but they will be a great deal more illuminating and informed if they are conducted by people who know particular things about, say, the Russians' historical fear of invasion, or the deep rooted tendency towards isolationism in American foreign policy (and the reasons for it), and more general lessons from history about the various ways in which societies have tended to behave. You do not need to have read Jane Austen to appreciate Margaret Atwood, but you can understand better and gain more from literature if you have some sense of its development, just as Frye has argued more specifically that understanding of literature can grow with knowledge of the Bible.[2] Discussions about the institution of marriage are not simplified by knowledge of different cultural practices and historical attitudes, but they must necessarily become less dogmatic and parochial.[3]

(4) A presumption in favour of materialistic and technocratic values

My previous point was that there is an ahistorical and acultural bias in our educational provision, that seems to arise simply from a failure to see that cultural and historical awareness enhance the open-mindedness and fullness of understanding that we claim to be concerned about.[4] But, of course, any proposal to put more weight on the historical aspect of intellectual traditions, and on subjects such as literature, does face a further challenge from those who regard these as less vital than various more utilitarian studies.

Here we encounter the only one of the six assumptions that involves a conflict of values and a challenge to the ideal, as opposed to a failure to see that what we are doing does not square with the ideal. Educators themselves are not on the whole guilty of inconsistency here, for it is primarily politicians and parents, rather than they, who value what may be seen as practical studies highly. Be that as it may, our schools are under considerable pressure to construct curricula and to teach with an eye to immediate and direct utility. In addition to long standing commitments to such subjects as typing, "shop," and home economics, we have recently seen great prominence given to such things as peace studies, sex-education, social studies, law, consumerism, and technology, quite apart from specific initiatives to turn the education of some students into a form of job-preparation or vocational training.

It would be foolish to denigrate these concerns wholesale, and it would be nonsensical to argue that education should not try to be useful. However, there is a fallacy involved in equating utility exclusively with what is directly and immediately useful to the economy of society in its current state. Things may be extremely and importantly useful, but only indirectly, in the long term, and perhaps to a wider set of objectives than the purely economic. Seemingly impractical and non-utilitarian pursuits, such as the development of aesthetic sensibility, may be extremely useful to society. It all depends what kind of a society we want, which takes us back to the ideal. If we want autonomous, intelligent, and liberal minded citizens, because we believe that they will make possible a better society (economically as well as morally), then the development of aesthetic understanding and appreciation may be a necessary and useful objective. This preoccupation with immediate utility may be a good preparation for society as it is, but it has little obvious relevance to our ideal. More strongly, it may be argued that it is far from clear that it is desirable on its own terms: preparing people for specific jobs, or developing a specific and limited repertoire of industrial skills, could only be effective on straightforward economic terms, if we could predict and anticipate future economic and industrial needs considerably more accurately than we have succeeded in doing so far. As many businessmen now concede, and as the Japanese, the leading industrial nation, have long proclaimed in theory and practice, the economic and industrial welfare of the nation is in safer hands if we produce young adults who are well educated in the broad liberal sense, than if we seek to produce specifically trained individuals. (Though it is important to add here that the Japanese should probably be seen as having a broader conception of utility rather than as being intent on a liberal education.)

But, while I believe that the argument against immediate utility on the grounds that it does not in fact prove useful on its own terms is strong, I would prefer here to put the emphasis directly on the issue of competing value. Providing people with information about contemporary social issues, such as sex or technology, is a poorer ideal than developing their minds. There are other things to be said on this matter, such as that sex-education may all too easily turn into indoctrination or that peace studies are incoherent when they are not based on a thorough understanding of history, moral issues, and people, which will be dealt with below. For the moment, I merely note that a preoccupation with information, technology, and vocational training is another factor that inhibits our ability to educate for the ideal.

(5) A presumption that values are relative

We are plagued by an incoherent relativism. The concept of relativism is not entirely straightforward. There are various distinct types of relativist theory, and some involve complex and sophisticated concepts.[5] But what I have in mind here are those views that assume that we cannot make objective value judgements. That is to say that we cannot reasonably take it to be a fact that something is superior to another, as opposed to it being a matter of the mere opinion of some individual, group, or society.

On the face of it, such a view is counter-intuitive. Surely we all make some value judgements that we are convinced represent a truth rather than mere opinion? Pele was a great soccer player; Shakespeare was a great writer; torture is morally odious. These judgements may be disputed and they may be difficult to establish as unquestionably true. But they are not, on the face of it, mere opinion. Insofar as they ever make such judgements and believe them to be true, the vast majority of those who think they are relativists are not consistent. I shall argue that in any case relativism in this sense is untenable. Nonetheless, a lot of what we say and do in education betrays, and only makes sense on, the assumption, ill-founded as it may be, that value judgements are relative. Not so long ago a number of educationalists explicitly maintained as much, some even arguing that all truth was relative, that things were as we perceived them, and that everything was the product of a dominant ideology, rather than the way things were as a matter of objective fact.[6] This extreme and explicit view is less common today. But still we do things in school that do not appear to make any sense except on the assumption that what matters is how you see things, and being sincere and consistent, rather than on how things are and what can be shown to be the case by appeal to objective criteria and standards. For example, values clarification programmes are exclusively concerned with subjective evaluations, and eschew any attempt to judge individual responses in terms of their truth. Again, a quite common reluctance to correct children's work or to select curriculum material on the grounds that it is more worthwhile than other material, is partly to be explained in terms of a reluctance to admit that we can say "this is poor, that is good." (Though there are certainly other factors at work here too.)

In calling this flirtation with relativism "incoherent," I am referring to the fact that we are blatantly inconsistent on this issue. On the one hand, we refuse to say that certain books should be studied because they are superior to others, refuse to correct or improve children's stories, or refuse to explain to students that their opinions on matters of value are sometimes false or incorrect. But at the same time our society in general (and sometimes our schools) takes up a firmly objectivist stance: the same people, very often, who would not venture to criticise students' essays as poor or their beliefs as incorrect, will state dogmatically that we should have censorship or that smoking is anti-social. I shall argue that serving the ideal requires that we better understand and assert the objective criteria of quality that do in fact exist in most areas, and that allow us to distinguish between the true and the false, the good and the bad, and the reasonable and unreasonable. A concern to develop autonomous individuals is not only to be distinguished from a concern to develop people who believe that everything is a matter of opinion; it actually requires that people come to understand the criteria for judgement that are inherent in various activities. To achieve the ideal, we have to develop an understanding of standards of excellence and criteria for truth. Our failure to act firmly and consistently on this matter is, therefore, another cause of our failure to succeed in matching the ideal.

(6) A presumption that the scientific mode is the most developed and best mode of inquiry

Finally, we are hampered by the dominance of the scientific paradigm and by the authority of the social sciences in our educational theory and research. I should make it clear at once that I am neither anti-scientific nor out to attack the social sciences as such. Some of the questions that scientists, sociologists, and psychologists investigate may be real enough; much of their work may be entirely praiseworthy, and many of their conclusions may be true and of considerable importance. That is not the issue. What is of concern is the extent to which people are dominated by the model of the scientific mode of inquiry, so that they sometimes cannot take other forms of inquiry seriously, and either insist on treating all questions scientifically or else simply ignore some questions as if they were neither real nor significant. Thus, for some people, reality begins and ends with what can be observed by the senses. But this is to ignore the philosophic-artistic dimension of man, which is self-evidently one of his dintinguishing characteristics and arguably what makes him human. Mankind conceives, imagines, creates, intuits, and so forth, and who is to say, even in this day and age, that his soul is not the single most important fact about him? But the soul, the fears, the aspirations, the loves, the ideals of man cannot get the serious attention they are due, if it is either assumed that they do not exist or else they are treated on a par with directly observable entities.

The social sciences do not have to be treated as if they were a species of the natural sciences, despite their name, and, of course, many sociologists and psychologists favour techniques of inquiry of an informal variety that draw attention to the different nature of the problems they deal with. Some go even further and effectively treat their study as a form of philosophy. But the bulk of educational research, including work in the social sciences as it pertains to education, is still dominated by the natural science model. What this means in hard currency is that most problems are treated as if they can be examined by rigorous observation of external factors, and problems and solutions that are not in this mode are given less attention. But that means that crucial questions such as "what should our aims of education be?," "what is it to be creative?," "what does it make sense to do to promote autonomy?," are either ignored or reduced to different questions which can be empirically treated (such as "what do people think our aims should be?"), often without apparent realisation of the shift. I think it also fair to say that, such is the caché of scientific inquiry, we tend to accept the conclusions of scientifically conducted research uncritically, as if the fact that a reputable process of inquiry has been adopted guarantees the truth of the conclusion. (Another example of confusing the quality of the process with the value of the product.) What this can mean in practice is that a particular style of teaching is adopted on the grounds that researchers have found it effective, without our realising that it has not been found to be effective for the purposes of furthering the ideal, for the simple reason that determining empirically that a certain teaching strategy promotes autonomy and understanding may not in fact be possible, and certainly wasn't the focus of inquiry. To conduct such an inquiry it would obviously be necessary to produce a clear account of what understanding and autonomy involve, and because of the kind of concept they are it is simply inadequate to conceptualise them in directly observable terms. But if they are not the kind of thing that lend themselves to observation, how can one empirically survey them? The conclusion to be drawn is not, as those wedded to the scientific paradigm are prone to conclude, "well in that case we can't cope with them," but rather to rely more on reasoning, intuition, impressionistic judgement and the like, which are equally capable of revealing truth, and are the appropriate forms of inquiry for certain kinds of concept.

My thesis is, then, that the ideal of producing autonomous, intelligent, sensitive, creative, imaginative individuals with broad intelligence and understanding, and of a tolerant and liberal disposition, is one that is nominally widely shared in our culture, and can be defended as a worthy ideal both in itself for individuals and for the ultimate good of society. But while most of us say that we value such things, our educational practice and theory is for a large part not conducive to the ideal, because we have not fully understood the ideal and hence what it implies. Six things in particular seem to crop up time and again to get in the way of sound thinking on the matter: first, we tend to assume that the qualities we are concerned with are generic rather than context specific; secondly, we assume that they are skills that can be developed by exercise, without recognising that they involve understanding and dispositions; thirdly, we are prone to emphasise the information and process dimensions of thought and pay scant regard to the value of understanding ideas in terms of their historical and cultural setting; fourthly, there is a bias in our society towards immediately serviceable skills and knowledge that is counter-productive on its own terms and at a variance with the ideal; fifthly, we are too reluctant to make judgements of value ourselves and to teach students to distinguish the good from the bad; sixthly, the only kinds of proposition we are inclined to take seriously as objective are scientific ones, and we therefore very often treat issues inappropriately as if they were amenable to scientific resolution, when they are not. I shall attempt to elaborate on and justify these contentions in the remainder of this book, arguing that we cannot hope to get far towards realising the ideal, if we continue to accept these assumptions, which are anyway false and confused.

At the moment, because these errors dominate educational thought, we have elementary schools that do not make as many intellectual demands, or stretch the industry and imagination of the child as much, as they might. Superficially, considerable emphasis is placed on the emotional relationship between teacher and children and on developing a caring, supportive atmosphere, on instilling basic social information, and on fostering creativity and imagination. (Reading, writing, and numeracy are, of course, still regarded as central to the curriculum at this level.) However, little thought seems to have been given to what is actually involved in the concept of caring or the closely connected question of what kind of caring matters and how best to develop it. Similarly, what passes for creativity and imagination, and the implicit presumptions about what needs to be done to produce truly creative and imaginative adults, have not been adequately considered. Arguments about and research into the teaching of basic literacy and numeracy suffer from a failure to address the conceptual questions and to draw conclusions from sound *a priori* reasoning, combined with too ready a reliance on empirical research which is questionable, not for technical, but for conceptual reasons. (There is something bizarre about a world or even a national stage on which different school districts adopt wildly different approaches, each claiming empirical validity for what they do. Either the truth is that within broad limits it doesn't much matter what we do, or a great many pieces of research are dramatically flawed. If the latter is the case, it is high time that we became a little more critical of empirical research in general.) What seem to be noticeably down-played in our schools are a concern for application to tasks, precision in performance, a solid grasp of basic rudiments of writing, reading, and number, and the instilling of the idea of criteria and standards that have to be met for the successful execution of any task or activity. To summarise in colloquial fashion: we know, from experience in certain schools today and in the past, that students, by the age of eleven or so, could be more knowledgeable, more rigorous in their application, and have better developed intellects, than, in general, they are or have.

We have a secondary system of schooling that is dominated by the idea of teaching generic skills (and correspondingly by the idea that good teaching is largely a matter of displaying various generic teaching skills), by a concern for "relevant" topics or matters of direct utility, and permeated by a crisis of nerve in respect of value and standards, thanks to an ill-conceived commitment to relativism (which it also preaches to students). There is relatively little emphasis on substantive understanding of particular worthwhile subject matter across a broad range and in depth. We talk of problem solving, not of grappling with particular problems, and of critical thinking not of thinking critically about specific important issues. We do not take active steps to initiate students into their historical, cultural, and literary heritage, and we do not develop a commitment to rigorous standards of debate, discussion, and inquiry. The result tends to be school leavers who may have proficiencies and self-esteem, may be easy going and pleasant, may have many other qualities, but who are not conspicuous for being able to talk about or cope with substantial issues and problems in life, personal, social, or political, in an informed, intelligent, open-minded way. They may have social and personal skills, they may be creative and they may be caring, but they are these things only in the senses of the words implied by the theory and research that lie behind them, and those senses are not adequate. Thus, they may have communication skills in the sense that they practice eye contact, etc. But is that really what communication is about? Is that really what matters? Would it not be preferable if they could communicate in the sense of understand other people, and make intelligent responses to them? If it would, then we are not doing the right kinds of thing in schools. It is not communicative ability in this sense that we have been concerned with or that our research has focussed on.

We have a university system that while it, too, obviously has its virtues (such as that it expands information, it promotes mastery of form and technical competence), is not notable for forcing the philosophical pace. It does not promote passionate commitment to truth, rigorous standards of inquiry, and understanding of the various different kinds of inquiry that are appropriate to different questions, or a willingness to challenge ideas and arguments at a fundamental level and an ability to do so in an intelligent and informed way. (Nor could it easily do so, given that the secondary school has not paved the way: there are times when it is difficult to avoid feeling that universities are doing the job that secondary schools could and should do.) Even philosophy courses are very often taught in the manner of scientific courses, heavily predicated on information and technique: students are not seriously addressing a question such as "what is justice?", but learning how conventionally to set out a response that is concerned with tabulating what various people have said about "justice."

The emphasis throughout our educational system and society at large falls on process, formality, and technique at the expense of content, substance, product, and appropriate treatment. But it is not sufficient to think in terms of going through a process; the question of its value depends upon the end product, and the question of what processes matter has to be determined by considering what they lead to. Formal qualities are empty, even assuming they make sense, unless they are applied within substantive contexts. Techniques have to be appropriately applied. A world in which having a Ph.D. qualification is a necessary condition for being a professor, in which having a degree in management is a necessary condition of being taken on as an administrator, in which application to graduate classes is partially dependant on verbal reasoning tests, in which theses have to have a literature review, no matter what the thesis is about or what type of thesis it is, tells its own story. And the consequence is inevitable: even Ph.D. students, nominally representing the apex of our educational system, while of course they can do some things very well, such as display technical mastery of particular research techniques, regurgitate with a wealth of detail the received opinion on a topic, write grammatical English (sometimes), construct an argument in line with certain accepted formal "principles," do, all too often, lack the human wisdom that those who are unashamedly sceptical about education and scholars accuse academia of lacking. They are not intelligent in any worthwhile sense of the word, not educated. They are technicians, whose trade is academics. They have not been immersed in literature and historical tradition, whereby their creative, imaginative, and critical abilities might have been nurtured. They do not understand a variety of important subject matters; they have not been taught to distinguish and deal appropriately with different kinds of question. They are not in a position to re-conceive their world, to display thorough understanding of it, or to challenge received dogma. They are not in a position to lead society, as true intellectuals should, in the fight against ignorance and folly.

If that, in broad and general terms, can be said to be the case with many of those who have pursued education all the way through our system, how safe is the future in the hands of people who by and large never even go to university? The majority of school leavers do not read, do not understand,

and do not feel, as truly educated persons should. They are in no position to contribute towards the realisation of the ideal, nor to withstand those who are leading us away from it.

Chapter 3

Giftedness: A Cautionary Tale

The placing of this chapter at this point may be briefly explained. Discussion about giftedness tends to embody both conceptual inadequacy and the errors of thinking outlined in the previous chapter. The result of this theoretical failure is, inevitably, practical problems. Few have a clear idea of what they are trying to do with so-called gifted children, and few schools are doing anything sensible. This chapter, therefore, represents a case study of an educational issue that is an embarrassing muddle because we have not worked out what we mean by "gifted," because we think in terms of it involving generic skill(s), and because we are inconsistent and confused about whether judgements of quality are relative or absolute, and subjective or objective. Following the broad overview that this topic allows, chapter four will examine specific intellectual qualities, chapter five affective qualities, and chapter six interpersonal qualities. Section I of this chapter, on the problem of definition, while it is strictly speaking a digression on method, is of extreme importance in the overall argument of this book, since it is maintained that educational research and theory is severely perverted by the widespread lack of understanding of the nature of conceptualisation and analysis.

I: The problem of definition

The current preoccupation with giftedness (sometimes referred to by other names, such as "exceptionality," "talent," or "special needs") is instructive in that it betrays a number of features that are common to debates about many educational issues.

First, the very fact of a new term being brought into play, even though, as we shall see, there is nothing new about the concept, is fairly typical of educational discourse.[1] Secondly, and again this is very often the case in educational debate, almost all the writing and research about giftedness focuses on the questions of how to teach and how to organise programmes for gifted children, rather than on the questions of what giftedness is and whether it is morally or educationally desirable to provide gifted children with a distinctive kind of education. Thirdly, the few attempts that are made to define the term are inadequate in one or more ways that are all too common in educational theory.

In this case there is no bias towards materialistic and technical interests, for those who write about giftedness, and most actual programmes for gifted children, are inclined to associate concepts such as creativity with giftedness and to emphasise artistic and intellectual matters. It is also not generally the case that giftedness is treated as a skill. But the remaining four of the six questionable presumptions outlined in the previous chapter can be seen to operate here. Giftedness is by and large treated as a generic quality. Proposals for curricula for gifted children tend, correspondingly, to ignore the idea of advanced and in-depth study of specific subject matter such as history and literature. The arguments advanced and the practical proposals implemented betray our uneasiness and confusion on the issue of the relativity of values. And the theoretical and research contributions to the topic either incongruously lean towards the scientific paradigm, or drift into an ill-disciplined and superficial amalgam of vague concepts, platitudes, truisms, and questionable assumptions. (For example: "there are many signs [of giftedness]. Does your child seem more curious and demanding than other children? . . . learn more rapidly . . . [appear] unusually creative and imaginative . . . more totally absorbed in what he is doing . . . display a greater readiness with words or numbers or musical phrases . . . have a particular facility with his hands . . . his body. If the child manifests any or all of these symptoms, it may well be that he or she is gifted and/or talented.")[2] Presumably, this is partly because the domination of the scientific paradigm has left few people properly equipped to deal with non-empirical questions rigorously and in the appropriate manner. Our researchers are familiar with creativity and intelligence tests, for example, but unsure what to do when it comes to talking about creativity, intelligence, or giftedness in some other less tangible sense. Naturally, therefore, much of the debate on giftedness, when it draws away from the attempt to treat the concept as a measurable entity, is noteworthy for its reliance on unanalysed concepts, lack of clear argument, and unsubstantiated opinion. What is meant, for instance, by the phrase "unusually creative and imaginative"? What is meant by the equivocal phrase "it may well be that he or she is gifted"? If these are meant to be signs of giftedness, as opposed to defining characteristics, where is the evidence to establish that they are?

The first three points made above are closely connected. Why has the word "giftedness" been introduced at all? The best and in ordinary life most usual reasons for introducing a new word or phrase are either that a new idea is being introduced or that the new coinage carries connotations or implications that other more familiar words for the same thing do not. In the developed natural sciences we are often introduced to new terms, and quite properly so, as new phenomena are observed or new theoretical concepts conceived. In ordinary language we similarly sometimes introduce new words to refer to new situations, events, or things, and sometimes coin words or phrases to refer to things that, if they are not actually new, gain a new significance or acquire new associations. Thus, in recent years, we have acquired or become familiar with words and phrases such as "black hole," "pheromone," and "social construct," to refer to things that we did not previously think in terms of. Colloquial words and phrases such as "yuppie" and "bonk" have also emerged, which, while they do not refer to new phenomena, carry new implications that in one way or another are suited to our current way of life and way of looking at things.

In education, however, we are constantly creating new words when it is far from clear that we are referring to a new idea or adding any important and legitimate connotations. What, for example, are "interfacing," "resource personnel," "catalytic agents," "creators of learning environments," or "the extrinsic dualistic organisation of coordinate administration"? Do these words and phrases really pin-point new ideas, concepts that hitherto we have been unable to refer to? They seem rather to be new names for familiar things, which can only serve unhelpful purposes, such as obfuscating, lending a spurious scientific respectability, and bringing fame to their progenitors. (Except the last example, perhaps. I have no idea what it is supposed to mean.)

The first question in respect of giftedness therefore is whether it is a term that really does introduce a new idea, or whether it is merely a new way of referring to a familiar concept. Should those who are interested in giftedness confine themselves to reading material that is catalogued under "giftedness," or would all that has been said about imagination, intelligence, and creativity be equally central to the issue and perhaps sufficient? The problem in this case is compounded by the fact that giftedness has not been adequately defined by writers on the topic, and different people take it to mean different things. For some people it is a term that is synonymous with intelligence broadly conceived; for others it is synonymous with the narrow view of intelligence that equates it with performance on an I.Q. test; for some it is a term that brings together concepts such as intelligence, creativity, and imagination, while for yet others it is supposed to pick out a unique not otherwise nameable aspect of human beings. Some define giftedness in terms of mental faculties, some in terms of achievement. Some conceive of it as a natural endowment, others as an acquired quality. But so long as it is the case that people mean different things by the term, do not fully clarify what they do mean, and in some instances do not mean anything new by it, nothing can be gained by use of the word "giftedness" except confusion.

Those who are familiar with curriculum guidelines for giftedness programmes, or books and articles on the topic, may be inclined to dispute my claim that giftedness has not been adequately defined. (They could scarcely deny that there are many different definitions.) It is therefore necessary to say a few words about different types of definition, and the sort of definition that is required if we are to make sense of our theory, research, and practice relating to this or any other issue. For the claim is not that there have been no attempts to define giftedness, but that those there have been are of the wrong kind, and hence inadequate.

There are, in the broad and loose sense of the word "definition," many different ways to define a term. Amongst the more familiar are: providing a brief explanation of the term in other words that are logically equivalent (as a dictionary typically, but not always, does), providing a synonymous word or phrase (as a thesaurus does), providing illustrative examples, providing similes, analogies, or metaphors, providing an account of how a word is used (as a dictionary does in the case of, e.g., "good," which is described as "a general word of commendation"), and providing a sociological account of the phenomenon in question.

Thus, we might say, following the dictionary, that "giftedness is the quality of being gifted, that gifted means being endowed with gifts, and that a gift in this context refers to a natural endowment, faculty, ability, or talent." Turning to the thesaurus, we could say that "giftedness" is "cleverness," "brilliance," "expertise," or "intelligence." We might say that gifted people are people such as Albert Einstein, Bertrand Russell, Vincent Van Gogh and Leonardo da Vinci (providing illustrative examples). Resorting to metaphor, analogy, and simile, we might say that the gifted are the crème de la crème, in Miss Brodie's phrase, that "when thou seest an eagle, thou seest a portion of giftedness" (William Blake actually referred to genius), or, paraphrasing E. M. Forster on creativity, that the gifted man "lets down as it were a bucket into his subconscious and draws up something which is normally" beyond people's reach. If we were to explain how the word is used, we might say "it is used as a summative term to refer to the qualities possessed by one who impresses us with his abilities." A sociological account would effectively define giftedness in terms of the specific qualities and achievements that are valued under this name in a particular society. Thus giftedness may mean one thing in America and another in Cuba.

While some of the above approaches have their value for certain purposes, and may guide us a little towards understanding the concept, none of them is the kind of definition that we need, for none of them clearly and unambiguously states what conditions have to be met for a person to count as gifted. And we need to know that, to know what conditions are necessary for a person to count as gifted and which of these necessary conditions are sufficient for someone to be classified as gifted, in order to fully understand what we are talking about, to ensure that we are talking about the same thing (or know when we're not), to allow us to recognise instances of giftedness, to allow us to evaluate it, to allow us to conduct research into it, and to allow us to recognise implications for teaching gifted people.

To say that giftedness refers to the possession of natural endowments, faculties, abilities, and talents begs more questions than it answers: what is meant by a natural endowment? Are there such things? Are the abilities that we in fact focus on in gifted people "natural"? Which faculties and talents are we referring to? A dictionary definition such as this does something to clarify the meaning of the word to those who are unfamiliar with it, but it does not help us to understand what constitutes giftedness or to determine whether particular people are gifted. (And that is to ignore the major question of whether, to what extent, and in what way, it is true that there are natural endowments, to which we shall return.)

Defining "giftedness" in terms of a synonymous word or phrase such as "creativity," "intelligence," "imagination," "alertness," or "quick wittedness" points us in some kind of direction. But it does not get us very far. Most alleged synonyms are not in fact truly synonymous. It is, for example, very misleading for the thesaurus to give "indoctrination" as a synonym for "education," since it was never an identical term and is now generally regarded as its antithesis.[3] Similarly, "wit," "fancy," and "inspiration" cannot all be true synonyms of imagination since they mean transparently different things. But the more serious consideration is that to define giftedness in terms of, say, creativity and intelligence, merely pushes the problem one step backwards. For what are these? What constitutes creativity? What do we mean by referring to someone as intelligent? (And, of course, by the same argument as we are using with reference to giftedness, it will not help to offer a dictionary definition of intelligence such as "quickness of mind," for that does not reveal the conditions that have to be met for a person to count as intelligent, which is what we need to know if we are to be able to recognise and make claims about it.)

To say that gifted people are like Einstein, does not tell us in what respects they are like him. Are they short like him? Capable of playing the organ, or what? We need to know what it is about Einstein that makes him an instance of a gifted person, rather than the mere fact that he is an instance of one. If we say that he, Russell, Van Gogh, and da Vinci are classified as gifted in terms of their exceptional ability, we have to ask again, ability in respect of what? What is the nature of this ability? What, if anything, are we saying about them other than that they did various remarkable things? Is that perhaps, rather than having some allegedly natural endowment, what we mean by being gifted? Am I gifted, then, if I am a remarkable proof-reader, regardless of the facts that that is all I can do well and that it is a skill that I learned? It does not matter, for the moment, what the answers to these questions may be. What matters is that until such questions are answered examples of gifted people do not help us to understand what giftedness is.

The metaphors and similes may serve to suggest something about the meaning of a term to people, but they do not in themselves help to explicate it. To make good use of metaphors you have to know in what respects they are supposed to hold: in what ways are humans animals, in what ways is my love like a red red rose? But until someone provides a clear and adequate definition of both terms in the simile or metaphor, it is impossible to answer the previous question. I can make sense of "The Assyrian came down like the wolf on the fold" only because I have a pretty clear idea of what the Assyrian is up to in the poem and what is meant by a "wolf coming down on the fold." But how can I extract the significant part of the statement that giftedness is like the "yeast in beer," if I know nothing about giftedness? Knowing that "making love is like walking in a field of flowers on a sunny day," while it may convey something important and true, is not going to help one understand what making love is, let alone how to recognise it or do it.[4]

A sociological definition, if it is scrupulously researched and well founded, can be extremely useful. To understand exactly what is involved in the Western idea of democracy, as revealed in institutional practice and social behaviour, and to see how this differs from the Soviet idea of democracy, is illuminating in itself and leads to a relatively specific account of the two concepts. However, it may well be that democracy as defined in our practices is not the same thing as our idea of democracy, whether we recognise as much or not. And we certainly don't want to be committed to defining all our concepts, particularly those that stand for things we value, in terms of how they have been institutionalised. We don't, for example, want to be told that marriage is to be defined solely in terms of the pattern of marriage as it exists today. (At any rate, I don't.) There is a more particular objection to be made to the idea of a sociological definition of giftedness, and that is that, precisely because there are conflicting and confused ideas of it about, our practice is similarly confused and contradictory, and one doubts whether a uniform and coherent definition could be extracted from observation of what we do in the name of giftedness.

While we are on this subject it would be advisable to review and dismiss four other practices which, though they are not actually types of definition at all, are sometimes treated as if they were or accepted as substitutes for definition. Tracing the etymology of a word, though it may throw light on its contemporary meaning, does not necessarily do so, and cannot be used as an argument to justify the definition of a word. Happiness, for example, derives etymologically from the word "hap" meaning chance, accident, or fortune (a meaning preserved in "happenstance"). But it is not the case that "happiness" today means "a sense of satisfaction occasioned by chance," and it would be idle to insist that that is what it should mean, when it is not what people understand by the term.[5] (This point has some relevance to giftedness, which clearly does have historical association with the idea of natural endowment. But does it necessarily have that association today? One rather suspects that one problem is that it does for some and not for others.)

Listing signs or symptoms that may indicate that a person is happy, intelligent, miserable, or relaxed is not the same thing as defining happiness, intelligence, misery, or the state of relaxation. At least, it is not necessarily so. We have to go carefully here, partly because the listing of traits or behaviours that suggest the quality in question is very common with reference to giftedness, and partly because of the widespread acceptance of the practice of providing behavioural definitions in educational research.

If a concept is itself essentially behavioural, if, that is to say, the word in question refers to a behaviour or set of behaviours, then obviously a list of behaviours may both define the term and provide a check list of signs that indicate the concept in question. Smiling, for example, can be defined in terms of observable physiological changes, and we might also choose to say that, if one's mouth is invisible but one's eyes are lit up, that is a sign that one is smiling. ("Behaviour" is interpreted fairly widely in this sort of context.)

There are some people who maintain that all concepts are properly defined in exclusively behavioural terms.[6] They define happiness entirely in terms of behaviours such as smiling, laughing, and eagerly engaging in activities. They do not do this simply for the practical purpose of being able to make firm categorisations of people as happy or unhappy. They sincerely believe that there is nothing beyond such behaviours. In no sense is there anything to happiness above and beyond such observable features. They thus deny that there are feelings, insights, understandings, perceptions, and sensations that neither are, nor are reducible to, behaviours, and they deny that any of our concepts, such as happiness, friendship, love, hate, and beauty are bound up with these non-behavioural phenomena, and as a result cannot be defined exclusively in behavioural terms either. Since, however, it is very rare, I will say no more about this extreme view.

By contrast, a very common view, thanks to the dominance of the scientific paradigm which requires that we observe, control, and replicate when researching, is that it is necessary to provide behavioural definitions of concepts that are acknowledged not to be behavioural in essence, for methodological purposes. Granted that "happiness" is not properly defined in terms of sparkling eyes, curved mouths, avowals that one is happy, and committed behaviour, if we are going to find out what makes people happy or what kinds of people are happy, then we have to treat happiness as if it could be defined in this way, otherwise we would be faced with the problem of observing the unobservable. The extent to which this view is ingrained in our thinking is indicated by the ubiquity of this kind of definition in educational research, the overwhelmingly greater attention given to so-called systematic, formal, or quantitative research than to ethnographic and other informal types of research, and the continued acceptance of taxonomies such as Bloom's and commitment to the idea of framing objectives in behavioural terms.[7] Nonetheless, the assumption that we have to use behavioural definitions for research purposes is false, and the damage done to our thinking and practice by accepting the assumption serious. There is no need to suggest that one should never adopt a behavioural definition or frame objectives in this way. But it is not true that one cannot observe or monitor that which is not behaviourally defined, and it is true that if one's research is based upon a behavioural definition of something that is not essentially behavioural, then one's research is into something different from what it claims to be research into. And that seems rather a drawback.

If it is the case that a concept refers to something that is not directly visible, then the researcher cannot see it with his naked eye. That is, after all, what "not directly visible" means. But, provided that the researcher knows exactly what he means by a word or what a concept involves, he can locate it by other, indirect, means. In the case of happiness, for example, there is a strong case for saying that it makes no sense to claim that a person is happy if he does not think he is, or to deny that he is, if he thinks he is.[8] If that were accepted (and whether it should be accepted is something that can only be decided by working out what "happiness" means, and whether what it means entails this conclusion), then it would follow that, provided everyone concerned agreed on what "happiness" meant and they were not lying (which are no more difficult conditions to meet than many others faced by empirical researchers), one could carry out a great deal of illuminating empirical research into causes of happiness and categories of happy people, without going anywhere near a behavioural definition. To take another example, in order to establish whether girls or boys are generally better educated at the age of seventeen, you do not have to define education in such behavioural terms as the number of hours spent in class, performance on standardised achievement tests, and familiarity with a list of great books. You can work with a definition couched in terms of concepts such as judgement and understanding, and locate these qualities by exercising your own judgement and understanding, provided that your definition of these terms is absolutely clear.

Conversely, if your research is based exclusively on smiling faces and the like, then that is what you are finding out about, not happiness. In order to relate it to the latter it will be necessary to establish something about the relationship between smiling faces and happiness. And that is logically inconceivable unless you are prepared to define happiness itself in the manner appropriate to its nature. (One obviously could not claim to have established a correlation between smiling and being happy, if one had not formulated a clear and acceptable definition of happiness in the light of which to conduct one's research.)

The consequence of our ignoring these simple facts is that educational theory and research are replete with "behavioural definitions" of concepts that are not true definitions of the concepts in question, but which are treated as if they were. It may be claimed, for example, that the research shows that the warmth of a teacher towards children is a very important factor. But, if the research was actually conducted by reference to various observable behaviours, then it does not show that a teacher has to be or feel warm; on the contrary, it shows that he has to engage in certain behaviours, regardless of what he actually feels.[9]

To return to giftedness, we may note that it is very common to find lists "summarising the characteristics of the gifted," including such items as:

1) The gifted develop their cognitive and basic skills early; they possess good memories.
2) They have special talents in one or more areas.
3) They are frequently curious.
4) They have a creative style.
5) They tend to deal at a high level of abstraction.
6) They are often interested in philosophical questions (e.g., "is the universe infinite?").
7) They are not always satisfied with rules and regulations.
8) They frequently have a unique sense of humour.[10]

Now where do such lists spring from? The fact that they are usually hedged about with qualifications ("tend to," "not always," "often," "gifted children display some or all of these qualities") suggests strongly that they are indeed meant to be no more than lists of indications that an individual may be gifted. But some at least are plausible criteria for defining giftedness. If a child did not display special talent in one or more areas, why on earth should we consider him gifted? Can one conceive of an incurious gifted person? Well, of course, that rather depends on what we mean by "gifted." What do we mean by "gifted"? If we have no clear answer to that, how could we possibly have established that a sense of humour frequently goes with being gifted, and how can we decide whether curiosity is a defining characteristic or a quality that is contingently related to giftedness? Thus, a list of signs that may betoken giftedness is to be distinguished from a definition of giftedness, and, in the absence of a definition, it is impossible to see how any such list could legitimately have been arrived at.

Many concepts in education are effectively defined by the instruments used to locate and measure them. The creativity and the intelligence that many educationalists refer to are one and the same thing as the ability to achieve a certain standard on particular tests. This procedure cannot be accepted as a way to define the actual concepts of creativity and intelligence, unless it were the case, as it is not, that there has been independent reasoning to establish the plausibility of such definitions. One cannot treat the business of setting up an observation schedule that allows one to count the number of kisses, boxes of chocolates, other presents, and words of endearment that one person gives to another, as engaging in the task of defining "love." "Love" does not mean doing these particular things, and if I want to engage in the task of arguing for a definition, I have to talk about why I am accepting some symptoms as criteria and rejecting others; I have to give reasons for presuming that "to love" means, amongst other things, giving people kisses. The setting up of an instrument that *de facto* incorporates criteria is not an instance of engaging in the business of defining. It merely stipulates a definition by arbitrary fiat.

Nor should we confuse talking about the causes, sources, or contingently related aspects of a phenomenon, whether these be social, psychological, physiological, or neurological factors, with defining the concept in question. When Hazlitt says that "the definition of genius is that it acts unconsciously" he is not in fact defining it, but making a claim about its source.[11] When people talk about the social conditions that produce giftedness, or the psychological type of gifted children, or the physiological and neurological states that accompany giftedness, they are doing something different from defining it, and something that they cannot seriously claim to be able to do in the absence of a clear understanding of what it is. Nor should we be satisfied with aphorisms of the type "genius is the infinite capacity for taking pains" or "genius is patience," for these likewise tell us not what genius is, in the sense of defining it, but how it comes about that people do the things that cause them to be accounted a genius.

All of the above may be regarded as ways of avoiding the need to proffer a definition of the term. What is needed is a statement of the criteria whereby we may ascertain whether someone is gifted, of the same type as the statement that a horse is "a solid-hoofed, herbivorous, perisodactyl quadruped, having a flowing mane and tail," such that, provided the definition contains no further terms that need explanation, we are in a position to determine whether a particular animal is a horse or not. The question of whether the criteria are themselves all readily observable, as is the case with horse, is quite distinct. If we are talking about a concept such as love, fairly obviously some criteria will not be directly observable. But they cannot be wished away. That's the way love is. An adequate definition of the term "giftedness" would be one that clearly enunciated the criteria that have to be met for someone to count as gifted, that fully and clearly explained the meaning of any other terms, such as "imaginative," that may come into the definition, that does not contain any internal incoherence or contradiction (for example, gifted people cannot both be exceptional and ubiquitous), and that does not have entailments which we cannot accept, (for example, if gifted people are to some extent naturally endowed, then we must accept that some people can never be particularly gifted).

We do not as yet have any such definition. This is widely recognised, but there is a curious reluctance to rectify the situation. McCluskey and Walker, for example, think that there is a "certain uniqueness about the phenomenon that defies analysis and renders any short definition somewhat sterile" and conclude that it is "a vague and intangible concept."[12] But there is some confusion here. It may be that "any short definition" would be sterile, but if that is so, it is because it is a complex concept requiring lengthy elaboration and explication. Why can we not have that? If it is intangible in the sense of by definition not capable of being fully explained in directly observable terms, then we must face up to that fact and explain it in the appropriate intangible terms. The fact that, for instance, the concept of happiness clearly has to be explained in intangible terms, in this sense, does not make it impossible to define (though it may make it more difficult to define). If "intangible" is taken to mean something like "indefinable" or indeed, the other word they use, "vague," then we have to face that fact too and do something about it. If a concept is confessedly vague, we cannot do much with it. If we cannot clarify it, we must use other concepts, for we cannot make confident claims about concepts that are not clear. Some concepts are certainly a great deal harder to get to grips with than others, some may even be interpreted in very different ways by different people, but no concept literally "defies analysis" unless it is incoherent in some way. (The concept of a "square circle," for instance, does defy analysis.) Assuming we are talking about something intelligible, then either we know what we are talking about or we don't. We can hardly rest satisfied with a lot of practical prescription for education resting on a concept that we acknowledge we have not adequately analysed, for that is to say that we know what we ought to do to foster giftedness, when we don't know what we are talking about when we refer to giftedness.

McCluskey and Walker also seem guilty of a common confusion between vagueness and generality. They believe that "every gifted child is unique." That may be true; just as every happy individual's happiness may take a specific unique form, so different people may be gifted in different ways. But, if that is so, it follows only that "gifted" is a general term, as are "goodness," "beauty," and "human." General terms do not have to be vague, however, any more than specific terms do. "Human," for instance, is clearly not a vague term, and while "goodness" and "beauty" are undoubtedly complex and difficult concepts such that many people's conceptions of them are vague, those whose particular interest it is to think about them are precisely concerned with clarifying them. So far as "gifted" goes, it probably is the case that for many people it is little more than a general term meaning "highly talented." But if that is so, then the term is not vague. Far from defying analysis, its meaning is very clear and straightforward. Unfortunately, if that is what "gifted" is taken to mean, it will not be a particularly useful term, since it is readily apparent that individuals may display varying degrees of talent, in various activities, in various ways, for a variety of different reasons. We would therefore need to concentrate on the myriad different species of giftedness to see in each case what we can discover about it, rather than to attempt to research giftedness itself. In just the same way knowing only what is true of all humans *qua* humans will not get us far. To determine policy and practice, we need to know about different types of human being, and about different aspects of being human.

II: The concept of giftedness

Most attempts to define "giftedness" go astray in one or more of the ways we have considered. For instance, Hobbs begins his foreword to *The Gifted Child, the Family and the Community*, which is entitled "who are the gifted?," by substituting the different question "how does one recognise a gifted child?"[13] His answer is that "generally [they] may be taller, heavier, and healthier than average children . . . may have a wider range of interests, and their moral and ethical values may be on a different level . . . [they are] often voracious readers." But provision of such a checklist, as we have seen, is no substitute for definition. Quite apart from the confessedly tentative nature of these claims, one must ask how anyone has arrived at these judgements in the absence of a definition. Abraham offers a checklist of 30 signs that indicate "considerable potential" in a child who scores well on at least half of them.[14] They include starting to talk and walk before the so-called average child does, having interests that are varied and spontaneous, having numerous hobbies, collecting things in an orderly manner, reacting to comments in a way that indicates a real meeting of minds, and being impatient and rebellious. But how could he conclude that a gifted child is likely to do such things, in the absence of a clear view of what a gifted person is? Or is it rather that these are supposed to be defining characteristics? Is the claim that we have evidence that gifted people usually do these things or that this is the kind of thing we mean by being gifted? In either case such a list is of little practical use given its tentative nature, the fact that it is neither exhaustive nor a list of necessary symptoms, and that many of the items require considerable analysis and interpretation themselves.   How does one determine, for example, that a child is commenting in a way that indicates "a real meeting of minds"?

Miller recognises that the implication of the typical dictionary definition is that "giftedness cannot be acquired" (since it refers to natural endowments).[15]   To some this would suggest that "giftedness" is an inappropriate word for what they are really interested in. But Miller prefers to redefine the word to suit his conviction that giftedness can be acquired. This is a somewhat peculiar tactic: if the word "gifted" means "having natural endowments" in normal usage, but we want to talk about learned and acquired characteristics rather than natural endowments, then why do we not do so? Why not simply ignore the word "giftedness"? Miller goes on to adopt Witty's view that a gifted and talented child is one "whose performance in any valuable line of human activity is consistently or repeatedly remarkable."[16] There is something to be said for this definition, even though it involves decisively changing the meaning of the word from that given in the dictionary, because it removes some of the problems associated with the dictionary definition. Giftedness in this sense is clearly something to be assessed by reference to achievement and performance, the question of natural endowments and the question of whether giftedness is a generic quality both becoming irrelevant. But if this is what giftedness is taken to mean, it follows that most of the claims made about giftedness have nothing to do with the matter, for most of the research on which claims are based was conducted in the light of a different view of giftedness, and there is no reason to presume that performance on I.Q. tests, the ability to walk at an early age, possessing a sense of humour and so on, have any bearing on whether a person is capable of consistently performing some important task in a remarkable way.

The U. S. office of education definition is worth commenting on. According to this "Gifted and talented children are those identified by professionally qualified persons who by nature of outstanding abilities are capable of high performance . . . children capable of high performance include those with demonstrated achievement and/or potential ability in any of the following areas: general intellectual ability, specific academic aptitude, leadership ability, visual and performing arts, creative or productive thinking, psychomotor ability."[17] The fundamental problem here lies in the ambiguity of the phrases "by nature of outstanding ability" and "potential ability." Is the implication that the ability of the gifted is a natural endowment or not? What is meant by "potential," and how is it judged if it is distinct from achievement?

It is possible that all that is meant is that some children can be seen to perform better than others in one or more of the distinct areas of activity mentioned. If that is what is meant, we face a problem in that the areas referred to are of different logical types: developing a good academic mind, developing psychomotor ability, and developing creative thinking are very different kinds of thing, and may have to be approached in radically different kinds of way. In some cases it is very far from clear what is meant: what, for example, is creative thinking and how does one either develop it or recognise it?[18] But, more to the immediate point, if this is all that is meant, the use of the term giftedness, and the associated idea that we are looking for a special category of person, is highly and unnecessarily misleading. It would appear that we are simply talking about distinguishing between more and less successful students in various areas, and that has been the task of the teacher since time began. The implication of this interpretation would be that "the professionally qualified persons" who make the judgements should be the teachers, those whose job it is to say that certain students have done good academic work, proved able leaders in the school, displayed creative talent, and so forth.

If, on the other hand, the suggestion is that we are looking out for individuals who, by virtue of some innate capacity, will prove to excel in one or more of those areas, even though there is no evidence of their achievement as yet, we face a totally different claim and one that begs some huge and crucial questions: are there innate capacities that significantly determine what an individual could hope to achieve in areas of leadership, visual and performing arts, and academic work? If there are, how can we successfully monitor these capacities? Are they generic capacities or specific to the various areas? On any such interpretation as this, the "definition" clearly presupposes the adequacy of things such as intelligence and creativity tests and implies that the "professionally qualified" persons referred to will be such people as educational psychologists. The way that most districts have responded to the definition indicates that they have · adopted this latter interpretation. But, as we shall see, there is little reason to accept its implications. In either case the U. S. office of education has not provided an adequate definition.

What has to be borne in mind is that the lack of clarity to be found in attempted definitions of giftedness necessarily runs through all the particular claims made about giftedness. Ann Weiner, for instance, tells us specific things about the reasoning and problem-solving needs and personal- and social-adjustment needs of gifted children.[19] But closer scrutiny reveals that she is actually telling us about the needs as she perceives them of 32 children who were brought to her and her colleagues by parents who wanted them to be "tested for giftedness." It is not simply that they therefore may not have been gifted. The sad truth is that there is no way of knowing whether they were. As Whitmore observes "identification procedures, in effect, define giftedness."[20] In other words, all the data about the characteristics of gifted children, their performance, their distribution through the population, the effects on them of different kinds of programming, have to be set aside. For the data are based on a variety of different pieces of research employing different concepts of giftedness, each of which may be incoherent or in some other respect inadequate.

In practice, the predominant view is probably that which equates giftedness with performance on tests of intelligence and creativity, perhaps supplemented by other standardised achievement tests. Characteristically, such tests are preferred by educational researchers to teacher assessments of student giftedness, because the latter, it is claimed, are shown to be extremely unreliable. Needless to say, closer scrutiny reveals that teacher assessments have been presumed to be unreliable because they do not have a strong positive correlation with the findings of standardised tests. We are caught in an extremely vicious, and rather dumb, circle: no serious attempt to work out what we mean by calling someone gifted is made. Instead we effectively and without consideration or argument decree that to be gifted is to perform well on certain tests. Any evidence that some people might be gifted even though they perform poorly on the tests, such as teacher assessment, is dismissed, thus necessarily confirming the definition. We will never escape this circle until we face up to the question of what we mean by "giftedness," "intelligence," and "creativity," and then consider the plausibility of the assumption that so-called tests of intelligence, creativity, and giftedness actually have anything to do with them. (Incidentally, the fact that teacher assessments are to some extent unreliable on their own terms, e.g., inconsistent, does not affect this argument. It may be the case both that teacher assessments are the only logically appropriate way to appraise giftedness, if it is defined in a certain way, and that their assessments will inevitably be imperfect in various respects.)

III: Nature or nurture?

The problem then is this: we have a lot of talk about giftedness, a number of ways of picking gifted people out, and a number of proposals and programmes for dealing with them. We also have a number of attempts to define the term. What we do not have is any agreement on what we are talking about, and no definition with which I am familiar has been of the right kind. That is to say, we do not have an account of giftedness that clearly sets out the criteria that have to be met for someone to count as gifted. But we need that, not only for the practical purpose of trying to pick out the gifted, but also to make research into the gifted intelligible. In the absence of a clear and uniform definition, we must question all research claims made about the gifted, for how can we make use of a researcher's claim to have discovered that gifted people are often the children of single parent families, if he has not stated clearly what he takes a gifted person to be? The only definitions that have been provided that are unambiguous are behavioural ones that are in themselves unconvincing. The most common examples of this type treat giftedness as equivalent to a good performance on various standardised tests, but it has not been shown that giftedness bears any relation to such performance, and it is not apparent why we should value such performance, whatever it is called. It is not true that we have to define giftedness in terms of directly observable behaviour. What we have to have is a clear idea of the concept, couched in terms of unambiguous criteria. When we have that, we have to consider whether what we are dealing with is in fact directly observable. If it is not, we have to make judgements as best we can in the light of the criteria.

The emphasis in writings about giftedness on how to teach the gifted, what arrangements to make for them, and what curriculum to provide can now be seen to be bizarre in the extreme. In the absence of a clear understanding of what giftedness is how can we make claims about how to treat gifted people?

One of the most perplexing problems in the area of giftedness is that of attempting to sort out what assumptions are being made about the question of whether it is an innate or an acquired quality. Certain authors do tackle the issue of whether giftedness is a product of nature or nurture directly, generally making reference to familiar research relating to intelligence, particularly that involving identical twins. Many adopt the reasonable conclusion that both heredity and environment are involved in the origins and development of intelligence and giftedness. It is arguable that environmental factors come into play even in the womb, and it is impossible to ignore a mass of *prima facie* evidence that all sorts of environmental factors, including teaching, make a difference to the individual's level of intelligence and, in so far as it is the same kind of thing, giftedness.[21] Yet, it is also reasonable to suggest that certain physiological conditions are necessary to the development of intelligence and giftedness (although that is not to say that being intelligent means meeting those conditions), and that a certain genetic endowment may likewise be necessary to various degrees of intellectual development. Brain damage, for instance, can clearly affect one's chances of becoming intelligent or gifted, and genetic factors may play a part in determining the state of one's brain. That being so, the view that nature and nurture both play a part is sensible. But it has the important corollary for educators that, while some may be particularly disposed towards development as gifted individuals, and while some may be effectively debarred from such development by inherited limitations, in general we may assume that the extent to which individuals develop their intelligence and giftedness is dependent on how their environment is shaped.

But, despite the fact that some people explicitly take this position, the bulk of our theory and practice surrounding giftedness, including very often the work of those who maintain this position, is confused and sometimes straightforwardly contradictory. For, if giftedness is presumed to be to any marked extent the consequence of how we bring children up and educate them, why do we lay stress on the idea of their potential? Granted that a severely brain-damaged child may be said to have no potential for giftedness, are we really in a position to distinguish amongst the majority of children between those who have potential and those who do not? If we are, then the implication must be that innate factors are crucial and far more significant than environmental factors. We should have to conclude that giftedness is on a par with physical stature, where there does seem some reason to suppose that individuals are destined to achieve a certain stature, provided that they are properly fed and exercised, but that all the food and exercise in the world won't make a tall person out of one who was genetically programmed to be small. Not only do we not have good grounds for assuming that intelligence or giftedness are like stature in this way (although to establish this point we would need to arrive at adequate definitions of the terms), but it is evident that such a presumption is at odds with the idea that giftedness is to a marked extent the product of environment. To put the point simply: if giftedness is largely acquired, focussing on potential is largely irrelevant, even if it were possible to detect it. If, on the other hand, it is largely a matter of innate potential, then we need to establish how to recognise potential and we should cease to talk as if the environmental issues were particularly important.[22]

Other indications that giftedness is widely presumed to be essentially a matter of innate natural endowment are the tendency to stress early signs of giftedness in children (such as learning to walk at an unusually young age), the widely accepted view that only "somewhere between 3 and 5 percent of the school population might be considered gifted,"[23] the notion of "the underachieving gifted child," and the very use of the word "gifted" with its clear implications of natural endowment in ordinary language.

If gifted adults are to any marked extent the product of education and upbringing, then it seems wildly implausible to imagine that whether people walk at an early age has got anything to do with the matter. It might be so, of course. God in his wisdom may have ordained it that only those who walk at an early age are capable of becoming gifted through education. But there is certainly no evidence that this is the case, and, as I say, it is on the face of it wildly implausible.

If giftedness is to any marked extent the product of education and upbringing, there seems no reason at all to assume that only a minimal percentage of people can become gifted. Here one could argue that if "gifted" is to retain connotations of being special and unusual, then, by definition, it has to be reserved for a minority. But there is a considerable difference between saying, as we would with "exceptional," that it is a term we confine to those who are pre-eminent, and saying, as we tend to do with "gifted," that as a matter of contingent fact we believe there are only a small number of such people. "Giftedness" may be exceptional, but it does not appear to mean that; it appears to have something to do with being creative, handling abstract concepts at a young age, being interested in philosophical questions, and a number of other specific abilities, none of which need necessarily be confined to 5 percent rather than 95 percent of the population. Only if giftedness is essentially innate and fixed, would it make sense to assume that a certain percentage of people are gifted and there is nothing we can do to alter the figure.

An "underachieving gifted" person is a straightforward contradiction in terms in so far as being gifted is a product of education and upbringing, for to have become gifted through these or any other environmental channels is to have achieved. Only if giftedness is the name of a determinate innate quality, a potential to achieve, does it make sense to claim that a person is gifted and underachieving.

It would seem, then, that while some state that giftedness is partly developed and acquired through education and upbringing, a great deal of the talk we engage in about it suggests the opposite: that we are dealing with an innate endowment which, if recognised, can at best be provided with a suitable environment in which to flourish, and which cannot be cultivated in those, the vast majority, who are born without it. Whatever our conclusion on this question may be, it is rather important to have one, for it makes some difference to the kind of programming for gifted students that makes sense. Should we presume that we are providing the kind of environment to allow their innate giftedness to flourish (rather as we provide light and water for the plant and leave it to do the rest), or providing the kind of educational environment that will help to make people become gifted (as we provide piano lessons to enable people to play the piano, regardless of what their genetic inheritance happens to be)?

It would not be reasonable to imagine that we could settle this issue, in terms of establishing the precise nature and weighting of innate and acquired qualities and characteristics, here and now. It is, after all, a long-standing, complex, and highly contentious issue.[24] One might wish that writers on giftedness would show more interest in and understanding of the subtlety and complexity of the debate, but one cannot expect them necessarily to have resolved it. However, it can be pointed out and emphasised that for practical purposes a clear and important conclusion can be drawn. While much of the rhetoric about giftedness is predicated on the idea that it is innate, reasoning shows that, though there may be some innate factors at work, our attention should be focussed on those aspects that are acquired through the environment, particularly through education. We should proceed as if giftedness were the product of learning and the environment, even if in some respects it is determined by innate factors. That is so because education and other environmental factors clearly play a major part in the emergence of gifted people and those are factors over which we have control. Insofar as some preconditions of giftedness are innate there is nothing we can do about them. Talk of taking the appropriate action to ensure that such innate potential is not wasted translates into talk about nurturing, which is to say talk about environmental factors. But in any case, it is necessarily the case that environmental factors play a significant role in the emergence of giftedness, given that it is defined in terms of doing certain things well.

One may point to certain examples of gifted individuals, such as Mozart,

Hummel, and John Stuart Mill, whose youthful precosity at first glance appears to keep the case for regarding giftedness as a natural endowment alive. But closer consideration leads to the conclusion that this is not so. In Mozart's case, his musical talent, evident in his earliest years, is not matched by any other obvious talents. A gifted musician he may have been, in a number of possible senses, but a gifted person he was not. Hummel was gifted in more ways, but his talent in the sphere of writing, like John Stuart Mill's intellectual talent, has to be seen as significantly the product of education. It really doesn't matter, for practical purposes, whether their genetic make-up was remarkable and related to their subsequent achievement, for what is certain is that one does not become a gifted philosopher without doing philosophy. It is worth adding that such people were from the moment of birth subjected to an environment that drove them towards achievement in their respective fields, and that, in any case, the children whom we tend to classify and treat as gifted bear very little resemblance in point of perceived characteristics and achievements to them.

It may certainly be said that individuals such as Hummel, who proved to be gifted in a number of areas, provide *prima facie* evidence of the existence of some kind of innate drive. Such a drive might be identified with Renzulli's "cluster of traits" associated with "high levels of task commitment."[25] But it remains debatable whether this drive or cluster of traits is innate, since it is equally plausible both in terms of logic and the empirical evidence to suggest that it is the product of environmental factors such as encouragement, reward, and expectation. Furthermore, even if there is an innate disposition to do the kinds of thing, including applying oneself energetically, that lead to the display of giftedness, once it is admitted that an unsuitable environment may destroy or render the disposition impotent, we are back with the inescapable consequence that what we do is what matters. Hummel's drive therefore needs to be nurtured and he has to learn things in order to direct that drive into gifted activity. It is also evidently the case that we have no plausible way in which to identify either his giftedness or his drive other than by reference to his gifted performance, for the only evidence that people have drive or commitment is that they exhibit it in relation to some activity. Trying to determine whether the fourteen-year-old Hummel is gifted by referring to the typical check list of signs of giftedness will not get us far. In the first place the guide lines for interpreting such lists are far too vague to lead to any certain deductions. In the second place it remains quite unproven that any of the items, other than those that are part of what being gifted means, are symptoms of giftedness. In the third place, as it happens, Hummel betrayed none of the symptoms, so far as we know. Nor would the use of I.Q. tests or creativity tests have helped, since there is no evidence to support the contention that gifted composers necessarily perform well on these tests. On the other hand, there is one test we could have applied to Hummel: we could have listened to his first piano sonata, completed in his fourteenth year.

Hummel may be said to have had a drive and a facility to do a number of things besides compose. But even in his case we have no reason to suppose that he would have been equally disposed to commit himself eagerly to fishing, the study of nuclear physics, or running an industry. Most "gifted" people are more like Mozart in that their drive and facility is relatively limited. Nor is this surprising, for one's drive can only take one so far: to shine as a historian, as a leader of men, or as a used car salesman, involves, in each case, particular kinds of understanding. Whatever the truth may be about the nature and extent of natural endowment, the recognition and development of giftedness require focussing on what individuals have done and can do by way of learning.

IV: The erroneous assumptions

I turn now to the question of what lies behind all this uncertainty and lack of clarity surrounding giftedness, over and above the crucial fact that we do not have an adequate definition of the term. Why do we find it so difficult to explain exactly what we mean by giftedness, in such a way that the confusions and obscurities noted would be resolved and we would know what criteria have to be met for someone to be properly classified as gifted?

Part of the answer surely lies in the dominance of the scientific paradigm and a corresponding lack of philosophical competence and awareness. When we do provide a clear definition, we do so in terms of observable or directly testable abilities, because we have become unthinkingly imbued with the idea that that is the only kind of definition that is clear, objective, and useful, and we lack the philosophical acumen to see that that is not true and to tackle the job of providing a more suitable analysis of the concept. The definition of education as "the intentional transmission of worthwhile knowledge, that involves cognitive perspective and is not inert, in morally acceptable ways" is, for example, perfectly clear (though it might require more detailed elaboration for those who are unfamiliar with it) despite the fact that it is not couched in terms of directly observable behaviours or measurable characteristics.[26] Whether it is "objective" depends upon what "objective" is taken to mean. Certainly it is not "objective" in the sense of directly observable and measurable, which is effectively what "objective" is sometimes taken to mean, thanks again to the dominance of the scientific paradigm. But that is a most peculiar idea of objectivity, and to presume that definitions should be objective in this sense is to beg the question at issue. On the other hand, if objective is taken in its more usual sense of "undistorted by emotion or personal bias" and "relating to the way things are rather than how we feel about them," there is no necessary reason to assume that this definition of education is not objective. It may be the case that this concept is more indeterminate than some others. It is, for example, clear that, even if we accept the definition given, there is room for disagreement on what constitutes worthwhile knowledge, and it is quite possible that two individuals should both be accounted educated despite the fact of being possessed of different knowledge. It is certainly the case that education is a normative term, which is to say that part of what we do when we describe someone as educated is indicate our favourable appraisal of that person, and that therefore to judge someone to be educated is partly evaluative. But once again the fact that value judgements and general rather than specific criteria are involved, while it may make such definitions harder to frame and substantiate, does not necessarily make them arbitrary or subjective in the sense of the product of emotion, bias, personal prejudice, or chance. They may still be assessed in terms of objective standards of reasoning.

As to whether it is useful, that depends on what we want it to be useful for. It is not particularly useful for the purposes of trying to make direct instantaneous observations of people to see whether they are educated or of trying to measure how educated they are. But then "being educated" isn't that kind of phenomenon, so why should we allow ourselves to be driven to misdefining it, in order to enable us to make instant observations and measurements? The definition is useful, however, extremely useful, for the purposes of coming to a clear and accurate understanding of what education is and talking and acting intelligibly in respect of it. If we were in general more receptive to and capable of producing this kind of definition where appropriate, much of the muddled talk about giftedness would have been avoided.

A second major factor that accounts for many of the questionable and unclear things that we say about giftedness is the erroneous assumption that the names of mental concepts refer to generic qualities. Thus, intelligence, creativity, and giftedness are the names of faculties that we possess or lack to some degree, just as we possess internal organs such as the liver, the kidneys, and the heart, or external qualities such as dark hair and legs. The first thing to be said about this view is that it is simply a mistake to assume that every word must refer to some entity, and in the case of human attributes it is a further mistake to confuse mental concepts with physiological and physical ones. We have, in a literal sense, brains, eyes, and hearts. But we do not have imaginations, understandings, intelligences, or giftednesses in this sense, any more than we have a broken heart in the literal sense when our lovers reject us. There is no entity giftedness: there is no part of our body or brain that is giftedness. If somebody has a problem with his liver we can operate on it or replace it. But if somebody is having problems with being gifted, we cannot similarly operate on his giftedness. There is nothing there to operate on. In extreme cases we operate on a brain that may be effectively inhibiting a display of giftedness or indeed normal intellectual activity; but this is rare, and in any case involves operating on a physical organ that is necessary to gifted or any other kind of mental activity, and not on giftedness itself.

The word "giftedness" is an abstract noun that we have introduced as the name of a fictional entity, in order to enable us to talk about such things as the causes, the origins, the sources, the needs, and the demographic distribution of people who are gifted. And people who are gifted are people who do things in a talented way.[27] That is to say, they are people who are noteworthy in that they do things particularly well, which in turn means that they meet the standards of excellence appropriate to particular activities to an inordinate degree. There may or may not be physiological or neurological conditions that are necessary to or detrimental to an individual's capacity to do things well, just as there may or may not be genetic or environmental factors that increase or decrease the chances of someone doing things well. But we are not referring to those factors when we use the word "giftedness." "Giftedness" does not mean "a certain neurological state of the brain." What we mean by a gifted person is one who is exceptionally talented, and the only logical ground for ascribing giftedness to a person is that he does things exceptionally well. One obvious implication of this is that, whatever may be the case about certain innate factors, physiological or neurological, hereditary or acquired, which may limit or increase the likelihood of a person becoming gifted, giftedness itself is at least partly the product of learning, for one has to learn both what the standards of excellence are in various activities and how to do particular things well.

The second point to be made about the assumption that giftedness is a generic quality also follows directly from the meaning of giftedness. It is that giftedness is *not* a generic quality. That is to say, people are not necessarily gifted in all or even many respects; they may, for instance, be merely gifted piano players or gifted golfers. It is indeed a general term, for a person can be gifted in one or more of a variety of different activities in each of which their giftedness will take a specific form, determined by the standards of excellence appropriate to the activity in question. Each particular display of giftedness is a species of the general attribute, just as a beautiful painting, a beautiful symphony, and a beautiful woman are all instances of the general term "beautiful," but take a particular form in each case.

But a general term is not the same thing as a generic term, and giftedness is not a generic term as, for example, compassion is: we do not call a person compassionate if he is only compassionate towards his children or his next door neighbour. To be credited with compassion one must display compassion in one's dealings with people generally, and, though the circumstances that call for it may vary and what one specifically does to indicate one's compassion may vary, the nature of compassion itself does not alter. This is because "compassion" is defined in terms of feelings of pity for the suffering or misfortunes of others, rather than in terms of what one may do to show that one has such feelings, and all instances of compassion are alike in involving such feelings. But giftedness is not defined in terms of specific criteria that are always necessarily involved; it is defined in terms of standards of excellence that necessarily vary. All compassionate people should, by definition, experience the same kinds of feeling in all of a variety of situations; for to be compassionate means to experience certain kinds of feeling in all of a variety of certain kinds of situation. But all gifted people do not necessarily display this kind of uniformity, because being gifted does not mean having particular kinds of experience or doing particular kinds of thing. It means doing whatever you do do particularly well, and what is involved in doing things well varies from activity to activity.

On the face of it this point seems sometimes to be acknowledged by those who discuss giftedness. The U. S. office of education account of giftedness, for example, explicitly says that giftedness may be displayed in any of various areas, "singly or in combination," such as general intellectual ability, leadership ability, and creative or productive thinking. Getzels, in the same spirit, widens the scope of the concept by adding the further areas "talent for mechanical achievement, talent for social achievement, and talent for altruistic achievement."[28] And it is probably fair to say that most writers on the subject would endorse McCluskey and Walker's explicit statement that "there are many kinds of giftedness . . . people are not all the same; they have different kinds of abilities. That is, there are many forms of 'giftedness'."[29]

However, these straightforward and seemingly explicit statements are contradicted by the way in which these and other authors then proceed to talk about giftedness. If it is agreed that there are many kinds of giftedness, then why do we concentrate our energy on talking about giftedness, rather than about gifted mathematicians, gifted historians, gifted hostesses, and gifted soccer players? If it is agreed that there are many kinds of giftedness, then why is most of the argument about curricula for the gifted focussed on organisational questions, such as whether they should be segregated, streamed, or provided with enrichment classes, rather than about what areas to develop giftedness in and what kind of curriculum would be suitable for gifted physicists, gifted historians, and so forth? If it is agreed that there are many kinds of giftedness, then why do programmes for teachers of the gifted concentrate on generic courses on "the nature and needs of the gifted," "the education of the gifted," and "materials and methods in the education of the gifted," rather than on courses in "teaching gifted historians," "education for gifted scientists," and "materials and methods in the education of gifted mathematicians"?[30] Why is so much emphasis placed on general signs or indicators of giftedness, such as attention span, speed of learning, wide variety of interests, and early development, rather than on demonstrated ability in particular areas? Why is so much weight placed on tests of intelligence and creativity that are conceived of as tests of generic ability? Why is Renzulli's view that "giftedness consists of an interaction among three basic clusters of human traits—these clusters being above average general abilities, high levels of task commitment, and high levels of creativity," widely respected?[31] For he is explicitly referring to generic notions of ability, commitment, and creativity, and he goes on to say that "gifted and talented children are those possessing or capable of developing this composite set of traits and applying them to any potentially valuable area of human performance," which explicitly indicates that in his view giftedness is a generic quality, such that the individual who is gifted can do anything well. On closer scrutiny even the U. S. office of education view is heavily imbued with the idea of generic abilities, for, while it refers to various areas, it will be seen that these are not classifications of different kinds of specific activity, but themselves involve putative generic abilities. It implies that some people are gifted intellectually, some academically, some in respect of leadership, and some in respect of productive thought. But in fact some people are gifted at certain intellectual operations and not others, some people are gifted in some academic areas and not others, some people are gifted leaders of boy-scout groups but not business groups, and some people think productively about marketing but not about ethical issues.

We see then, that, while superficially it is conceded that giftedness is not a generic quality like tolerance, the nature of which, by definition, is such that if one has it one will display it in all manner of situations, virtually everything else that is said about giftedness reveals that we cannot fully rid ourselves of the idea that it is a generic quality. We cannot face up to the fact that being gifted is a matter of being able to do certain particular things exceptionally well, and that therefore developing giftedness is a matter of enabling individuals to learn to do things well. Even when that is acknowledged, we are tempted to revert to the idea of generic ability, presuming that there is some innate quality in individuals that renders them more able than others to learn to do things well in general.

The literature on giftedness, taken as a whole, perpetuates the idea that giftedness is something that individuals possess or lack, to whatever degree, as a consequence of being the persons they are. It is admitted that one's tendency to display it can be encouraged or inhibited (for that is the rationale for laying on some kind of programme for the gifted), but it is never doubted that giftedness is given only to a few or that its occurrence is due to something about the individual, whether occasioned by genetic factors, early environmental factors, or a combination of the two, rather than to the nature of their education. Gifted programmes are not designed to make people gifted, but to stimulate and encourage those who are gifted. Nobody is so foolish as to maintain that all gifted people will display their talent in all areas of human activity. But the implication of giftedness theory is that gifted people could display it, given the appropriate conditions, in all manner of areas, and that they will display it across the spectrum in certain broad areas, such as academic activity or personal relations. If this were not the implication, why should we talk about giftedness without qualification, rather than about being a gifted writer of detective stories, a gifted shopkeeper, or a gifted gardener? But not only is it a matter of empirical fact that giftedness is usually displayed in a limited range of activities, much more serious is the point that the idea of giftedness as a generic quality doesn't make sense.

So far as the empirical facts go, it is a matter of simple observation and common experience that most individuals are gifted in some areas and not in others. Furthermore, most people are not even gifted across the spectrum in respect of any of the broad areas usually listed by those who write about giftedness. Very few people are gifted academics or gifted leaders without qualification. They are gifted at some academic subjects or gifted at displaying leadership qualities in certain kinds of situation.

More importantly, the idea that somebody is gifted, period, is unintelligible. It makes no sense to say that a person is gifted but not gifted at anything, since being gifted means doing some thing(s) exceptionally well. Since the range of human activities is enormous and extremely varied, there is no *a priori* reason to suppose that a person who is gifted in some respects will necessarily be gifted in others, and, as we have just said, as a matter of empirical fact people seldom are gifted in respect of all human activity. It is nonetheless conceivable that a person should be. But what is not conceivable is that a person should be gifted in respect of all human activity purely and simply in virtue of some innate quality called "giftedness," because the competence and understanding that are necessary to displaying giftedness in most important areas of activity have to be learned. If I am a gifted historian or a gifted skier, it is because I have come to understand what is involved in history or skiing, and what the criteria or standards of excellence are in either case, and learned how to do either one.

In short, giftedness is not a generic quality in the sense of an ability to do any manner of thing exceptionally well, with which certain individuals are blessed and which it is our task to locate and foster. Giftedness is specific to various activities, and, while some people may prove to be gifted in a wide range of activities, and while there very possibly are certain conditions of the brain and of early upbringing that have to be met if a person is to become gifted, giftedness itself is the product of acquired competence and understanding. If we could set aside our lingering flirtation with the idea of generic ability, we would see the absurdity of our attempts to detect giftedness in the abstract in young children, and would be able to turn our attention to the more appropriate task of selecting curriculum content and teaching it in such a way as to promote the kind of competence and understanding in worthwhile activities that directly leads to the development of particular kinds of giftedness.

The whole issue of giftedness is also imbued with the hesitancy and confusion that surrounds our attitude to value judgements, in particular our uneasy adherence to relativism. On the face of it, concern for the gifted involves the antithesis of a relativist view. For, whatever else giftedness implies, it implies that some individuals are superior to others in certain respects and should be treated differently as a consequence. But the matter is not quite as straightforward as that. For, while on some views the percentage of gifted children is very small, the natural tendency of broadening the areas in which giftedness may be displayed to include such things as psychomotor ability and talent for mechanical achievement, and of maintaining that a child is gifted if he scores high points on some of a list of thirty or so items as varied as "above average height," "has spontaneous interests," "likes school," "creates jokes," and "prefers the companionship of older children," is to suggest that giftedness may be fairly common.[32] It is as if, having focussed on a particular small percentage of children, we feel embarrassment at such transparent elitism and do everything in our power to suggest that in one way or another many children may be gifted.

It is impossible to sort out this particular matter at this juncture, because, of course, the question of how many people are gifted is dependent for its answer on how giftedness is defined. It may well be that if giftedness is defined in terms of performance on certain standardised tests, something like five percent of the population are gifted, whereas, if it is defined in terms of a check-list of thirty odd signs, a far greater number will be. But, however that may be, one thing that clearly follows from what has been said about giftedness here is that, since giftedness is to a large extent developed by education, there is no necessary reason why most children should not prove to be gifted in some respect or other.

The issue of values now becomes important, for, given that giftedness may be displayed in anything from poker playing to psychiatry, we surely have to address the question of what, ideally, we want people to be gifted at doing. It is the fact that this question is virtually unaddressed in the literature, combined with the fact that some of the tests and signs of giftedness referred to seem so ineffably trivial, that highlights our reluctance to come to grips with the issue of whether we do or do not believe that some pursuits are more worthwhile than others. Yet as soon as we acknowledge, as preoccupation with the gifted suggests we do, that judgements about people's relative ability are not simply idle preferences or arbitrary whims, but can be grounded in reason and can be matters of fact, we should surely accept the corollary that similarly objective judgements may be made about the worthwhileness and triviality of various pursuits. Why should we be interested in gifted thieves, gifted gamblers, or gifted golfers, for example? Is it more important to be a gifted mathematician or a gifted football player? Is it of any particular concern to us that a child should be gifted in respect of performance on creativity tests? Would we perhaps have reason to be more concerned about developing a gifted musician?

I shall pursue this question in subsequent chapters. Here I want only to point out that one of the most obvious and important questions relating to educating the gifted has been entirely neglected, presumably because of the difficulty we seem to have in seeing that value judgements are not simply a reflection of personal preference, and that some things are as a matter of fact more important than other things. That question is: "what are the educationally worthwhile areas in which we want to develop giftedness?" Is, for example, the view that giftedness is equally important in respect of academic subjects, leadership ability, and psychomotor ability acceptable? Is it true?

V: Programming for the gifted

The fact that the question of what is educationally worthwhile is not being addressed is one major criticism of the debate concerning the nature of programming or curriculum for gifted children. But there are others.

There are many different views on this issue. Some are logically unproblematic, but seem to make talk of giftedness largely irrelevant. For example, whatever the motivational, social justice, and educational efficiency merits of the proposal may be, it at least makes sense to say that at a certain age some children, having been introduced to various pursuits, show better grounding in and more talent for some of them than others do, and that these children should therefore be presented with a different, more demanding, curriculum in respect of those pursuits. That is a straightforward argument for setting by subjects. Such a policy may highlight the uneasy tension between our egalitarian preference for comprehensive schooling and our recognition that some students are superior to others in various specific respects. But it makes sense. On the other hand, this argument and policy do not require and would not be helped in any way by reference to the notion of giftedness.

Most other current proposals however do not make sense. For instance, topping up the curriculum of gifted children with enrichment classes, whether subject specific or general, or establishing a gifted stream, are practices that are hard to justify. If a child is more advanced in mathematics than his peers, then what he needs ideally is a class of similarly advanced students. Topping up his regular class with a more advanced one has some merit, but only in that the advanced class provides what he needs. His boredom and frustration in the regular class will presumably intensify. Streaming makes little sense because few people are gifted across the board. And most absurd of all is the idea of non-subject-specific classes for the gifted tacked on to the regular classes, especially when we add the corollary notion that there may be specialist teachers of the gifted without reference to any particular sphere of activity. Of course some teachers are more experienced with and interested in gifted children than others, just as some teachers prefer dealing with secondary or elementary children. But a preference for and experience with a particular group is not the whole story. Whether or not it is the case that, in order to teach secondary level history, you need to know more about history than you do at elementary level, as some would maintain, it is evident that an essential requirement when teaching gifted children is understanding sufficient to the purposes of teaching unusually advanced or able students matters of unusual depth and complexity. In other words, teachers of gifted children need to have a high level of understanding of whatever it is that they are going to teach. One must therefore be gravely concerned about enrichment classes for the gifted that are not predicated on any particular sphere of interest or competence on the part of either students or teachers. If some children happen to be gifted in that they are more competent at maths, physics, and history than their peers, what is the point in leaving them in regular classes, but giving them two extra lessons a week in which they do some something different such as discuss social problems, music, or literature at an allegedly more advanced level? Their regular lessons remain inappropriate, their capacity to show giftedness in the new areas is not established, and the teacher's ability to teach children gifted in the new areas is not established. To cite a specific example from British Columbia: what sense is there in taking nine-year-old so-called "gifted" children out of language arts classes, in which they are by no means necessarily particularly advanced, in order to encourage them to "brainstorm" about pets with a teacher whose qualifications for teaching the gifted do not include any particular knowledge of pets, language arts, or critical thinking?

If we add together the points so far made we see a bizarre situation in which different school districts select gifted children by quite different means, involving quite different criteria and *ipso facto* different conceptions of giftedness. They also treat gifted students in different ways, but the differences of treatment and programming are not logically connected to their different conceptions (which would at least make sense, even if it would be confusing). On the contrary, they are the product of the usual political and administrative processes, drawing selectively on research and theory that in all probability was conducted in the light of a different conception of giftedness. We thus have some children selected because they do well on an I.Q. test, others because they have proven academic ability, others because they are the children of one-parent families or learnt to read at an early age, all referred to as gifted, and then, perhaps, in a somewhat arbitrary fashion, provided with extra lessons on no particular subject matter, taught by people with no particular understanding.

What we should be doing is determining the extent to which particular children are gifted in one or more educationally worthwhile area, and then providing them with teachers who are capable of teaching the subjects in question at a higher level and in a way that challenges and engages them.

The above remarks about programmes for the gifted can be made without reference to the intractable problem of whether some people are or are not blessed with an innate genetic endowment that allows or propels them to attain heights of achievement that others could not. For it has not been denied that there may be such an endowment. All that has been emphasised is that being gifted means being able to display unusual talent in some one or more endeavours. Whatever the truth about the relative importance of nature and nurture, it is beyond dispute that except in very rare cases of brain-damaged individuals, we can take active steps to enable people to become more gifted in virtually any area. If this were not the case, it is difficult to see why we should bother to teach at all. Gifted people, as should be becoming clear, are not a distinct species, they are just people who are better at doing certain worthwhile things than others. Since we can take virtually any child and improve his musicianship or his mathematical ability to some extent, we know that we can increase giftedness in virtually all children.

Having a clear understanding of what giftedness means allows us to make sense of arguments about how to detect it and what to do with gifted students. Whether I.Q. tests, critical thinking tests, or creativity tests are appropriate depends upon what the connection between them and being gifted may be. They are clearly not direct tests of giftedness, because a typical I.Q. test or creativity test does not presume to test people's talents in respect of certain worthwhile activities. Whatever value they may have (and this will be discussed in subsequent chapters), it is evident that there are more appropriate and more revealing tests—namely tests of ability in various specific spheres. If you want to know whether a person is a gifted mathematician or musician you test his mathematical or musical competence, because such competence is what giftedness refers to. Similarly, if you want to estimate which of several students are likely ultimately to be more gifted mathematicians or musicians, the sensible thing to do is test their current competency. This indeed is not foolproof: different individuals develop interests and talents at different times and in response to different stimuli. To write somebody off at the age of eleven as relatively poor at mathematics may prove mistaken. That is a very serious problem facing any process of selection in education. It was in fact one of the objections to the 11 + system of examination in Britain that led to the break up of a tripartite system in favour of the sort of comprehensive schooling that is endemic in North America. Nonetheless, if you are going to select, this is clearly the appropriate ground on which to do it. Besides which, even if a test of mathematical competency may prove inaccurate in the long run, if it is well constructed it should have a certain immediate validity. That is to say, if, out of a group of twelve-year-olds, half have clearly mastered the current material better than the other half, that seems good reason to provide them with a different curriculum of some sort in the immediate future.

The major problem in all this relates to the timing of examination and selection. When should we start differentiating among students? Theoretically, I.Q. tests and the like have the advantage that since they relate to timeless innate capacity they can be administered at any time. But in fact they do not relate to timeless innate capacities of any real significance (see below). The common sense answer to the problem would appear to be that testing should be on a regular basis: at the end of each year, for example, students' relative degree of giftedness in any area would be assessed, and they would be set for the following year in accordance with the assessment in various subjects.

I have called this chapter "Giftedness: a cautionary tale," because I hope it will be apparent to what extent talk of giftedness, which superficially seems to be in tune with the ideal outlined in the opening chapter, in fact militates against it, and does so for some of the reasons that were referred to in the second chapter. Concern for giftedness presumably arises out of a sense that there are in our schools many particularly able students who are not being engaged or stretched enough in intellectual and other respects; or, as we might put it in the present context, we are falling unnecessarily short of our ideal. Furthermore, giftedness, for most people, is a concept that goes beyond the vocational and technological bias of our age, being partially identified with concepts such as imagination and creativity, as well as intelligence. Thirdly, the recognition of difference and superiority implicit in talk of giftedness challenges some of our relativistic tendencies. If the call were simply for the cultivation and development of gifted students in educationally important areas, it would more or less coincide with the major aspirations of the ideal. In these respects, then, preoccupation with giftedness is welcome.

But in fact all the talk and action surrounding giftedness does little to advance the ideal. We are not monitoring our pupils' progress so as to bring out the best in them, but singling out students in a variety of ways, most of which have no obvious relevance to the matter in hand, and providing them with a variety of programmes, some of which are as aimless and futile as the provision of an afternoon's general discussion a week to top up the regular curriculum, and few of which have any bearing on actively developing understanding and capability in defined important areas.

At the bottom of this grotesque confusion lies the false assumption that giftedness is an attribute possessed by some rather than others, which is generic (that is to say which indicates one's potential competence in any area), and which can be developed and enhanced by giftedness classes and giftedness teachers without reference to specific contexts. But there is no such thing as giftedness, if that means a fixed capacity to do things well. All that there are, are individuals who at given points in time can display more or less competence and talent in performing various activities. All that we can do is determine what activities or areas of study are important, and seek to match the level and style of our teaching to the varying degrees of student competence. And in order to maintain and enhance levels of competence, we have to develop students' understanding in particular areas.

As I said at the beginning of the chapter, it is not at all clear that the word "giftedness" needed to be introduced into the debate, since it does not in most usages appear to mean anything new, and it is confusing to have it used in a variety of different senses. If we are to use the word, it is clear that as educationalists we should be concerned about giftedness. We should be attempting to detect it in children, to identify and evaluate the various areas in which they display it, and to enhance and promote it. But given the nature of human beings and what education is, that does not lead to the conclusion that we need experts in giftedness. It leads to the conclusion that all teachers should be interested in giftedness, and the whole curriculum should be geared towards it. For the promotion of giftedness in educationally important spheres is precisely what schools are for. However, we would remove a great deal of incoherence and equivocation, if we were to rephrase that sentence and say instead: "Teachers should be concerned to teach children such things and in such a way that they become gifted in a variety of educationally important spheres."

Whatever the truth may be about there being some innate potentiality that allows of or limits the possibility of an individual ultimately proving to be gifted in some respect(s), it is certain that we can contribute to the development of gifted performance in individuals by teaching them in ways that enhance their understanding.

Chapter 4

Intellectual Qualities

I: Brainstorming

"Giftedness," as we have seen, is a very general term. For some it covers intelligence, creativity, and imagination, but, even when its meaning is less wide than that, it remains a broad term covering a range of talents over a spectrum of activity.

We do of course need general terms on many occasions for all sorts of practical reason. Sometimes we want to talk about what is true of all members of a class (e.g., animals), and for convenience we need to be able to refer to the class rather than have to itemise all the different members (e.g., pigs, chickens, hedgehogs). However, the thorough understanding and control of an issue or topic is not facilitated by concentrating on general concepts. This is not to be confused with the point that we require clear concepts. That is obviously true. If our idea of intelligence or education is unclear, muddled, or confused, it is not going to be possible to talk sense about it. But even if our ideas are clear, if they are also all general or broad, then, by definition, we cannot say very specific things. Art criticism, for example, that was based exclusively on broad terms such as "beautiful," "effective," and "creative," would be harder to follow, harder to assess, and less illuminating, than it would be if we could also make use of more specific ideas such as "shape," "colour," and "perspective." Indeed, the development and refinement of disciplines and areas of study can be seen as a process of articulating increasingly specific concepts.

One of the problems with our discourse on intellectual qualities is that it is conducted largely in terms of general concepts such as giftedness, intelligence, imagination, and creativity, so that we fail to come to grips with important questions about different types of giftedness, different aspects of intelligence, different facets of imagination, and different spheres of creativity. If creativity is what we are concerned with, then we may find ourselves lumping the successful pop-singer together with the Nobel prize winning physicist; yet, as educationalists, we need to raise all sorts of question that call for distinguishing between these two examples of creativity. (We do not necessarily have to conclude that one is less important than the other, but we do need to consider that question and others, such as their relative educational significance or the extent to which either can be developed or enhanced by schooling, that are not helped by the identification of both types of activity as creative.)

A further problem is that much of what has been said in the previous chapter about giftedness is also true of other broad intellectual terms frequently encountered in educational debate, such as "critical thinking," "problem solving," "brainstorming," "thinking skills," and "intelligence." Most of these terms superficially seem to refer to qualities that coincide with the values incorporated in the ideal. The frequent use of such words suggests that we are strongly committed to rationality as one educational aim. However, the way in which these ideas are conceived, and hence the way in which they are treated in practice, very often involves the same kinds of error that we have encountered in examining giftedness.

Definitions of these terms, though sometimes more clearly articulated than those typically provided by advocates of giftedness, are, for the most part, equally varied, equally unclear, and similarly of the wrong kind. For example, there are different accounts of what intelligence is, each one carrying different implications for how we should proceed if we are to develop it. Some of these accounts are ambiguous, incoherent, or unclear. Some, though clear in themselves, are questionable because they define the concept in terms of performance on tests that have not been independently shown to test intelligence. And others are not couched in a way that indicates what conditions or criteria have to be met for a person to count as intelligent, but rather in terms of examples, similes, metaphors, and synonyms.

"Brainstorming" provides a good example of confused definition. The verb "to brainstorm," which is incidentally still not recognised by the latest editions of certain reputable dictionaries, derives from the noun "brainstorm." Historically that appears to have been a pejorative term: a person was described as having "a brainstorm" when he went over the top in some way, or began acting or talking insanely. But educationalists, providing another illustration of their tendency to create unnecessary jargon, determined to treat the noun as an alternative for "brainwave," which, by contrast, has honorific connotations. Traditionally, a "brainwave" is a "good idea." But the word "brainwave" also carries the connotation that the "good idea" is the product of unexplained and sudden insight or intuition. No doubt brainwaves may tend to occur more often in the minds of those who have some knowledge and understanding, so that strictly speaking they are not totally inexplicable flashes of inspiration. Nonetheless, the clear implication of the word is that one's ideas or solutions come through instantaneous insight or recognition, rather than as a result of determined calculation or conscious reasoning. If this connotation is carried over to the new honorific sense of "brainstorm," we end up with the verb "to brainstorm" meaning to generate valuable and powerful insights or intuitions spontaneously.

That is more or less what some (probably few) educationalists do take the word to mean. David Pratt, for instance, defines "brainstorming" as "the generation of ideas . . . involving free flowing creative thought and spontaneous non-critical expression of ideas."[1]

But, if this is what brainstorming means, then the idea of programming brainstorming sessions or of teaching people to brainstorm is plainly incoherent. If to brainstorm is to suddenly see the light (come up with a good idea, a practicable solution, etc.), without the benefit of organised argument and reasoning, then how can one possibly choose to engage in it, or purposively set about it? To organise a brainstorming session, to issue the command "let's brainstorm," can mean nothing, beyond the negative points that there shall be no agenda and no attempt to sort the problems out by rational argument. A class that sets out to brainstorm is a class that sets out to have inspired insights. But, by definition, inspired insights don't come to order.

In other words, while the idea of a brainstorm in the sense of a brainwave, is perfectly clear and coherent, even if the change in vocabulary serves no obvious point, the idea of brainstorming as a planned activity or of brainstorming to order is logically contradictory. Nor are logical points such as this simply matters for scholarly disquisition: they make a great deal of practical difference. Faced with serious issues to discuss in school and actual problems to solve, there are teachers and administrators who will in all seriousness herd people into a room and expect them to have intuitive insights to order, rather than tackle the issue or problem in a rational way with the benefit of information and understanding that is provided in some organised way. This is not to say that some occasions that are labeled "brainstorming sessions" may not in fact be productive. It is to say that the idea of brainstorming as a purposive activity is a nonsense, and therefore, not surprisingly, many such sessions are unproductive and futile so far as their declared purpose goes.

Most educationalists take a slightly different and more particular view of brainstorming. Parnes, for instance, adapting Osborn's work, produces a list of rules that have to be adhered to closely in a brainstorming session, which is quite representative and widely known.[2]

The most emphatic rule (implicit in the previous conception too) is that all proffered ideas should be treated as acceptable and criticism on any count is absolutely barred. Others are that modification of, or combination with, other ideas that have already been produced is to be encouraged, quantity of ideas should be sought, and odd or unusual ideas should be particularly welcome. There are also a number of more specific general ploys that are listed that may be useful ways of dealing with a seemingly intractable problem. For example, it is suggested that it may sometimes be productive to think in terms of substitution, rearrangement, magnification, or reversal. Thus, if the problem is "what to do with a class whose teacher cannot maintain discipline," thinking of some kind of substitution might lead us to propose that a new teacher be substituted or that some of the students be replaced by students from another class. Reflection on the category "magnification" might lead us to propose that "class size could be increased, as could number of teachers, number of assignments, or magnitude of punishment or reinforcement."[3] Other comparable strategies include Gordon's idea of presenting the group with an abstraction rather than a specific problem, such as the problem of storing things in general rather than the specific problem of parking cars, and Baldwin's "webbing," which involves a particular strategy for recording information.[4]

Approaches such as these effectively define brainstorming in terms of the rules, strategies, and techniques proposed. To brainstorm is to do these things. Brainstorming in this more specific kind of sense has been widely adopted in both industry and schools, and a number of claims have been made for its effectiveness. Parnes, for instance, asserts that individuals working alone and following the principle of deferring judgement (i.e., not worrying about quality of ideas) produce from 23% to 177% more good solutions than they do when simply left to come up with good ideas in any way they choose. It has also been claimed that individuals who have been involved in brainstorming sessions may increase their scores on creativity tests.[5]

But it is difficult to regard such claims as particularly significant. If brainstorming activity does correlate with improved performance on creativity tests, this may well be because creativity tests typically test the same kinds of thing as are valued in brainstorming. For instance, as we shall see, creativity tests generally focus on the generation of a large quantity of responses without regard to quality, and they are often scored by reference to the unusualness of responses. Furthermore, if, as I shall argue, creativity tests do not in fact relate to true creativity and do not appear to measure anything of educational value, the fact that brainstorming contributed to improved performance on them would be of no particular importance.

As to Parnes' conclusions, one can well believe that people who have *any* strategy to follow would tend to produce more good ideas than those who are simply told to produce good ideas. But the real difficulty with making sense of this claim is the fact that determining what counts as a good-quality solution is exceedingly problematic, and no account is taken of the varying complexity and importance of ideas. Parnes' research certainly does not establish that those who engage in brainstorming sessions tend to produce objectively better solutions to important real-life problems than others, either during such sessions or subsequently as a result of having engaged in such sessions.

Brainstorming in this sense is based upon the ideas that a situation in which one's suggestions have to meet certain standards of quality and may be criticised is likely to inhibit people, and that having some set of general ideas about the ways in which one might modify a proposal (e.g., magnification, reversal) may help one to achieve some modification. Both are reasonable enough ideas, and one would therefore expect people who engage in brainstorming sessions to become more self-confident and more productive of ideas. Nor would it be particularly surprising if many brainstorming sessions culminated in some useful and unusual ideas. But what seems equally clear is that whether a session does lead to valuable conclusions depends also upon the knowledge and understanding that the participants happen to have. The techniques and strategies alone cannot lead to success. Sooner or later the proposals have to be evaluated. Yet such an approach explicitly teaches that it is the process of one's thinking that matters, rather than the quality of it.

As Child remarks, "the central aim of the method is to produce some lasting habits of ideational fluency in the children, though this aim has never been validated."[6] The main reason that it has not been validated (or invalidated) is that no research on the matter could be convincing until the concept of "ideational fluency" is adequately defined. If it is defined in terms more or less similar to those that define brainstorming, if, in other words, ideational fluency is characterised in terms of the generation of many ideas, without reference to their quality, then it is likely that extensive brainstorming will contribute to it. But then the value of ideational fluency must be seriously questioned. If on the other hand it is defined in terms that include reference to the generation of good ideas in relation to important matters, it is evident that, whatever the value of brainstorming, ideational fluency is dependent on knowledge and understanding of important subject matters and the criteria of quality in various spheres.

Preoccupation with brainstorming is a good example of our misplaced belief that education can be profitably looked at in terms of process, without explicit concern for the context in which the process has to operate. We have to brainstorm about something, just as we have to think about something, be imaginative about something, or be creative about something. That being the case, two crucial questions about any instance of brainstorming (thinking, imagination, etc.) are: what is the nature of what we are brainstorming about and what are the criteria for quality of ideas in this sphere? We may accept that there is some value in sometimes taking children's ideas seriously, even when there is no merit in them; we may accept that it is sometimes useful to get a lot of ideas out on the table without too much concern for their appropriateness, value, or quality; and we may accept that it is sometimes a useful exercise to listen to other people's ideas and try to make some positive contribution to modifying them rather than to shoot them down.[7] But one cannot do any of these things in a vacuum. The question therefore becomes whether we want to have special occasions (brainstorming sessions) when we exercise these habits for their own sake in contexts that do not require any particular complex and worthwhile knowledge or understanding, or whether we want to incorporate these techniques judiciously in the context of trying to teach people to understand important things and to get them right. It is apparent, therefore, that the issue of relativism also comes into the picture here. For, those who truly believe that there is no such thing as "getting it right" and who consequently judge the individual's "ideational fluency" purely in terms of quantity, lack of inhibition, and unusualness, will naturally and correctly approve a strategy that is explicitly designed to encourage those characteristics. But once we concede that there is such a thing as objectivity, even in the domain of values, then the value of brainstorming itself becomes highly questionable

The issue of relativism will be explored more fully below. Here it will be sufficient to observe that, since, on the face of it, 2 x 2 does equal 4, storing cars in plastic bags suspended from the ceiling is not a sensible suggestion for coping with the parking problem, and restoring a teacher's discipline in a class by substituting another teacher avoids the problem rather than solves it, the view that there are no objective criteria for the quality of ideas and solutions is counter-intuitive. Three immediate conclusions can be drawn from the recognition that there is in principle a distinction to be drawn between good and bad ideas: first, the quality of ideas is at least an additional criterion that we ought to be concerned with. Secondly, the empirical question of whether brainstorming strategies, which explicitly ignore the question of quality in the process, nonetheless improve people's ability to end up with unusual and good ideas, can only be determined by research that clearly sets out the criteria for quality in various domains. Thirdly, while it is possible that the practice of brainstorming develops habits that may contribute to the generation of good ideas, it is logically inconceivable that it should achieve this aim in and of itself. Nobody can be expected to come up with a good and appropriate idea or solution to a problem in an area where they lack understanding of both the subject matter or facts and the criteria for determining quality. Individuals who understand nothing about morality and medicine are not in a position to brainstorm their way to good ideas about the problem of overpopulation, nor to recognise a good idea if one happens to crop up.

But what are we to conclude more generally about the desirability or otherwise of brainstorming? First, it is necessary that any particular teacher or school that contemplates promulgating it as a specific kind of activity should be clear what they mean by it. If they mean "the spontaneous generation of good ideas," without further qualification or explication, they may as well forget about it, since the concept of a planned session for the spontaneous production of ideas is contradictory, and there can be no coherent talk of good ideas in the absence of talk about criteria for establishing what ideas are good. If they mean the production of ideas, without regard to quality and without regard to any specific techniques or procedures, it is difficult to see any reason for encouraging the practice. What is the inherent value in asking people simply to say anything, without any attempt to evaluate or assess what they say, and without any attempt to help them say anything of quality or even to help them say something? And what conceivable grounds are there for supposing that the habit of doing this, once cultivated, will lead to any beneficial consequences? If, however, they intend to adopt certain specific rules of procedure and techniques to govern the process whereby ideas are initially produced and subsequently modified, we move on to the next point.

We have no reason to reject out of hand the suggestion that people's capacity to solve problems and generate good ideas may be enhanced by habituating them to the practice of throwing out as many ideas as possible, without being inhibited by concern for criticism from others or the quality of the ideas themselves, and by encouraging them to adopt various specific techniques such as modifying a previous idea, looking for some way of substituting one element, or considering minimising some element. It may be the case that individuals who are schooled in this way are more successful than those who are not in coming up with creative ideas in business, imaginative solutions to personal problems, helpful ideas for social reform, and wise political advice.

However, while it may be the case, there is not a shred of empirical evidence that it is the case. None of the research into the effects of brainstorming has been conducted with respect to adequately elucidated concepts of success in such areas. Furthermore, the insistence on cultivating the use of such techniques in sessions devoted exclusively to that end, rather than in the context of studying specific matters, is entirely unexplained. And it may be added here that the various lists of rules and techniques provided by different advocates of brainstorming (which do not differ a great deal) are surprisingly limited. There are not in fact only some eight or ten strategies of the type "try substitution" that one might employ, so why do we emphasise a particular small set of strategies at the expense of others? Why, to revert to the major point, do we not adopt the view that teaching of particular subject matters would be improved by the judicious encouragement of these techniques, from the generation of a quantity of ideas of whatever quality to the attempt to employ substitution, rather than the view that brainstorming is a distinct and separate activity?

The answer to that question brings us to the third and most important conclusion. We treat brainstorming as an activity in itself, because we cannot rid ourselves of the misleading idea that good thinking is a matter of certain processes that can effectively be divorced from any particular context. But that is not true. The characteristics of brainstorming are at best part of what is necessary to become adept at generating ideas, unless one categorically argues that generating ideas should be defined simply as saying something, never mind how foolish, incoherent, irrelevant, obscure, or contradictory it may be. Educationalists have no reason to be interested in promoting that conception of generating ideas. Since we are concerned ultimately with good ideas, it is evident that we must be concerned with more than mere brainstorming. But not only does the generation of good ideas involve understanding and concern for meeting criteria of quality, in addition to the characteristics involved in brainstorming, it is also the case that the specific techniques alluded to take a different form and can only be applied in the light of understanding of various contexts. The principles of substitution or maximisation cannot be interpreted unless one knows what one is talking about. The consequence is that brainstorming sessions are inevitably confined to dealing with topics of supposed general knowledge (or confined to those with specialist knowledge of a particular topic). And the consequence of that is that all the brainstorming in the world cannot in itself make a person more able to come up with good ideas about complex and important issues that require particular understanding. Good thinking may certainly be said to involve processes, one of which may be brainstorming. But the idea of developing the process on its own does not make sense. The process has to operate in conjunction with some subject matter, and it takes a different particular form in relation to different kinds of subject matter, quite apart from the fact that it cannot get off the ground where there is no understanding.[8] Therefore the partial contribution that the techniques of brainstorming may conceivably make to good thinking, is only made in respect of the kinds of thing one brainstorms about. Furthermore its value lies only in its use as an initial activity to get things started. Once the ideas are on the table, any educational progress is going to depend upon dealing with them in a rational coherent manner.

Adding all this together, one must say that the good sense in the idea of brainstorming amounts to little more than the observations that sometimes people are too inhibited in trying out ideas that are superficially silly but which nonetheless may lead us somewhere, that explicitly encouraging them to produce such ideas may help towards overcoming the inhibition, and that, having been presented with a superficially rather strange idea, there are various ways in which one might try to modify it to get something of value out of it. Each of these is a reasonable observation. But they lead only to the conclusion that in our teaching generally we should take account of them. They do not lead to the conclusion that there is any value in the idea of brainstorming sessions divorced from the rest of the curriculum, or that there is any coherence in the idea of brainstorming as an ability divorced from particular understanding that enables one to brainstorm about something particular. Nor can they serve as a substitute for the observation that a more important, because logically necessary, aspect of generating good ideas is a thorough understanding of the domain in question. It is not very difficult to get a good historian to brainstorm about the origins of the second world war and to do it well. It is impossible to get a "good brainstormer," who does not happen to have any historical understanding or knowledge, to do it at all, let alone to do it well.

These simple facts would not have been obscured, if we were not deeply, perhaps unconsciously, wedded to the ideas that teaching people to think well is a matter of teaching them processes of thought, without regard to specific content, that abilities such as brainstorming are generic, such that the ability to do it in one situation means you have the ability and can exercise it in another, that thinking can be analysed entirely in terms of skills and strategies that can be perfected by exercising them, as opposed to understanding and judgement which cannot, and that the issue of quality in responses should be played down, because the question of quality is a matter of subjective opinion.

II: Critical thinking and problem solving

One difference between giftedness and critical thinking is that, whereas much of the writing about giftedness makes the contentious assumption that giftedness is largely a matter of innate endowments, most of the writing about critical thinking does not. It is widely assumed that people develop as critical thinkers as a result of instruction and being called upon to practice the manoeuvres and strategies to which they are introduced. This is certainly a clearer and more coherent position than the view that it is an innate faculty. Critical thinking, on anyone's view, unlike brainstorming, implies thinking of quality, sustained periods of reasoning, and reasoning that conforms to rules of logic and standards of excellence. A critical thinker is one who can reason logically about an issue and detect flaws or confusion in unreasonable argument. Since one has to learn the rules of logic and the standards or criteria of sense in various domains, both what they are and how to recognise them, it is evident that developing critical thought will not simply be a matter of exercising an existent faculty, as body building involves exercising already existing muscles. It will largely be a matter of bringing people to understand, and then allowing them to practice displaying that understanding. While the literature on giftedness meanders uncertainly between the contradictory assumptions that giftedness is innate and that it is the product of teaching and other environmental factors, the literature on critical thinking tends to ignore the question of what innate factors may be necessary prerequisites of becoming a critical thinker, and to concentrate on the question of what we can do to develop it. And quite reasonably so, since whatever necessary prerequisites there may be, they are plainly very widely distributed. We have no reason to suppose that the vast majority of students could not in principle become good critical thinkers. It is a matter of what we do to make this possibility occur.

But now we come to a major and erroneous assumption that is common to our thinking about giftedness and critical thinking. It is an error that largely accounts for the fact that our preoccupation with critical thinking, which ought to be of crucial importance to achieving our ideal, is not in fact so, and may even be counter-productive. This is the assumption that a developed critical faculty is a generic quality. The assumption that individuals are (or become) more or less critical, period. The idea that if you are (or become) a critical thinker, then you are a critical thinker, whether you are discussing your marriage, the ozone layer, or King Henry VIII. Only on this assumption would it make sense to adopt the kinds of strategy that avowed champions of critical thinking espouse in teaching for critical thinking, only on this assumption do our critical thinking programmes make sense. But this assumption is plainly false, and consequently a great deal of what we do to advance critical thinking in schools is largely time wasted.

The error consists in failing to see that critical thinking is context bound. Just as one has to display gifted qualities in some one or more contexts for it to make sense to claim to be gifted, so one has to be critical about something, for it to make sense to claim to be a critical thinker. This observation, which has often been made before, is sometimes countered by the response: "Well, of course we know that. We know that one has to think about something, if one is going to claim to be thinking. But our programmes always do involve thinking about something. Indeed, they could not fail to do so, for the very reason given: since it is inconceivable that people should be thinking, but not thinking about any thing, it follows that our programmes must be getting people to think about something." This response is entirely reasonable, so far as it goes. But it misses the point of the criticism.[9] That point is that not only must critical thinking be about something, but also, as a matter of empirical and logical fact, the ability to be critical in one context does not vouchsafe the ability to be critical in another. (Furthermore, from our point of view, that something should be educationally significant.)

Empirically, few can fail to be aware that many people who by any definition are good critical thinkers in their chosen area of expertise are not so in various other areas. Lots of people who talk about politics with erudition and logic, talk absurdly about education or medicine. Many people who display manifest critical ability in their private life, talk nonsense about ecology. But the significant point is the logical one: this is inescapably so, since one cannot be a critical thinker in an area or on a topic where one lacks information and understanding. To make an intelligent contribution to a topic, you not only need to know some facts (have some adequate information), you also need to be able to apply the rules of sound reasoning; and the form those rules take, the question of what constitutes sound reasoning, varies from subject matter to subject matter and with different kinds of question. My powers of critical thinking are practically non-existent when it comes to discussing a ballet, although I am a person who tries to avoid contradiction, who can distinguish valid from invalid syllogisms formally, and who eschews non-sequiturs. I know so little about ballet that not only am I hampered by lack of information (e.g., how has this ballet been staged before? was that a difficult step for a dancer?), much more seriously, I am incapable of detecting contradictions, non-sequiturs, and invalid syllogisms in ballet talk. In short, if I am to contribute as a critical thinker to discussion about ballet, I need to understand the nature of ballet and the concepts that are central to it. Without that understanding, even were I to gather information on the topic from others, I am literally incapable of distinguishing between good and bad reasoning on the matter.[10]

So, while it is true that critical thinking programmes have a content, the question becomes what kind of content is it, and is there any reason to suppose that it will help people to think critically in other contexts? The problem is that, whatever the content may be, it is inevitably going to be limited and partial. And in fact the situation is worse than it might be. For not only is the content limited, as any curriculum selection is bound to be, but critical thinking programmes also typically choose the wrong kind of content, if the intention is really to expand students' powers of critical thought.

Although critical thinking programmes differ considerably in point of detail, their logic remains essentially the same. This is true even of the two main types or categories that can be distinguished: those that are more or less identical to courses in logic, and those that are based upon the examination of a variety of specific problems and examples of reasoning.

Those courses that are essentially courses in logic will seek to introduce students to the rules of logic, enabling them to learn their names, to understand them, and to recognise them in abstract form. For example, students will be introduced to the idea of an argument of the form, "If all As are B, and C is an A, then C is a B," and taught that this is a valid form of syllogism, so that any specific piece of reasoning that follows this pattern will be valid. They will be taught, by contrast, that "All As are B, this is a B, therefore it is an A" is invalid. They will be taught the distinction between validity and truth: an argument may be valid, but its conclusion untrue, perhaps because its premise was false. They may be introduced to the law of the excluded middle, which states that "for any statement p, the statement 'p or not-p' is true as a matter of logical necessity," and come to understand what this means. A typical course in logic will in fact be rather more sophisticated than my few examples suggest, but this will be its nature: recognising, understanding, and naming patterns of good and bad reasoning. (A course in logic will very likely involve consideration of specific examples of the abstract rule. I shall consider the value of examples below, when discussing the second type of critical thinking programme. The differences between symbolic, formal, and informal logic are not important for our present purposes.)

Now it is clear that critical thinkers do have to be able to follow these and other similar rules and principles. For these are the rules of logic, of sound reasoning, of critical thinking. The question is whether studying them directly, in this abstract way, is a sensible way to go about developing observance of the rules. There has been research related to the empirical question of whether individuals who have studied courses in logic end up displaying more logical ability than those who have not. But this can be discounted, not just because it has been inconclusive on its own terms, but also because it has by and large been ill conceived—not surprisingly, since to conduct acceptable research on this matter would require arriving at a satisfactory conceptualisation of what is to count as a person with general logical skill. Given the basic point that we are here concerned with, that you cannot display logical powers except in various contexts, a decision would have to be made about what contexts mattered when judging people's general ability.

More important, then, are these points that do not have to be empirically established, since reasoning shows that they must be so:

i)one does not need to be able to name a logical rule to be able to recognise it;

ii)one does not need to be able to formulate it in abstract terms to be able to abide by and recognise it in specific cases;

iii)one cannot apply the abstract rules if one does not understand the form that they take in particular kinds of discourse; and

iv)one cannot reason logically about subject matter concerning which one is ignorant.

Millions of people who have never heard the phrase "law of the excluded middle" or "valid syllogism" can nonetheless argue about specific things in a way that observes the rule and conforms to a valid syllogistic pattern. Similarly, millions who could not set about presenting the bones of their argument in formal terms, perhaps simply through lack of any experience of so doing, can nonetheless present a specific argument that is formally acceptable. But on the other hand, nobody could organise his argument about, say, papal infallibility in valid syllogistic terms without some reasonable understanding of the concepts central to Catholicism. And nobody, however logical, could argue logically about the value and merits of fly-fishing, if he knew nothing about fly-fishing.

From the first two points we may conclude that studying logic is not necessary for being logical; from the latter two we may conclude that it is not sufficient. In other words one does not have to study logic to be logical, and it is certainly not enough to do so. Whether it may nonetheless be worth doing as part of a wider programme designed to enhance critical thinking, we shall consider in a moment.

The majority of critical thinking programmes and courses involve the introduction of logic, but firmly embed it in concrete examples. Basically the structure of such courses consists in exercises in recognising valid argument and invalid argument in the context of particular problems or passages of reasoning. The difficulties here are these:

i)Typically, the problems or passages are brief, isolated, fragments of argument.

ii)Typically, they are, if not always fictitious, of no real immediate concern to the students. (They are not their problems; it is not their argument.)

iii)Typically, they do not involve specialist knowledge or information.

iv)Typically, they do not involve unfamiliar concepts or, more significantly, developed and sophisticated networks of concepts pertaining to some particular kind of inquiry.

For example, students may be presented with an excerpt from a newspaper editorial or a textbook example of a short piece of reasoning, and asked to exercise their powers of critical thinking in detecting poor reasoning of various sorts. The first two criticisms, though frequently made, are not perhaps devastating in their implications. Nonetheless, if the presumption behind all this is that practice makes perfect (at least when combined with guidance and instruction), it is worth noting that the practice tends to be confined to brief isolated passages of argument, whereas *bona fide* critical thinkers have to detect logic and illogic in lengthy disquisitions as well as short paragraphs; they also, ideally, have to exercise it when their passions are aroused and they are discussing issues of genuine importance to them. There certainly are people who can display critical powers only when they are not directly involved in an issue, and that is not good enough for our purposes. I would conclude that the first two features of critical thinking programmes are somewhat unfortunate, since they militate against the aim of preparing people to be critical in involved and lengthy arguments on matters of concern to them, but that they are not crippling in their implications for such a programme.

The other two features, however, surely are. It is understandable that a programme devised for students in general should not be burdened down with specialist terms, complex concepts peculiar to particular subject matter, or arguments that presuppose familiarity with sophisticated disciplines such as aesthetics, ethics, or mathematics. But the fact that they are not merely confirms and underlines the central objection to such programmes: one cannot display one's logical powers or one's skills of critical thinking in areas that one does not understand. If the programmes avoid complex and important domains of thought, they are not preparing people to think critically about complex and important issues. By the same token, such programmes do not prepare people to display critical thinking in general. For the only sense that can be made of the claim that somebody is a critical thinker in general or without qualification, is that the individual can as a matter of fact think critically about everything, and that presupposes understanding everything. But critical thinking programmes do not attempt to provide understanding of everything. On the contrary, as we have seen, they are at best empowering people to reason logically on narrowly focussed, brief, non-specialist, non-complex matters. As with courses more heavily biased towards formal logic, there may be some value in this, but it is evidently not the case that it leads in and of itself to the ability to think critically about important matters.

If there were no obvious alternative, one might nonetheless welcome any such attempt to promote critical thinking. At least these programmes do seek to get students to be logical and rational about something. In addition they may ignite and develop the desire to be logical. But there is a transparently obvious and superior alternative —namely to dispense with courses in critical thinking conceived of as a process that is essentially the same in any context, and instead to encourage critical thinking in the context of significant and powerful areas of thought.

There is a need to select certain subject matters that are thought to be more important in the affairs of men than others. This will obviously involve some argument and may not be easily or unanimously resolved. (Nor is it essential that it should be here.) But the kind of thing that may be argued is that it is rather more important that people should be able to think critically about politics, environmental issues, or the quality of personal life, than about baseball, detective stories, or gardening. And that therefore schools should centre their attempt to foster critical thinking on the former set of subjects rather than the latter. Whether the reader would categorise the examples in the way that I have is not immediately important. My present concern is with the general point that the ability to think critically about politics does not necessarily entail the ability to think critically about detective stories, and vice versa. Therefore, unless the view that value judgements are relative and it doesn't matter what activities people are able to think critically about is substantiated, we have to make a decision as to what we want students to think critically about.

One criterion in making such judgements is the intrinsic value of various activities. Another arises out of the fact that some subjects are defined not simply in terms of their subject matter, but also in terms of dealing with a logically distinctive kind of question. Thus ethics is not simply about moral matters, as angling is about fishing. To understand ethics is to understand how to reason in relation to moral matters, and reasoning in moral matters is both distinguishable from reasoning in, say, scientific, aesthetic, or religious matters, and of all-pervasive significance: you can ask moral questions about history, science, or indeed angling. But you cannot ask angling questions about morality. In order to understand ethics, and hence to think critically in this domain, you have to understand the central concepts of ethics and to appreciate the kind of reasoning that is appropriate in this sphere. To recognise what is logical in ethics you have to understand its concepts, just as you do in angling. The difference is that the former is more complex, more important, and of wider application.

The criterion of logical distinctiveness may prove less contentious than the criterion of intrinsic value. Whereas it might be disputed that angling is a more trivial pursuit than the study of politics, it surely cannot be denied that only certain subjects have these twin characteristics of being pervasive and requiring a specific kind of understanding. Much work has been done on this kind of issue, and I therefore feel no qualms about suggesting that morality, aesthetics, philosophy, mathematics, natural science, and history, represent the obvious subjects that display the traits in question.[11] Any involved discussion about a particular issue of complexity and importance is likely to touch upon questions in one or more of those areas, and people will not be able to reason critically about the moral, aesthetic, scientific, mathematical, philosophical or historical aspects of the argument, if they have not been brought to a thorough understanding of these difficult areas.

More will be said about the specific kind of content that the school curriculum should have below. My remarks here have been confined to making the point that critical thinking is misconceived as being a generic ability and a process that takes the same form in any context. Consequently, critical thinking programmes do not teach critical thinking *per se*, but rather critical thinking about a somewhat arbitrary and non-specialised set of problems. Such an approach must necessarily be insufficient for producing people who can think critically about various particular important things, and it is not necessary to that aim, since the little that may be said to be common to all instances of critical thinking, such as the desire to be critical, can be equally well developed in the context of studying the various particular important areas.

It is not necessary to say much about problem solving, since the logic of the situation is substantially the same as it is in the case of critical thinking. Our unthinking, perhaps implicit but nonetheless real, commitment to the idea that being a critical thinker is a matter of mastering processes rather than mastering subject matter in a certain kind of way, is evident here also. As is the related presumption that the ability is generic. We set up problem-solving exercises in our schools, as if to become proficient at solving some problems made one proficient at solving all. But this is simply not true, as should by now be clear. If we want people to be good problem solvers, we have to ensure that they can solve problems that matter in real life, and that requires giving them the substantive information and the specific kinds of understanding necessary for coping with the key kinds of question we face when we encounter real problems. Playing about with such programmes as de Bono's lateral thinking exercises will be as much use, no less no more, than concentrating on crossword puzzles or detective stories would be.[12] All three approaches demand that we perform critical exercises, but all three in themselves generate at best only facility with the material they provide, and that material, in its different ways, is relatively insignificant in terms of thinking critically about the serious and important issues of life.

In addition, de Bono's approach re-introduces the problem concerning the quality of ideas we encountered with brainstorming. It is a feature of his conception of lateral thinking that students should produce unexpected or original solutions to problems and that the question of whether these are correct or incorrect should not arise. But if their quality is irrelevant, why should we value the exercise? Only if a contingent connection could be established between exercise in generating any ideas and the ultimate tendency to generate good ideas, would we have reason to adopt this kind of activity in schools. There is no such evidence, and it is most implausible to suggest that there might be a connection, for the reasons given: good ideas depend on understanding. Understanding doesn't grow on trees, it is context specific, and this kind of problem-solving activity (sometimes referred to as divergent thinking) explicitly denigrates the importance of understanding. But the concepts of a "good idea" and "understanding" are inextricably intertwined. In ignoring one, we necessarily ignore the other.

III: The concept of skill

The emphasis so far has fallen on demonstrating that critical thinking and problem solving are not generic qualities any more than giftedness is, and in indicating that what we do when we lay on programmes specifically designed to promote them is a disservice to our ideal and at odds with what we want to achieve. They are context specific concepts and that means that they are things to be developed in particular contexts. That being so, we have to determine the appropriate contexts and teach those matters in a way designed to develop critical and problem solving students in those areas.

But there is another feature of talk about critical thinking that is important. This is the tendency to refer to it as a skill. Now a skill is fairly clearly and unambiguously a particular kind of ability. Not all abilities are skills. A skill is an ability, usually physical, that is discrete and improved by training or practice. Thus, standing on your head is a paradigm case of a skill: it is a physical ability; it is discrete in that it is self-contained; and, though it may be made part of a circus act, a lecture, a party trick, or whatever, it is an act in and of itself. It can be learned and once learned can be put to use in a variety of contexts. It is also something that one learns to do purely by practice. No understanding is either necessary or sufficient for the purpose of learning to stand on your head.

It is at once apparent that the use of the word skill to refer to intellectual operations involves a quite different sense of the word. To put it bluntly, thinking critically is not a skill. But since so many educationalists have adopted this manner of speaking, let us accept it for the purposes of this discussion. However, in accepting it, it is vital that we remember that it involves a quite different sense of the word. For, so-called intellectual skills are not discrete, are not physical, and cannot be perfected by practice alone. All of this is already implicit in what has been said: it should be quite clear from the above discussion that the fundamental point about critical thinking is that its exercise involves understanding and that the understanding required is of various different sorts. It is not an ability that can be divorced from any context; it has to be instantiated in, and takes a different form in relation to, various subject matters. And it is not something at which you get better simply by repeated exercise in any setting. What you get better at by practice is the particular type of critical thinking you engage in.

This particular error, the assumption that everything is a skill, runs through much of our educational thought and practice. It is not simply that our broad use of the term to cover two quite distinct types of skill is confusing. Much more than that, it is surely the case that part of our counter-productive practice stems from this erroneous categorisation. If we concentrated on the fact that critical thought presupposes understanding, we would not have failed to appreciate, that, since there are various kinds of understanding, we need to determine what things we want understood. And, as a consequence, we would never have become hooked on the idea of teaching critical thinking as such, as opposed to teaching people to think critically about history or about science or whatever. Referring to it as a skill lulls us into accepting the usual implications and connotations of that term. Skills are things that can be trained in and of themselves. If we can teach people the skill of wielding a pen, dribbling a ball, or operating a machine, and then leave them to decide when and where to put the skills to use, why, then we can teach people the skills of critical-thinking, brainstorming, and problem-solving in the same way, and leave them to apply the skills as and when they choose. But this is all nonsense—nonsense that might have been avoided, if we took more care with our language and our concepts and, specifically, did not regard as skills abilities that manifestly are no such thing.

The issue of our confused flirtation with relativism is also involved here. In one sense, as we have seen, critical thinking programmes are clearly not relativistic in their presumptions: they are designed to elicit from students responses that conform to the objective standards of sound reasoning, and to develop a tendency to abide by them. But the failure to see that there is more to being a critical thinker than simply going through a formal process, may be partly attributable to a reluctance to take seriously the idea that there are distinctive and objective standards of reasoning even in areas such as ethics and aesthetics.

I shall have more to say on this in a subsequent chapter, but here it will be sufficient to point out that whatever else may be the case, the notion that moral judgements or aesthetic judgements are simply a matter of subjective opinion, and that therefore all one can ask of someone is that they abide by formal rules of logic such as non-contradiction, is quite certainly mistaken. There are criteria for determining objectively whether a moral judgement is tenable that arise, as similar criteria arise in any other field or area, from the nature of the activity in question. Just as what makes a good football player or a good skier is largely determined by what constitutes the game of football or the activity of skiing, so what makes a morally good person or a beautiful painting is largely determined by what morality and art are all about. One may concede that experts in the latter two areas are less in agreement about the nature of their subject matter than, typically, are sportsmen about theirs. But that will not do away with the notion of expertise. It will not alter the fact that some ethical pronouncements are absurd and some well founded, and distinguishing between them is a matter of understanding this complex domain.[13]

Were we to keep this firmly in mind, to assert unequivocally that whatever the difficulty of establishing the truth of certain claims in areas such as ethics and aesthetics, they nonetheless are areas where we can distinguish the correct from the incorrect, the acceptable from the unacceptable, and the plausible from the implausible, in objective terms, we might be less inclined to spawn a curriculum that fails to tackle the issue head on, and fails to initiate students fully into these subjects so that they may be in a position to "get it right." In short, I suggest, our misplaced feeling that one doesn't get it right or wrong, so much as speak sincerely or insincerely, consistently or inconsistently, has played a part in our failure to see the importance of studying specific subjects such as ethics and aesthetics, and in our adoption of the false conclusion that, provided people have generic critical skills, they can cope with anything adequately.

In conclusion, there is no need to deny that some good may come out of some courses in critical thinking. There are such things as rules of logic and formal qualities of good reasoning, and such courses may well contribute both to making students aware of these, being concerned about them, being alert to them, and, more generally, being concerned with precision in thought. Furthermore, in so far as the problems and passages, the exercises that form the basis of the programme, are well chosen, they may cover important issues, and there is no inherent reason why the particularly important business of conceptual clarity and analysis, which is not usually to the fore in such programmes, should not become so.

However, my argument has been that our unreflective tendency to conceive of critical thinking as a generic skill, coupled with our uneasiness about the question of relativity, is what has led us to adopt programmes which, as they stand, are clearly not the most appropriate way in which to promote critical thinkers in the full sense. A critical thinker is one who, understanding not simply the formal rules of good reasoning, but also the particular form they take in certain particular kinds of inquiry, also has the knowledge and understanding requisite to make use of them in relation to various kinds of important subject matter. Theoretically a critical thinking programme could be elaborated to answer our needs: it could employ longer and more complex passages of argument, it could select material relating to issues and problems that were of real concern to students, it could involve the exploration of sophisticated modes of inquiry such as ethics and science, it could involve substantive bodies of knowledge and information, and it could demand an emphasis on conceptual work as well as the other aspects of logical thought. But, of course, if these elements were given the time and the attention they deserved, what started out as a programme in critical thinking, included in the wider curriculum, would expand to become the curriculum itself. And that is what we surely require: a curriculum that substantially consists of important subjects and basic and powerful forms of inquiry treated in a critical manner.

Chapter 5

Imagination and Creativity

I: Reason and emotion

There is a common misapprehension that those educationalists who value rationality as an aim necessarily have lukewarm feelings, and ignore the aims of educating people in respect of their emotions and developing imagination and creativity. That was not true of Plato, one of the pre-eminent rationalists of all time, whose view of the soul divided into three parts is sometimes misconstrued as the view that feelings and desires should be suppressed by reason.[1] Rather his contention was that feelings should be rationally ordered. Their dictates, demands, and impulses should be reviewed and organised by reason, with will-power being enlisted on the side of reason, so that the individual is motivated and inspired by a coherent and rational set of feelings and desires. It is not passion, emotion, and feeling themselves that Plato wants us to avoid, but being a slave to passion or a helpless victim of ill-coordinated emotions and feelings. It was not true either of an eminent rationalist of our own times, R. S. Peters, as the title of one of his books, *Reason and Compassion*, sufficiently indicates.[2] And it is certainly not true of me.

The assumption that those who emphasise rationality are hostile to qualities such as imagination and creativity, is partly due to our tendency to polarise the intellect and the emotions, and partly to a failure to conceptualise such things as critical thinking, emotion, and imagination adequately. Both of these faults, in their turn, arise partly out of our lingering commitment to a vague version of faculty psychology. We have not thoroughly excised the misleading idea that imagination, creativity, and critical thinking are activities we engage in with distinct parts of the brain, as digestion and blood purification are the functions of different parts of the body. We still talk as if we believed that imagination were a mental organ, akin to a physical organ such as the liver, so that the question of whether a person is imaginative is a question about the functioning of the imaginative part of the brain, just as the question of whether certain bodily functions are in order is a question about the functioning of the liver. And we do things in our schools, designed to develop imagination, that would only make sense on the assumption that such a view of the matter was correct. (It may be noted in passing that Plato has sometimes been regarded as an early exponent of faculty psychology. But his reference to parts of the soul was purely figurative. He meant that we can logically distinguish between people's desires, reasoning, and will-power, not that there are physically distinct parts of the soul responsible for each of these activities. He knew that that could not be so, because he recognised that these activities are not purely physical. They all in one way or another involve understanding.)

The tendency to polarise rationality and feeling is to be resisted.[3] Rationality, far from being opposed to feeling and emotion, actually involves them. To be rational is not simply to perform certain operations. The rational person is necessarily committed to certain values and standards. He cares about truth and accuracy, he is concerned about evidence being appropriate and reasoning coherent. He is offended by argument that is illogical or misplaced. An individual may prize rationality above all else, and consequently denigrate some particular feelings and emotions. But he cannot be hostile to emotions as such, because his prizing of rationality and his denigration of other things are themselves species of emotion. More generally, there is no reason why one who prizes rationality should not also value other things. Commitment to rationality is entirely consistent with commitment not only to commitment itself, but also to the values of caring, intuition, insight, imagination, creativity, and so forth.

Conversely, concepts such as intuition, imagination, creativity, and emotion are logically tied up with rationality. Having imagination, being creative, perceiving by means of intuition, and experiencing emotions are only possible in so far as one's reasoning is coherent. To those who are not familiar with it, this claim may seem strange. It is nonetheless the case, and our failure to recognise it lies at the heart of much confused theory and practice relating to these concepts. I shall elaborate on this throughout the chapter, but, in brief, the point is that if intuition, for example, is to be truly intuition, as opposed to idle fancy, absurd speculation, or idiotic brainstorm, then whatever the source or cause of the inspiration, it has to get it right. The intuition has to be reasonable. And if we are going to encourage and value intuitive insights, as why should we not, we have to be able to assess them and to discriminate between the sound intuition and the nonsensical claim to insight.

Our tendency to see mental qualities as processes, and to largely ignore the context in which they operate, naturally gets in the way here. Intuition is loosely thought of as a spontaneous and somewhat mysterious process. But one has to have intuitions about something or other, and the possibility of the process of intuition taking place is necessarily dependent on some prior understanding. It is inconceivable that I should intuitively see what my neighbour should do about her unhappy marriage or intuitively grasp the theory of relativity, if I don't know anything about my neighbour's life or physics. Intuition involves perceiving things without the conscious use of reasoning, but the fact that it is not conscious does not mean that reasoning does not lie behind the intuition. Therefore, what people are capable of intuiting depends to some extent on what they are capable of reasoning about.

Similarly, imagination, although it is often casually conceived as some kind of inspirational visitation or as the generation of some idea on no basis of knowledge or understanding, is clearly no such thing. Conceiving of anything is dependent on prior understanding and experience. On almost any view of imagination, such as that it involves the capacity to posit what is not the case or to invoke possibilities, the concept presupposes the ability to know what is the case or to distinguish between actuality, possibility, and impossibility. What we call imaginative conceiving is indeed to be distinguished in various ways from deductive reasoning, but it still has to be based on knowledge of some sort. And the quality of imagination still has to be assessed by reference to our rational understanding. Nor is creativity any different in this respect. Even those most prone to talk about creative impulses as if they were the spontaneous springing into gear of some unique faculty or the product of mysterious and unidentifiable inspiration, cannot reasonably deny that creative acts logically entail understanding, even if we concede that that understanding need not be explicit.[4]

Emotions and feelings, so frequently loosely identified with one another, are not in fact synonymous. Emotions are indeed a species of feeling, but not all feelings are emotions. An emotion such as envy is distinguished from a feeling such as pain precisely by the fact that the former involves some kind of understanding. One cannot experience envy without understanding oneself and one's situation in a certain kind of way. This is a logical, not an empirical, point. "Envy" means something like "a feeling of discontent and ill will brought about by consideration of another's advantages, possessions, etc." It follows that, if you do not perceive that others have certain things, if you cannot conceive of them as advantages, if you do not experience a feeling of resentment because you see the situation in a certain kind of way, then whatever you may feel, whatever your mood or state of mind, you cannot be experiencing envy. What makes your state of mind, whatever its "feel," one of envy is the fact that the feeling is occasioned by a certain perception of your situation.[5]

The ideal that we are concerned with, while it involves the aim of developing critical thinking and other aspects of rationality, is no less concerned about imagination, creativity, and the education of the emotions, because these are important aspects of intelligent thought and behaviour, and valuable in respect of advancing our knowledge and understanding, fostering and enhancing the quality of life, and developing sensitivity, sympathy, and tolerance. But while these concepts are distinct from purely intellectual ones, they nonetheless involve rationality to an important degree. Educational attempts to develop them must therefore take account of their rational element.

The failure to recognise that imagination is grounded in reason, and the related presumptions that imagination is a gift bestowed on some but not on others, that it is something that "visits" people rather than something that is consciously developed, and that it is an endowment that is strengthened by exercise, without concern for the context in which it is exercised, may once again be traced to some of the fundamental errors and misconceptions with which we are concerned.

However, as in the case of giftedness, one of the six noted characteristics of our current thinking is not in evidence here, and that is the bias towards materialism. On the contrary, those who proclaim the value of imagination (and the other concepts discussed in this chapter) evidently object to this bias. In calling for more attention to be paid to the fostering of imagination, they are calling not only for a more enlightened attitude to knowledge than is conveyed by those who emphasise information, technical skills, and vocational training, but also for the reinstatement of certain other values such as beauty, quality of life, and the realm of fantasy. They recognise, as did those apostles of the arts and crafts in the late nineteenth century, such as Walter Pater, William Morris and John Ruskin, that whatever the value of industrialisation and technology (and there is no need to scorn them, denigrate them, or deny either their intrinsic value or their usefulness to man), they will destroy us if they are not handled imaginatively and creatively, and they will not satisfy us unless they are complemented by an equal concern for our creative and artistic instincts.

The question is whether the way in which champions of imagination, creativity, and emotional development conceive these concepts, and hence the practical steps they propose to take to cultivate them, are acceptable. And the answer is no, to a large extent because the argument surrounding the concepts exhibits the other characteristics noted.

First, and most obviously, we tend to regard imagination and creativity as generic qualities and as skills, just as we do critical thinking. We therefore propose to perfect them by exercise, without paying attention to the question of the context in which they are exercised. We assume that what matter are the processes of imaginative and creative thought, and are quite content to see them exercised in relation to trivial material. Our practice reveals an inability to recognise that imagination and creativity involve understanding (and are therefore not strictly speaking skills), and that understanding of one kind of content does not entail understanding of other kinds of content (and therefore we cannot develop imagination and creativity *per se*, but have to develop imaginative and creative ability in various distinct areas, which means that we have to make decisions about what areas are important).

Secondly, our failure to establish a coherent and plausible attitude to relativism inhibits us from settling the question of what subject matters are most worth studying, and from treating student performance in various domains in a way that does justice to the standards of quality implicit in them. Many of the putatively imaginative and creative achievements of students are not assessed in terms of their objective quality. They are regarded as worthwhile achievements, simply because they are, allegedly, the product of the imaginative or creative process. Or, perhaps more commonly, the issue of their quality does not arise because they are exercises in relatively trivial areas. Either way, we do not see the need to arrive at an understanding of the objective criteria for determining good poetry, good fiction, or good science, as a necessary part of developing imaginative and creative poets, writers, and scientists.

Thirdly, the dominance of the scientific paradigm leads to much theory and research in this area concerning itself with something other than true imagination or creativity. This is particularly true of research into creativity, where two kinds of view are clearly distinguishable. On the one hand, there is a fair amount of writing and practice that is not scientific or disciplined in any way. This is the kind of view that refers allusively and loosely to creative processes, happenings, and inspirations, and that treats creativity as a form of sincere self-expression. On the other hand, there are standardised creativity tests and research instruments that treat creativity as a discernible quality (or, at least, treat discernible qualities as necessary and sufficient indicators of creativity) and as a quantifiable one. What both approaches have in common is a quite inadequate conceptualisation of creativity. The former makes it ungraspable; the latter makes it something other than what it is, as I shall demonstrate below.

Fourthly, the lack of emphasis on historical and cultural understanding that is a feature of the contemporary curriculum is of particular concern here. Imagination and creativity are by no means confined to such arts subjects as history and literature. They may be as important in science or mathematics as anywhere else. But these are qualities that have to be indirectly nurtured, rather than directly taught, and history and literature are the subject matters that deal with the story of human beings in all those respects that have not been hived off as academic disciplines. Therefore, if imagination and creativity are not developed in these subjects, we are doing nothing to develop people who are imaginative and creative in respect of the vital issues that are the concern of historians and fictional writers. In addition, as I shall argue, literature and history are necessarily creative and imaginative activities, while science is not necessarily (although it may often be so). Consequently they are areas which necessarily encourage preoccupation with imagination and creativity.

II: Education of the emotions

The education of the emotions is widely agreed to be of importance by rationalists and non-rationalists alike. The questions are what is the nature of emotions and what might be meant by educating them, such that the value in so doing may be seen to be self-evident?

We talk a lot about educating the emotions, but do not have any clear idea of what we should be doing about it in schools, because we have not thought out the conceptual issue. The topic provides a good illustration of the close connection between theory and practice. There is no shortage of people who disparage educational theory and maintain that decisions are best left to experienced practitioners. But the implied distinction is absurd. Theory and practice are as interrelated as rationality and feeling. The business of selecting one procedure rather than another and of assessing one practice as preferable to another is theoretical, so the idea of practice divorced from theory is unintelligible, unless we were seriously to advocate unreflective action. Nor are we going to advance far in our practice or be in a position to evaluate it, if we are not prepared to engage in the reasoning, the gathering and weighing up of evidence, and the argument about which aims are preferable, which constitute educational theory. It may be that much actual educational theory is garbled, poorly conceived, or badly researched. But the conclusion to be drawn is that it is poor theory that is the enemy of good practice, rather than theory itself, and the necessary solution is to start theorising soundly. It is therefore a useful lesson to see that our uncertainty as to what we should do about the education of the emotions stems in large part from our lack of clarity as to what it means and what it necessarily involves.

An emotion, as has already been said, is a particular kind of feeling. The salient characteristic of emotions, as distinct from other feelings, is that it is necessary that a person should experience some feeling because of the way in which he appraises or sees his situation. There is no reference here to cause and effect nor is the claim empirical. It may be the case that my jealousy is occasioned by the fact that my wife has taken a lover or that my happiness is due largely to my wealth. But whether wealth makes people happy or the loss of a loved one makes people jealous are contingent questions. However usual they may be, neither is necessarily the case: there are happy poor people and, I daresay, unjealous forsaken lovers. However, whatever may cause different people to experience various emotions, the meaning of emotional terms is such that it would not make sense to attribute jealousy (rather than envy, misery, or even stomach ache) to someone unless he perceives himself as being in a situation of a certain sort. (In this case the kinds of situation in question would obviously include, but need not be exclusively tied to, a situation in which one loses one's loved one to another.) Similarly it would not make sense to attribute happiness to someone unless they perceived their situation in a certain distinctive kind of way (broadly speaking, as being harmonious with their aspirations and desires).[6] Happiness may feel different from jealousy, though in truth there is not a great deal we can say about that, since we do not know what different people do feel when they experience various emotions. But, in any case, it is not the distinctive nature of the feeling in each case that defines the emotions. It is the distinctive nature of the understanding accompanying the feelings that does so. Whether the perceptions or understandings are accurate or true is not relevant: if it turns out that my wife has not got a lover, this will not alter the fact that I experienced jealousy when I thought she had. Nor will my happiness be less real, if it happens to be the case that I am deceiving myself and my assumption that all is as I would like it to be in my world is false. The crucial point is that particular emotions are defined in terms of some particular form of appraisal of a situation, some particular cognitive or intellectual perception or understanding.

Emotions such as jealousy, happiness, love, being afraid, envy, sympathy, compassion, and hate (as contrasted with simple feelings such as pain or pleasure, which may be experienced without any particular cognitive appraisal) are important in human affairs. They constitute potent motivations, and affect the sum of happiness and misery. The question now is what we mean by educating them.

There are various things that people might mean, particularly if they are not too concerned about the precise meaning of education. Some might think that a proper education of the emotions consists in suppressing them, others in rooting them out. Some might incline to the view that one should cultivate the ability to keep one's emotion hidden from public view—develop the stiff upper lip.[7] Others might think in terms of encouraging public display of one's emotions, so that emotionally educated people are identified with those who loudly proclaim their love and hate. Some might identify educating the emotions with cultivating strong responses and intense sensations of such things as jealousy and compassion.

There are a number of things that might be said for and against each of these ideas. But none of them is a good candidate for the meaning of "educating the emotions." Attempting to root out emotions so that people simply do not experience them, assuming it could be done, would be best described as exactly that. What has it to do with educating them? Teaching people to overcome or suppress their emotions, or to hide them, would be a species of training rather than education, and, furthermore, training a response to emotions rather than training emotions themselves. Those who are taught to advertise their emotional state may be said to have learned something, but it could scarcely be said that their emotions themselves have been educated in any way. Developing the individual's capacity for intensity of emotional experience may conceivably play some part in the education of the emotions, but it is certainly not the whole of it, and it is in any case not very clear what one could do to bring about this intensity in any direct fashion. Nor is it clear that it would be desirable. Intense experience of the positive emotions, such as love, might be worth cultivating, but intense experience of the negative ones such as hatred would not obviously be, so it is not the intensity of emotion in itself that we should be concerned with.

This last distinction provides a useful hint. Different emotions have different value, both in themselves and for various extrinsic purposes. To educate people in respect of the emotions should surely include enabling them to discriminate between them. Education of the emotions, if it is truly education, should enable people to distinguish between one emotion and another, particularly those such as envy and jealousy, or love and infatuation, which are easily confused. It should empower people to recognise their own emotional state and to classify those of others correctly. And it should qualify people to make sane and appropriate evaluations of the various emotions, based upon sound understanding of what they entail. What, for example, is wrong with envy and infatuation? Well, part of the answer will be found in a thorough understanding of what they are.

In view of the fact that emotions are, by definition, feelings or sensations logically associated with particular types of cognitive appraisal, it is evident that educating the emotions is essentially a matter of teaching people about the kind of appraisal that is associated with the various emotions (teaching them, in other words, what jealousy, love, and so on actually mean) and helping them to recognise particular emotional states in themselves and others. There is no point in trying to focus on the sensations themselves or to teach people what the feelings of jealousy and love are like, because we cannot directly locate or grasp the sensations themselves. We do not even know that the nature of our experiences are exactly similar (precisely because they cannot be isolated and paraded before us as colours might be). We may presume that if you and I are both in love we are both experiencing the same feelings or sensations. But we do not know that, and there is no means by which we could know.

Even sophisticated neural investigation would be irrelevant to this particular question, because, however closely sensations may be related to various neurological or physiological activities, they are not to be identified with them. It is not the feeling of pleasure itself that is monitored by measuring nerve and brain waves; it is at best the physical source of pleasure. Indeed, it is perfectly reasonable to suggest that your sensation of pleasure may be different from mine, even when the pattern of our neurological reactions is the same. Evidence of this kind will not affect the attribution of jealousy or love to people at all, for when we say that someone is jealous or in love we are not attributing a particular kind of sensation to them, as if referring to the various flavours of ice cream. We are saying only that they have some sensation(s) that accompanies a particular type of cognitive appraisal. It is, to repeat and stress the point, the type of appraisal conjoined with some sensation, never mind of what kind, that makes an emotional experience what it is and not another type. This leads inexorably to a conclusion that may be rather startling, if it is unfamiliar: to understand what love is, and to be able to distinguish it from lust, infatuation, friendship, and to be able to recognise it in oneself or others, is not a matter of trying to find out what people who have been in love have felt, so much as a matter of increasing intellectual understanding—a matter of exploring and understanding the many various and subtle situations that are correctly characterised as involving love.[8]

It follows that, if we want to educate people in respect of emotions, we should not be giving primacy to the sciences. The natural sciences increase our understanding of the physical sources of sensations, but not of emotions themselves. Psychology is engaged in the altogether different task of inquiring into such things as what may cause people to love one kind of person rather than another, and what kind of behaviour people in love tend to engage in.

We have to make people aware of, and develop understanding of, the kinds of emotion that can be experienced. Since the majority of the emotions are complex concepts, and since they are not the exclusive concern of any academic discipline, it seems beyond serious cavil that we must proceed to educate the emotions through the study of philosophy, literature, and history.

Philosophy addresses itself directly to the conceptual questions, seeking to provide greater understanding of the nature of emotion itself and clear and coherent definitions of particular emotions. Literature explores the concepts indirectly, but nonetheless most usefully and subtly. Novelists and poets enrich and illuminate our understanding of love, jealousy, hate, envy, etc., by their detailed exploration of particular instances. A novel such as Arnold Bennett's *Riceyman Steps* is, for example, a sustained study of the emotional state of miserliness. The reader is led into the mind of the miser and brought to understand what it is like to be a miser. No empirical study of the contingent facts about misers could conceivably provide such insight, if only because that would not be the purpose of such a study. History inevitably deals with emotions, because history is concerned with the story of human activity and that activity includes emotional experiences, responses, and motivations. It is important too in that it provides some understanding of the way in which emotions may take different forms in different times and places, some emotions even passing out of view in particular cultural settings. This is because different cultures have different views of the world, and the kinds of cognitive appraisal that they are capable of may therefore vary. For instance, the experience of jealousy is only logically possible in a society that has some sense of personal possession. Cultures that have a minimal notion of possession will be equally unlikely to feel jealous. And obviously the specific nature of the type of cognitive appraisal that is associated with a particular emotion will vary in different societies. The concept of love, for example, has quite certainly varied both culturally and historically.

We learn what love, hate, jealousy, and so forth are by acquiring a keen sense of what kinds of situation are associated with them. Somebody who is familiar with Greek literature thereby comes to understand the Greek conception of love. Understanding the concept does not necessarily enable one or cause one to fall in love (à la mode Grecque in this example), but it allows one the possibility of so doing, and enables one to recognise it for what it is. No doubt people have been sexually aroused by one another, attracted to one another, bored or interested in one another, since time began, with or without any developed understanding. But they cannot have been in love, until some association between sensation and a certain type of situation has been consciously articulated; for it would not count as love, if it did not involve the fact of seeing one's situation as being of a certain sort and associating feelings with that particular perception. Our capacity to love is enhanced by, and largely dependent on, being able to classify what might otherwise be a sensation of anything from heartburn to exhilaration, as love.

It is not a necessary condition of identifying and experiencing emotions that one should study philosophy, history, and literature. Plenty of cultures prior to the Greek initiation of historical inquiry in the fifth century, and plenty of illiterate people today, experience emotions. They may acquire the requisite understanding from conversation with friends, from films or television, or any other source of information you care to mention. But if people are to have a full and subtle understanding of emotions, and to develop sophisticated and accurate conceptions of them, so that they can deliberately seek them out or shun them, and recognise them in all their manifold and subtle varieties, then they need access to the most discriminating and varied delineations of the emotions. The study of philosophy and literature is important, because it is, or should be, a study of the best that has been thought and said about the various emotions. The study of history should promote the awareness of shifts, developments, and contrasts in conceptions over time and place that is necessary to combat the chauvinistic dogmatism, the unimaginatively narrow and exclusive conceptions, of so many people, and hence to increase tolerance and sympathetic understanding.

The objection to a diet of Barbara Cartland romances, detective stories, magazine questionnaires on the extent to which you are in love or jealous, and television soap operas such as *Dallas*, is that they portray emotions in very simplistic, crude, and stereotypical form. They encourage people to conceive of love and other emotions in limited ways, and hence presumably lead people to seek an unrealistically limited kind of love, and to make misleading and puerile judgements about the emotional experiences of others. By contrast, those who have immersed themselves in fifth-century Greek culture, medieval culture, and eighteenth-century culture, who are familiar with distinctions between French, Indian, and North American culture, and who have read widely amongst novelists and poets of quality, have, by definition, been introduced to a wide range of intricately explored types and examples of the various emotions. Can it be seriously disputed that Plato, Chaucer, Shakespeare, Graham Greene, and Margaret Atwood understood a thing or two about the forms that emotions such as love and jealousy may take, and that he who wants to increase his own understanding would be well advised to partake of their wisdom? He, on the other hand, who is not interested in what kinds of love there may be, nor in whether he is truly in love or in whether his friends are jealous or afraid, can content himself with a pop-psychology manual, which will teach him that he's in love if he doesn't eat his breakfast, sends flowers twice a week, and gets an erection when in bed with his partner. And he can ignore the question of whether his friends are jealous or afraid until they beat him up or run away.

To summarise: the education of the emotions consists in providing people with a good understanding of the various emotional concepts. It should not be confused with indulging the emotional outbursts of children or suppressing them, nor has it got anything to do with sentimentalism or self-expression. It must proceed by means of studying the subject matter in question. That could in principle be done in a variety of ways, but the richest store of wisdom on the subject is to be found in the work of those who have provided the most subtle exploration of the concepts of the various emotions. We seem increasingly to turn away from making the study of history, culture, and literature a cornerstone of our curriculum. One can only presume that this is partly because our failure to face up to the questions of what emotions actually are and what educating them must therefore entail, has blinded us to the importance of these subjects in this respect. More particularly our tendency to see emotions as internal processes, as sensations or feelings, rather than as essentially linked to understanding, and our tendency to look to psychological theories of emotional development which are based on a different and misleading conception of emotion, have led us astray.

III: Imagination

We value imagination. In itself it is thought to be an attribute to be proud of; in the arts it is an essential part of quality; in all areas it is recognised as an asset, for it is imaginative scientists, lawyers, and engineers who provide us with the breakthroughs. But because we are prone to conceive of imagination loosely as an entity and a functional capacity of the brain that can be developed by exercise in any context, we are also prone to believe that the way to develop imagination in schools is to call for its exercise in and of itself—to let it rip, so to speak, without concerning ourselves with the context in which it is operating, the material or subject matter wherein it is exercised. Schools that overtly praise imagination and that encourage imaginative work in any and all activities, are thought to be doing the appropriate kind of thing.

Up to a point, there is some reason in this. Imagination does need to be exercised if it is to blossom, just as critical thought does. And one can exercise it in any context, as one can critical thinking. But just as there is no generic skill of critical thinking, so there is no generic faculty of imagination, and to exercise the latter in trivial matters is as valueless as to exercise the former on trite and irrelevant material. There is the further problem with imagination that people tend to talk as if it were an innate faculty that merely needs to be called forth or encouraged to show itself in order for the exercise to begin. But this is a fundamentally mistaken notion. The new born baby does not have a faculty of imagination waiting to be developed. Imagination does not exist at that stage. There is no entity, physiological or of any other sort, that is imagination. There is therefore no thing, initially, to be developed or cultivated. Imagination is a quality that only becomes possible with the development of understanding and learning. It is an attribute that people develop in themselves as a consequence of the way in which they make use of their learning and understanding, rather as speed is not an entity waiting to be exercised, but a characteristic that individuals acquire as a result of the way in which they come to move.

I have already referred to the fact that ostensibly faculty psychology has had its day, even amongst psychologists. I might add that the burden of what I have to say here was eloquently elaborated by the philosopher Gilbert

Ryle forty years ago in his book, *The Concept of Mind*.[9] But it may be felt that recent research which suggests that one side of the brain accounts for our rational and deductive abilities, and the other for the visual, perceptive, and imaginative abilities, shows that we are wrong to persist in saying that mental concepts do not refer to parts of the brain. I must therefore stress that this view is mistaken and involves the original misconceptions of faculty psychology.

It may be the case that the display of imagination, calculative ability, and creativity, for example, are each connected to one side of the brain or the other, such that damage to one half of the brain will impair ability in some respects but not in others. So much may be accepted for the purposes of this discussion without quibble. And indeed for all I know, and for all it matters to the issue at hand, it may be the case that in the years to come we will be able to associate various abilities with more specific parts of the brain. Now it certainly follows from this that a certain state of a certain area of the brain is a necessary condition of the exercise of a certain ability. In much the same way, the existence of an unimpaired leg is a necessary condition of walking naturally. But just as it does not follow that having legs is the same thing as walking, so it does not follow that having a certain part of one's brain in good working order is the same thing as being imaginative. Ryle's fundamental point, and one which, I suggest, despite various criticisms that have been leveled against his work, is plainly correct, is that the names of our various mental concepts all involve reference to the manner in which we think and understand. As such they neither are supposed to nor in fact could refer to physical organs. A brain is not a mind, and understanding and thinking are not parts of the brain but activities that we use the brain to engage in.

It is true that the way in which we speak suggests otherwise. That, I am suggesting, is part of the trouble. We do say that "he has imagination" or "his imaginative faculty is strong," as if there were an organ of imagination akin to the liver or the kidneys. But whereas if there is something wrong with the kidneys we go directly to them and remedy the problem in some way, removing them or transplanting them if necessary, we all know very well that, if there is something wrong with somebody's imagination, we don't start slicing up the brain. Similarly, if something is wrong with somebody's sense of humour, we don't in normal circumstances start wondering about the physical state of their brain. No doubt an etiolated brain could lead to loss of humour (for we acknowledge again that a brain in good functioning order is necessary for the exercise of any mental capacity). But, by and large, when people lack humour, if we do anything, we do the sorts of thing that come into the category of teaching and educating them. And that is what we have to do in the case of imagination. Not teach or instruct "it," still less start meddling about with the brain, but teach and educate people in such a way as to encourage them to use their brain imaginatively. We teach them to do things in an imaginative way.

When we talk of a person having imagination, and superficially suggest that he is possessed of some inner element or organ, what we actually mean is that he performs certain kinds of operation in a certain kind of way. The abstract noun imagination is derivative on the adverbial form "imaginatively": there is no more substance to the imagination than can be extrapolated from the notion of doing things imaginatively, just as there is no more substance to the idea of speed than can be abstracted from the idea of doing things fast. The proof that this is so is to be found in the fact that we have no reason to call a person imaginative, except on the condition that he does things imaginatively, and the fact of his doing so is a sufficient condition for calling him imaginative. Thus the necessary and sufficient condition of imagination is doing things imaginatively. It simply doesn't matter, so far as the meaning of imagination goes, what is going on in the brain, because "imagination" does not mean "a particular pattern of neurological waves." Nor should the point that having imagination means doing things in an imaginative way be confused with a species of behavioural definition. I am not suggesting that imagination should be defined in terms of certain specific and observable behaviours such as providing a certain number of answers on a creativity test. I am suggesting that the meaning of the term is that we do things in a certain kind of way, but I have not said that the way in which we do them can be characterised in purely behavioural terms. What remains true is that, if we were to say "he has imagination," even though he never did anything imaginatively, we should be talking nonsense, just as we should be if we refused to acknowledge that he was imaginative, despite the fact that he did things imaginatively.

The question now becomes, in what way does a person have to do things to be accounted imaginative? My answer is that he has to "have the tendency and ability consciously to conceive of the unusual and effective in a variety of particular contexts."[10] If a person is inclined to and able to reason in this way, then he is imaginative. (Note that use of the phrase "reason in a certain kind of way" does not make this a definition of a process. We are not talking here about whatever processes people who are imaginative may go through, not least because we know practically nothing about that. We are talking about what it means to be imaginative, and what it means is "to be inclined and able to conceive of the unusual and effective." The definition is in terms of product or achievement, and not in terms of experience or process.)

Imagination must involve conscious conceiving of ideas because it is a peculiarly human concept. Machines such as word processors might themselves produce, or be made to produce by the now proverbial barrel of monkeys, works and ideas that we would be prepared to classify as imaginative. But if the product is randomly produced, mechanically produced, or, in short, not produced as a result of a conscious intention to achieve some such thing, we surely wouldn't want to call the monkeys or the machine "imaginative." Pretty impressive, no doubt, but not imaginative. Imagination, like all mental concepts, presupposes consciousness of what one is doing. There would be no obvious reason to call a person imaginative, for instance, purely on the strength of insights garnered in a trance or under hypnosis. This is one reason why the tendency to attribute mental concepts to machines, however sophisticated, makes no sense.

There must also be some consistent and long term tendency to produce the kinds of idea and solution in question (not, be it noted, a tendency to be imaginative, for we cannot include the word we are trying to define in the definition), for imaginative is a dispositional term. One is not imaginative, simply because one has done something imaginatively. One has to show that one characteristically performs in this kind of way, to deserve the label.

But the crucial elements in the definition are the criteria of unusualness and effectiveness. A person who continually states the obvious, offers predictable solutions and well worn ideas, and in other respects barely strays from the familiar and well-known, is scarcely to be regarded as imaginative. There will sometimes be severe problems in determining whether particular conclusions are unusual, but the difficulty in determining whether somebody is imaginative by this criterion should not be confused with difficulty in determining what the word means. It is sometimes difficult to decide whether a person has sufficiently few hairs to count as balding, but that doesn't make the meaning of balding elusive. But the products of the imaginative person's reasoning must be effective as well as unusual, for we do not mean by imagination simply the capacity to produce unusual but bizarre, absurd, or useless ideas. We have other words for that kind of ability such as "fancifulness" and "whimsicality." Again there may be many difficulties in the way of determining whether certain ideas are efficacious, but that is not an objection to the definition.

In short, if "imagination" is to mean something clear, specific, distinctive, and worthwhile, and to be defined in a way that accords with normal usage, rather than to be some vague emotive slogan, an unneeded synonym for something else, the name of something of no obvious value, or defined in some new and idiosyncratic fashion, it must meet the criteria of consciousness, inclination, unusualness, and effectiveness. They are necessary conditions of imaginative thought, and taken together they are sufficient.

That being so, it will be at once apparent that imagination cannot be a generic quality or ability, for the criteria of unusualness and effectiveness vary from context to context. What makes for an unusual and effective solution (and hence an imaginative one) to a town planning problem has to be determined by different criteria (and very likely by different kinds of criterion, which is different) from those that will be relevant to an unusual and effective solution to a philosophical problem. There is no necessary reason why a person who is imaginative in one area should be so in another, and his capacity to be so in either one will be partly determined by his understanding of the area in question. We do indeed often refer to people as imaginative without qualification as to the respects in which they are imaginative, and this tends to reinforce the misleading idea that imagination is a quality that, if one has it, is generic. But evidently what we mean by the unqualified use of the adjective is that a person is imaginative over a wide range of areas that we deem to be of significance and importance. Nobody is going to judge people "imaginative" without qualification on the strength of their tendency and ability to come up with unusual and effective ideas in respect of trivial pursuits such as playing marbles or baking biscuits.

Perhaps I had better rephrase the last claim, since some educationalists seem inclined to do exactly that. I had better say that, while a person may reasonably be described as an imaginative marble player, it would seem quite ludicrous to suggest that he is therefore an imaginative person without qualification, unless one wrongly assumed that since he is imaginative in this area he must also be capable of being an imaginative philosopher and physicist. Furthermore, if imagination is to be ascribed equally, without qualification, to a certain kind of marble player and a certain kind of physicist, then one questions the so far unquestioned presumption that imagination is necessarily of value. Some imagination, on this view, would be of great worth, some would be trivial, and some, such as the imagination of the torturer, would be downright evil. It is altogether clearer, less confusing, and more in accord with the facts of the matter to insist that imagination is always context bound, and the presumption should be that, when a person is described as imaginative without qualification, they have shown that as a matter of contingent fact they can display imagination across a spectrum of important areas.

Given that imagination means this, it follows that in order to nurture it we have to give students understanding of the various spheres in which we think it most important that they display imagination. Once again, then, we see the crucial importance of determining what subject matter is important and teaching it. It is also necessary to teach the subject matter in such a way as to bring students to an understanding of the criteria of quality inherent in particular fields. Imaginative scientists, imaginative poets, and imaginative spouses alike have to appreciate and recognise what makes for good science, good poetry, and good spousely behaviour, because, we have said, we do not count people as imaginative if their ideas, while unusual, are ridiculous or poor ones. It makes no sense to talk of doing anything directly to or with the imagination (cultivating it, exercising it, encouraging it, etc.), until a certain level of understanding has been achieved, because prior to that "it" does not exist. And, when people acquire the understanding that allows them to be imaginative, it makes no sense to talk of developing imagination in itself, or to presume that a person who is imaginative in one field will necessarily be so in another.[11] Whether it is reasonable to posit a general factor of imagination, common to all instances of imaginative thought and behaviour, or not, the fact remains that imaginative acts are dependent on specific contextual knowledge. If there is a general factor of imagination, we do not know how to locate it, strengthen it, or do anything else with it, whereas we are able to take steps to promote and cultivate imaginative thought by ensuring a sound basis of understanding.

This basis of understanding is, of course, only a necessary condition of imaginative behaviour. It is not sufficient. Many people who have a good grasp of various subject matters, a sound understanding, do not strike us as being particularly imaginative. But, because we are not dealing with a skill in the true sense of the word, we cannot teach people how to proceed imaginatively as we can teach them how to multiply or how to operate a lathe. Imagination has to be nourished, cultivated, and encouraged, rather than instructed, instilled, or trained. We have to proceed indirectly rather than directly, by such means as explaining the meaning of imagination and illustrating specific instances of imaginative work, by feeding the imagination with examples of unusual and unfamiliar information and material, and by showing that we value imagination. A thoroughgoing relativism is quite incompatible with concern for imagination, for if there are no standards of quality in poetry, no criteria that distinguish good from bad poetry, then anything unusual that anybody writes would count as imaginative poetry. That would not only render imagination of no obvious value or interest, but it would also involve an incorrect conception: imagination does not mean the capacity to produce unusual work of no quality.

A curriculum concerned with the development of imagination therefore has to involve those subject matters in which we are particularly concerned to see imagination displayed and those that are most likely to foster the imaginative spirit or disposition by opening up the mind to the variety and complexity of human experience. As to which subject matters are important, there is nothing to be added, at this point, to what has been said in discussing critical thinking. The issue will be addressed directly in the chapter on Curriculum Content. But, while imagination is by no means confined to the realm of the arts, the study of literature and history do have a special value in this respect, because these are the subjects that, *par excellence*, open the mind to the fact of variety and feed it with strange and unusual ideas. To study the world of the Aztecs, to read the story of Ulysses, to become familiar with the culture of Indonesia, or to read the novels of Charles Dickens, is to be led to realise something of the possibilities open to man, is to engage with imaginative treatment of themes and issues, and is to turn the mind away from the idea of life as a series of closed problems to which the solution may always be found by sound calculation. History and literature are particularly informed by imagination, they credit it, they trade in it, they celebrate it, and they insistently call for it, even as they proliferate ideas and information which one needs in order to proceed imaginatively. The point, in a nutshell, is that a good novel or a good history is necessarily an imaginative work. A good maths textbook is not necessarily imaginative, and the imaginative maths textbook does not feed the imagination except in respect of mathematics. We can only hope to foster imagination by adding to our understanding some experience of imaginative work.

The idea of exercises in imagination, without qualification, is incoherent. In practice, therefore, classes explicitly devoted to imagination encourage its exercise in relation to trivial activity. (If it is related to a serious body of knowledge such as history or science, then it is not a class in imagination, but a class in history or science calling for imaginative study.) Treating student products as imaginative when they are merely imaginary is confused. Our tendency to advocate such practices and our failure to insist on a curriculum based on certain important subjects, including in particular history and literature, to be taught in ways that draw attention to the imagination, that encourage imaginative treatment, and that inform people about the criteria of quality that are a necessary part of imaginative activity, can be traced to our failure to conceptualise imagination adequately, our tendency to see it as a generic skill, and our unwillingness to grasp the thorn of relativism.

IV: Creativity

Creativity is another value that nominally we share, and another concept that for the most part is crassly misconceived. Some educationalists cheerfully assert that "creativity . . . . is one of those concepts that is virtually impossible to define."[12] That, however, is mistaken. If it were impossible to define in any way, it would have no meaning, and we would be well advised to stop talking about it. But in fact it has been defined quite satisfactorily by numerous philosophers.[13] The problem is that educationalists by and large ignore the philosophical work and proffer definitions of their own that are either of the wrong sort or inadequately carried out. If one thinks of creativity as a process, for example, then it will indeed be "virtually impossible to define," because what we refer to as the creative process is something that we have no way of getting to grips with. Unless we mistakenly identify the process with some neurophysiological activity, what we are referring to is a necessarily unobservable phenomenon. (It is a mistake to identify neural activity with the creative process, because being creative does not mean that one's brain is being activated in some particular way, as was argued in relation to imagination.) We do not know anything at all about the process itself as such, nor could we. It is the name we give to an undescribable, unexplained, putative process that for all we know takes a different form with different people on different occasions. Small wonder, then, that creativity in this sense is undefinable. It has no specific meaning.

But if we are concerned about what it means to be creative, then there is no problem about defining it clearly. The reason that most definitions are unacceptable is that they are poorly worked out. For example, Bruner has defined creativity in terms of the evocation of "effective surprise" in oneself or in others.[14] But such a definition merely substitutes one obscure phrase for another: what is a feeling of effective surprise? How does one recognise it and distinguish it from feelings of effective awe, amazement, or stupefaction? What is meant by "effective"? Is it plausible to identify creativity exclusively with this ill-defined feeling? Am I creative merely because I startle my audience with my outrageousness (or would such startlement not count as a feeling of effective surprise)? Which and how many people have to be effectively surprised for my actions to count as creative? These and other similar questions might be answered, and, if they were, in a clear and careful fashion, then we would be approaching an adequate conception of creativity, perhaps. But the questions are not even recognised, much less answered, and the result is a concept that to all intents and purposes has not been defined.

One of the most well known "definitions" is provided by E. Paul Torrance. Creativity, in his view, is "becoming sensitive to or aware of problems, deficiencies, gaps in knowledge, missing elements, disharmonies and so on; bringing together available information; defining the difficulty or identifying the missing element; searching for solutions, making guesses or formulating hypotheses about deficiencies, testing and retesting these hypotheses and modifying and restating them; perfecting them and finally communicating the results."[15]

Closer consideration reveals that this is not in fact a definition at all, but a hotch-potch list of activities in which creative people may engage. The activities themselves stand in need of as much definition as the term creativity. What is meant by "becoming sensitive to . . . deficiencies"? What kind of "searching for solutions" or "modifying" of hypotheses are we talking about? More fundamentally, it will be noted that this "definition" is couched in such a way as to betray the by now familiar assumption that creativity is a generic quality: reference is made throughout to the business of "identifying missing elements," "making guesses," "searching for solutions," and so forth, as if they were activities one could become good at without regard to specific contexts.

Quite apart from such specific inadequacies, one must question whether this is in fact remotely the kind of thing that we have in mind when we distinguish between a creative composer such as Mozart or a creative scientist such as Einstein, and the uncreative John Smith. To be sure, Mozart and Einstein will have been sensitive to problems, will have searched for solutions, and modified hypotheses. But is that what we are referring to when we call them creative? Besides, it is reasonable to suppose that John Smith too engages in these activities. It has of course been maintained by some that "creativity" is not a term that should be confined to a few remarkable individuals, and that we are all creative to some degree. It should be emphasised that such a claim is not an empirical one, but a conceptual stipulation. It involves changing the meaning of the term so that it may truthfully be said that we are all creative. But what is the point of such a move? We do not need to call the business of being aware of problems, making guesses, and restating hypotheses "creativity," we confuse ourselves by introducing a new and different meaning for the term, and we render the concept so broad and imprecise that there is not much we can do with it. We also challenge the normative implications of the term. Creativity is generally thought to be a particularly noteworthy and estimable quality. Why should the mere business of thinking, aspects of which is what Torrance's account really seems to describe, which is common to all, be regarded so favourably? Surely, at the very least we want some reference to the quality of thinking involved?

Since the logic of creativity is very similar to that of imagination, we can be relatively brief about sorting out this conceptual confusion.[16] A creative person is one who, in one or more areas of life, intentionally produces something of originality and quality, to some extent consistently. It must involve intention, since we should not be inclined to attribute creative qualities to a person whose ideas or artifacts, however good, are clearly the product of accident, any more than we should be inclined to think of shrimp as creative just because they are found in some pretty pattern on the shoreline. A person may accidently produce works which, by extension, we classify as creative, but, while his "painting" produced by the accidental knocking over of tins of paint may conceivably be a work of art, he assuredly does not deserve to be called creative. (He might be, if he deliberately decided to knock the paint over in order to produce a picture, but that is different.)

Consistency of some sort (to precisely what degree is unimportant here) is also required. To call someone creative is to attribute some kind of ability to him, and we do not recognise something as an ability if it cannot be repeated. I do not have cricketing ability if I consistently fail to score runs, merely because on one occasion I score a century. I am not to be accounted a creative thinker, if I only ever had one good idea.

The domain in which one produces is not important to the definition of the term. It may be ideas, artifacts, or effects on other people, for example, and the ideas, artifacts, and effects may be of many different kinds. People may be equally creative in respect of their handling of people, their handling of bank balances, or their handling of musical composition. But we do not draw the conclusion from this that creativity is an ability that, in so far as one has it, one may put to good use in any sphere. On the contrary, we draw the conclusion that the capacity to be creative depends partly on knowledge of a sphere, and therefore has to be developed in particular contexts. As has been noted in respect of other concepts, while the meaning of the word creativity remains the same whether we are talking about creative mathematicians or creative horse-riders, the form that creativity takes, the criteria for determining that a person is creative, differ from one sphere to another, so that one cannot meaningfully develop creativity *per se*. There are some minor elements in being creative that, being common to all particular forms, may indeed be developed in any sphere and utilised in all. For example, a creative person is, amongst other things, one who is disposed to look for imaginative solutions, and it may be that such a disposition can be developed in any sphere and carried over to others. But nobody can be creative in a sphere he does not understand.

The criteria most to be emphasised are those of quality and originality. If a person's poetry, solution to an administrative problem, or mathematical deductions are unoriginal or of poor quality, then why on earth would we want to call him creative? Why should we want to use any honorific term, since there is no obvious value in recycling familiar ideas or propounding silly ones?

If we turn our attention to school practice, we can identify two common trends, which, for convenience, I shall label the expressionist and the scientific. The expressionist school of thought promulgates education for "creativity" that takes the institutionalised form of boldly entitled "creativity lessons" or more specific courses in creative art, creative writing, creative reading, or whatever it may be. The characteristics of this school of thought include either ignoring the criteria of originality and quality or arguing that these should be interpreted subjectively, and emphasising criteria such as sincerity and spontaneity. In other words we are dealing with a quite different concept of creativity from that which has just been outlined. Now, I am less concerned to argue that this is a confusing and unnecessary misuse of the word "creativity," than I am to argue that such practices are not educationally of much worth. It *is* a misuse of the word, for creativity does not mean "the sincere expression of one's feelings or ideas," it is unnecessary since we have other words such as "self-expression," "spontaneity," and "sincerity" that are perfectly adequate, and it is confusing, since one can never be sure what is meant by the term, if it is allowed to have a variety of distinct definitions. But surely of more immediate concern is that such practice has little or no apparent value.

The idea of "lessons in creativity" makes no sense strictly speaking, since one cannot teach creativity or practise being creative without qualification. One has to practise being creative in some particular respect. Of course, that being a matter of logical necessity, such lessons will have an identifiable content. But the implication of calling them "lessons in creativity" or "creativity hours," rather than lessons in creative writing or creative maths, is that it does not matter in respect of what creativity is displayed. But it does matter, for two reasons. First, some activities may be inherently trivial and have no educational worth, and secondly, developing creativity, even in the particular sense of self-expression, in one context will not necessarily promote it in others. One must therefore ask why we should value the idea of children being left to do as they choose with sand, paint, or dressing up clothes. No doubt young children will always engage in such play and gain benefit from it in terms of satisfaction, discovery, increased confidence, and self-esteem. But what has it got to do with education? And while we may certainly want to encourage children to express themselves freely without being constrained by criteria of quality, do we really want to allocate special lessons to the pursuit of this objective, so that a clear distinction is drawn between self-expression without formal restraints, and study? It would seem more appropriate, in the context of schooling, to integrate our concerns for a degree of self-expression and a relaxing of the demands of quality into our teaching generally.

This point applies equally to more specific lessons in creative writing, creative drawing, or creative mathematics. There is little to be said for encouraging the idea that there is, on the one hand, the regular English lesson in which one learns to read and write in accordance with various rules and standards, and, on the other hand, the creative writing lesson in which one simply expresses oneself. For this suggests, what is the very reverse of the truth, that self-expression is to be contrasted with the ability to write according to the rules. On the contrary, one cannot express oneself except through mastery of some set of rules.[17]

This brings us to the fundamental objection to creativity conceived of as synonymous with self-expression. Not only is it misleading to suggest that self-expression can take place meaningfully without reference to rules and standards, it is also anti-educational to encourage activity that has no concern for criteria of quality. "Creative poetry" cannot even be poetry, if it ignores the criteria of good poetry. For the criteria of good poetry arise from the criteria that define poetry. Education involves bringing people to understand certain important and worthwhile pursuits. To encourage children simply to express themselves is to teach them the false doctrine that it is valuable to do that, to perpetrate the misconception that self-expression is the product of a sincere desire to express oneself alone, and to promulgate a host of works and activities of no obvious merit. A "creative" poem that meets no standards of poetic expression is not worth having.

It may be said that, while it is true that creativity implies standards and criteria of quality, we are forgetting that work may be creative from a child's perspective, even if it is agreed that it is not creative by adult standards. A poem that would not impress us much from the pen of Keats, might be noteworthy from the point of view of a fourteen-year-old. It is certainly true that what is regarded as good work may vary depending on who produces it. But this line of argument is not helpful here, since we are dealing with a conception of creativity that involves no reference to quality of any sort. If the different view that children's creativity should be defined by reference to criteria of quality appropriate to their age were adopted, we should naturally welcome the encouragement of creativity in that sense. Though it is worth adding that it is not empirically the case that students who are creative in this sense (i.e., good in comparison with their peers) necessarily end up as creative adults. The truly creative composers, writers, and scientists were not all good students during their school days.

In short, some of what we do in schools is misnamed as creative and has no obvious value, educational or otherwise. True creative writing, creative mathematics, and so forth would involve understanding of the nature of these activities and adherence to the criteria of quality built into them.

The scientific school of thought is most evident in creativity testing, and the use of such tests as exercises to develop creativity and as research instruments. Such tests take many specific forms, but whether students are asked to list possible uses for an old tin or a brick, to make pictures out of circles or other shapes, to solve a number of brief and isolated problems or puzzles, or to provide suitable titles for the outline of various short stories, their logic and the problems inherent in the idea of such tests remain essentially the same.

Features that are common to all such tests include the use of material which belongs to no substantive discipline or subject area, the absence of assessment in terms of quality, (or, if present, assessment by no clear criteria), and an emphasis on the quantity of response. Thus, individuals are judged to be highly creative simply in virtue of the fact that they list more uses for an old tin or a brick, complete more circles, or provide more plot titles, than others, without reference to the quality of their contributions. When a qualitative measure is introduced we are faced with the problem of how to judge whether a response is suitable: by what criteria does one determine whether listing "as a bed warmer" as a use for an old brick, or "as a watering can" for an old shoe box, are good responses? How does one decide whether a particular plot title or completed circle is of good quality? There are two problems here. One is that as a matter of fact most creativity tests do not clearly specify how such judgements are to be made, and sometimes they turn them into further quantitative exercises. The other is that it is difficult in the extreme to say how sensible criteria of quality could be introduced since the activities in question are so formless.

They are, of course, deliberately formless, because this type of creativity test is based upon the misconception that there is something called the creative faculty that exists independently of acquired understanding, and therefore the tests are deliberately conceived in such a way as to minimise the effects of learning and knowledge. But whereas there are ways of determining what counts as good poetry or good maths, because these are reasonably well defined activities, there is no obvious way of determining what makes for a good use of a brick or a good picture made out of a circle. The result is that scoring is usually straightforwardly quantitative: the more responses the better. When a qualitative element is introduced, as it is with the plot title test, scoring is based on the intuitive judgement of the tester in conjunction with a quantitative element. (Consequently, we, who rely on the tester's findings, have no idea how the judgements were made or whether we would agree with them.) Occasionally what purports to be qualitative turns out on closer inspection to be quantitative. For example, one research instrument scored children's responses to the task of completing a picture out of two geometrical shapes by reference to the originality and appropriateness of the responses. But originality was defined in terms of extent to which a response was uncommon in the sample, and a necessary condition of appropriateness was taken to be providing a response that conjoined the two shapes.[18]

To put it bluntly, so-called creativity tests in fact test the student's ability to produce rapidly a large number of responses in relation to an inherently trivial task, without concern for the quality of the responses. This "ability," if such a word is appropriate, clearly has no inherent value and nothing to do with creativity in the true sense. Why should we care whether children are more or less prolific at thinking of uses for a brick, and what has this got to do with being a creative poet or mathematician? It is not even as if there were any convincing evidence for a positive correlation between performance on creativity tests and subsequent creativity. Logically there could be no such evidence until researchers begin to carry out their work with a proper definition of creativity. For how could one reasonably claim to have established that high performance on a test correlates positively with subsequent creative activity, in the absence of a separate and clear definition of creativity?

A great deal of the research concerning the characteristics of creative people is circular. For example, research has been conducted into the question of what the characteristics of creative architects may be, and the conclusion drawn that they are characterised "in terms of the ability to achieve through independence rather than through conformity."[19] But one would not select an architect as an instance of a creative architect in the first place, unless one presumed him to have the quality of independence as opposed to conformity. What happens in such research is that the empirical and the conceptual are not properly distinguished. There is the empirical question of what creative people are like (e.g., do they tend to have red hair, to come from happy homes?), and there is the conceptual question of what it means to be creative (e.g., does one have to be original?). We cannot properly examine the former question until we have settled the latter one. The fact of the matter is we are trying to conduct empirical research in this area with inadequate conceptions, and consequently we have no pertinent data.

To summarise: "creativity," which at the level of a dictionary definition means "having originality of thought, showing imagination," has to be more precisely defined, if we are to be able to make meaningful and precise claims about it, recognise it, foster it, act appropriately in relation to it, and research into it. In particular, if we wish to retain the implications of value in the term, if we are to continue taking it for granted that it is a good thing, we have to be able to give some account of it that indicates that it is indeed of value. Much of our talk, practice, and research in this area is conducted in the absence of any such adequate definition. Two notable and conflicting results are that some of our procedures are based on a vague identification of creativity with self-expression, and others are based on a very specific identification of it with the ability to produce many responses to fairly trivial tasks, involving a minimum of knowledge and understanding and no criteria of quality. The nature of creativity is in fact such that, whether there is or is not some general innate factor of creativity, creative activity is dependent upon the ability to understand and meet the standards of excellence implicit in various particular subject matters. If we sincerely care about producing creative people, we need to develop people's capacity to produce original and good work in various important areas, and therefore need a curriculum that focuses on worthwhile subject matter, and produces understanding of the nature and criteria of quality in the various subjects, while at the same time encouraging independence of mind and originality. Our failure to see this can be traced to the erroneous beliefs that creativity is an inherent generic ability, that it is to be defined in terms of process rather than the treatment of specific material, that it can be empirically discerned and measured, rather than its products appraised or judged, and that there are no objective criteria for judging somebody's work to be creative.

V: Insight and intuition

In discussing imagination and creativity, I have been at pains to combat the idea that these are the names of mysterious processes or faculties that spontaneously and cheerfully go to work on any material they encounter. On the contrary, to be imaginative or creative involves having understanding of subject matters and consciously making use of that understanding.

There are, however, certain terms such as "insight" and "intuition" that do, by definition, refer to the sudden and spontaneous realisation of a truth. These qualities are indeed serendipitous. They pick out a phenomenon that one can hardly deny, namely the accidental hitting upon a fortunate (and hence by definition desirable) discovery of one sort or another. Nor would I wish to appear to despise or denigrate such occurrences. But precisely because we are here referring to accidental achievement, and to realisations that come upon us suddenly, there is not much that we can say about their workings and not much that we can do to promote them directly. If we could describe the reasoning process whereby we arrive at an intuition then it would not count as an intuition; conversely, we do not describe the moment of recognising the solution to a problem in geometry as an intuition, if it follows a process of rational deduction.

If an insight is something that suddenly hits us, rather than the end link in a chain of conscious reasoning, then we cannot practice having insights. We have to wait on their emergence. However, it surely is the case that even these concepts are favoured by a well prepared mind, and it must be the case that assessing the relative merits of various insights and intuitions is a rational business. It is difficult to see how people who have no understanding of personal relations, a particular social problem, or history, are going to be in a position to gain a sudden insight or intuitively recognise the appropriate thing to do in respect of their personal relations, the social problem, or a historical crux. And it is certain that establishing that the insight or intuition is sound will require some understanding of the nature of the area in question. You may intuitively hit upon an explanation of Alcibiades' conduct in fleeing from Athens to Sparta in 414 B. C., but to establish the wisdom of your insight we are going to need to get involved in the history of the period, and we will need to be good historians. You may intuitively recognise that you should apologise to the person sitting opposite you at dinner, but to establish that you are correct will require some reasoned explanation and understanding of the situation.

The upshot of this discussion must be that if we want creative, imaginative, and intuitive people, then we must start providing people with a thorough understanding of those areas in which we are particularly concerned to have these qualities operate, and with a grasp of the criteria of quality inherent in the various areas. Preoccupation with such concepts is not to be dismissed as a preoccupation with vague and arty frills and fancies. They are not to be seen as concepts opposed to and at war with the more demanding, tougher, and realistic concept of rationality. Nor is it sensible to classify these concepts as aesthetic and contrast them with more practical ones. Nobody in his right mind wants to destroy technology in the manner of the Luddites, or to pretend that industrial and material considerations do not matter. But we do want to ensure that technology is utilised creatively and imaginatively, and we do want to insist that beauty and other artistic and aesthetic values are also important. There will always be the question of the quality of life, as well as the question of maintaining life.

But if we are to produce truly creative and imaginative people, people whose emotions are indeed educated, and people who can be expected to have useful insights and intuitions, then we must cease to move uneasily between vague ideas of innate faculties that may blossom without the development of understanding, and impoverished conceptions defined in terms of quantitative measurement of trivial performances. We must teach people certain bodies of knowledge, such as science, mathematics, and ethics, in such a way that they come to understand the nature of the discipline, as well as acquire information, and appreciate what makes for a well conducted scientific inquiry or a well reasoned moral judgement. In particular, we must emphasise the study of history and literature, for whereas a great deal of the importance of studying science and maths lies simply in having understanding (so that many good scientists are not particularly creative, but are none the less important for that), writers and historians are inevitably concerned with imagination and creativity. Every writer aspires to be creative and imaginative, that is to say to produce original good work, for there would be no point in writing a novel or poem that was not distinctive. Furthermore, these are the subjects that feed the imagination by providing the stories and examples of man's striving for new horizons.

It is true that, in order to promote creativity and imagination, we must encourage students to display these qualities, we must allow them to exercise and practice them, and set up an environment in which they feel free to take risks and experiment. But such requirements must be met in the normal course of events. We do not want certain lessons designated as "creative" or "imaginative". We want the whole curriculum treated in this way and designed to encourage these qualities. But encouraging them does not imply taking a holiday from discipline. On the contrary, it is essential that study be conducted in a disciplined way and be subject to objective evaluation according to criteria appropriate to the subject matter. Nor should we confuse the notion of objective evaluation with quantitative measurement. There is no inherent reason why objective evaluation should not take the form of judgement and appraisal, and in some cases it will be necessary that it should do so. Thus if we want creative poets, we had better teach students what poetry is, and draw their attention to the criteria that determine whether something is poetry, and hence whether it is good poetry.

The fundamental reason why so little of what we do in the name of creativity and imagination has anything to do with it, is that we are wedded to the false assumptions that these are innate generic skills or faculties and that what matters is the process rather than products or achievements that meet clear standards of quality.

I should make one final comment that is of relevance to my treatment of other concepts in this book as well as the ones considered here. I have argued that creativity means something specific, and that there are other unacceptable conceptions in existence. This raises the question of who I may be to determine the true meaning of creativity. The answer is that all definition starts by trying to accurately portray how a word is used or understood in common parlance, but ends by stipulating a particular sense. The important questions are whether the particular conception an individual offers is clearly and coherently articulated, and what the implications are in respect of such things as whether it has value, and whether we can recognise or research it. It will make little or no difference to the argument if some readers choose to say that they do not mean by "creativity" what I mean by it. Whatever we call it, we are not contributing to the development of useful and original thinking by encouraging children to think of uses for old tins, to play with colours at whim, or to engage in typical problem-solving exercises. However we define the word, the assumption that there is an innate creative talent that can be encouraged to blossom without the development of understanding is neither plausible nor coherent. The kind of creativity and imagination that we require presuppose disciplined understanding and knowledge.

Chapter 6

Interpersonal skills and values

I: Caring and other social skills

There is wide agreement that what are frequently referred to as "interpersonal" or "social skills" are important and that our educational system should develop them. We want people to get along with each other, to set others at ease, to communicate effectively, to conduct themselves appropriately, and to feel confident in social intercourse, both for the advantages this brings in terms of the smooth functioning of social life, and for the satisfaction and absence of frustration, embarrassment, and unpleasantness that it brings to individuals.

Where the rules of social intercourse are many, clear, and dogmatic, as has been the case in many societies, the problems of misunderstanding are minimised. The more social behaviour is regulated and ritualised, the easier it is to ensure ease and efficiency in human relationships. However, our commitment to an open society, and to the values of autonomy, freedom, and tolerance that are integrally bound up with it, makes it hard for us to accept too many demands and conventions. We rely less on specific rules and rituals, and more on individual interpretations of general principles than closed or tribal societies do. We still expect certain kinds of behaviour rather than others, but these are conceived in broad terms such as "showing respect for others" or "being polite," rather than in terms of specific behaviours. The individual has to rely far more on judgement, and less on the guidance of specific precepts of conduct. One consequence is a far greater degree of variation between people's ability to handle social situations of various sorts than some societies have had to face. To continue for a moment to use the educational jargon of our time, some people lack various "social skills" to a greater or lesser extent, and we therefore need to take active steps to develop them.

What is in dispute is whether such qualities as being able to communicate, being caring, being a good listener, and being a good mixer are properly to be called "skills," and whether referring to them and treating them as "skills" is not detrimental to the aim of fostering and promoting them.

It will be recalled that a skill is an ability than can be perfected by training and exercise of the ability itself, without regard to the particular context in which it may be put to use. If we extend the meaning of the term to cover all manner of abilities, then we must at least avoid treating different kinds of skill as if they were of the same kind. In particular, it is vital that we do not treat things such as creativity or critical thinking as if they were skills in the sense of abilities that can be perfected by practice and exercise alone, without regard to context. As we have seen, they involve understanding, and one cannot expect to develop creativity or critical ability in any particular domain, without promoting understanding of that domain. For the sake of clarity, therefore, I shall confine myself to the use of the word "skill" to refer to a physical, discrete, and trainable ability.[1]

It would seem clear that such characteristics as being able to communicate, being caring, and being a good listener are not skills in this sense. There may be some genuine skills involved in the larger concept, as, for example, there are skills involved in being a good soccer player, even though being a good soccer player involves other qualities such as reading the game, commitment, and anticipation, which are not skills. Thus, looking people in the eyes, asking questions in certain ways, shaking hands firmly, smiling, and taking up points made by one's interlocutor, may be regarded as skills. That is to say, they are behaviours or performances that can be drawn attention to, practised, and exhibited in and of themselves. One can practise shaking hands firmly, become proficient at it, and make use of the skill whenever it seems appropriate to do so. One can learn to look people in the eyes, by deliberate practice, just as one can learn to wear a smile. And since what is meant by "asking questions" and "taking up points" here are formal and routine procedures, they too can be drawn attention to as discrete acts and deliberately practised. But, while it is therefore true that there are some social skills, it is far from clear that they are particularly important from the point of view of social and interpersonal relations, and it is absolutely clear that there is a great deal more to the business of successful human intercourse than the mere display of such skills.

The claim that these skills are important is at best a contingent truth.

That is to say, it may be the case that, by and large, people feel more comfortable and at ease when they are in the company of people who smile a lot, provide a lot of eye contact, and repeat what is said to them. But it certainly isn't the case that people necessarily feel this way. There are people who do not feel at all comfortable when held in eye contact, and who are frankly irritated by conversations with people who insist on going through the formal motions of varying their questioning technique or picking up *verbatim* on what is said to them. It is therefore arguable that promulgation of these skills represents an attempt to establish certain rituals, rather than an attempt to meet the needs of social intercourse. It is not that good social communication necessarily requires such practices, but that we choose to perceive these as some of the procedures that should go to define good relations, just as, at other times and places, spitting, wearing a tie, or standing up at the entrance of a lady, have been regarded as aspects of good social behaviour. Of course, if our society decides to treat smiling or eye contact as aspects of good behaviour, it will follow that the ability to exercise these social skills becomes a social asset. But that does not establish that they are skills that are in fact necessary to good communication or good social relations. The more important point is that, even if they do have a part to play, it is a very small part of what is important in respect of social and interpersonal behaviour, and the exercise even of these minimal skills requires judgement if it is to be effective. Not only does one need to do rather more than smile, engage in eye contact, and vary one's questioning technique, if one is to prove oneself a good listener, communicate well, or live up to the label "caring"; one also needs to be adept at deciding when to smile, when to engage in eye contact, and when to ask questions in a particular way, if one is not going to make a complete fool of oneself. Understanding of some kind is therefore a prerequisite even of the proper exercise of these *bona fide* skills. In particular, understanding of the nature of a culture is required, since what is an effective technique or form of communication varies culturally. In Japan, for example, the appearance of openness that is a norm in Canada, is regarded as utter rudeness. Understanding a culture, of course, in turn requires historical, literary, social, and political insight.

If we focus directly on the larger concepts of caring, communicating, and getting on with people, we see that they cannot be defined as skills. To be a caring individual, or, as I should prefer to phrase it, to be a person who cares about others, is not simply a matter of *doing* anything: it involves feeling about people in a certain kind of way, and, if it is to be of any use, it involves conveying to others an awareness that one does care. To some extent conveying the impression that one cares is achieved by engaging in particular behaviours. Nobody is going to believe that I care about him, if I ignore him, for example. But engagement in specific behaviours alone is not going to get us far, particularly if such skills become a routine part of our social conventions. If I am to convey to people the idea that I care about them, I must do more than look directly at them, encourage them to talk, and smile or look suitably pained on their behalf. I must persuade them that, beyond these conventional responses, I understand what they are saying and am sympathetic to them, I am interested in their problems and share their enthusiasms. That will not be possible, unless I do have some understanding of them as individuals and of what they are saying. And if I am actually going to care about these people, as opposed to making a good job of seeming to care, then in addition to understanding them, their situation, and what they are saying, I have to have a certain disposition or set of emotions in respect of them.

Being caring and being able to convey that one cares require understanding of people and situations in general, and understanding of particular people and situations as well. Caring draws on the qualities of creativity, imagination, and critical ability, which, as we have already seen, are themselves heavily bound up with understanding. The same may be said of communication, listening, and the various other concepts that interrelate and overlap with one another in this area. Good communication, if it is really that, is not and cannot be exclusively a matter of mastering certain procedural skills. One may appear to communicate well by hiding behind various techniques and behaviours, and indeed that is precisely what we would seem to encourage by an emphasis on skills of communication. But one is not actually communicating well, unless one both understands the people and the subject matter being discussed and manages to convey this to the other people present. Nor is one a good listener simply by virtue of executing certain behaviours, which, let us assume, do at any rate convey the impression that one is engaged and listening intently. A good listener is one who truly hears, understands, and takes an interest in what is said. It has not been established that the skills of listening and communication that are popularly emphasised are necessary to being a good listener in this sense. But, if they are, it is clear that they alone will not get one far: understanding is required in order to make appropriate use of such skills, and, in addition, one has to understand both the individuals and the subject of discussion.

In short, our current practice in respect of these interpersonal concepts, insofar as it treats them as skills or sets of skills, does very little to enhance people's capacity to care, to communicate, or to listen. It treats them, once again, as processes or generic abilities, as if caring about people and communicating with them were general talents that one either has or lacks, and that are to be defined in terms of the motions that one goes through. But it is not the case that one is generically a caring person (to whatever degree): we care about some people and not about others. No doubt some individuals care about more people than others, and the former might be regarded quantitatively as more caring. But that will not alter the fact that caring is not a quality that, if one has it, one will automatically generate in any company. One has to care about somebody or something. Consequently one cannot cultivate caring in a vacuum. One has to bring people up to care about particular people and things. To do that you have to give them reason and understanding, as well as instill a certain disposition.

Caring is not generic, it is not a process, and it is not a skill. Nor is it a concept that we can focus on without examining the issue of relativism and values. Caring does not mean accepting anything. It involves making judgements of value about who is worth caring for when, and what one should do in particular situations given that one does care. What, for example, does a caring individual do when faced with a situation in which a married couple with whom he is very friendly are separating, one very reluctantly and in ignorance of the fact that the other has a new lover? The answer doesn't matter. What does matter is that to act in a way that is based on genuine caring, and to show that one cares, is going to involve, not various formulaic behaviours, but trying to understand the individuals, the situation, the practical problems, the moral ramifications, and the likely consequences of various actions. Without such understanding one will not be able to show that one cares, nor to claim that one cares, because if you care you should be determined to understand the situation correctly.

Our concern for social and interpersonal relations should therefore involve a modicum of interest in developing some basic (and in this case correctly labelled) skills. It should also involve setting an example by way of exhibiting attention, affection, and other dispositions. But an attack on the problem that goes no further than that, or that is limited to encouraging friendly interpersonal relations in the classroom and developing these relatively trivial skills, cannot achieve our aims. To do that we have to provide understanding. Those people who can most truly show care and consideration for others, and who can most truly communicate, are those who have wide understanding of people, situations, and subject matter, and whose grasp of that understanding is imaginative and critical. Nor is this thesis affected by empirical claims to the effect that many well-educated people have been uncaring and uncommunicative. For this is not an empirical claim. It is a matter of reasoning, and reasoning tells us that, while the most ignorant of people may care and the most well-educated may be social misfits, the appropriate thing to do, if you wish to increase the chances of people communicating effectively, showing care and consideration for others, and managing social situations skilfully, is to equip them with information and imaginative understanding. No one can be expected to tolerate, care for, or communicate what they do not understand.

II: Values clarification

Values clarification purports to be a way of developing people's understanding in respect of values. And so, in a limited respect, it does. But, owing to certain defects in the theory that lies behind it, and because it is limited in what it is concerned to achieve, use of values clarification is an extraordinary way for us to set about approaching the ideal of a citizen body that is well-informed, articulate, and critically autonomous in respect of values. It would be wrong to suggest that it is totally without rhyme or reason or that it can achieve nothing of value, but we have to remember that planning curricula and organising our programme of teaching is a matter of selecting between alternatives. Values clarification may not be entirely devoid of merit, but it is inferior to another perfectly feasible approach to education in respect of values.[2]

The main thrust behind the advocacy of values clarification seems to have been the desire to replace a dogmatic initiation into received opinions or values, sometimes amounting to indoctrination. Proponents of values clarification believe that pushing certain values down children's throats is anti-educational, unacceptable because values are not matters of undisputed fact, and, anyway, largely counter-productive. In all of this they are probably more or less correct. The specific form of particular values clarification programmes differs, but, as is the case with creativity tests, the essential pattern remains the same. The programme consists in presenting students with a wide variety of hypothetical problems and questions involving value judgements, and requiring them to take a stance on the issues and to explain their reasons for so doing.

There are many points that might be raised here that it is not necessary to examine in any detail. For example, the fact that the problems encountered, even though they may be realistic or drawn from real life, are, like those involved in critical thinking programmes, not the actual problems of the students and may be of no interest or consequence to them. They tend, as again they do in critical thinking courses, to be treated in isolation from any wider context. On the other hand, many people have expressed concern that some of the issues discussed strike too near the bone, and may lead to grave embarrassment for students. There are also conflicting claims about the empirical evidence for what is achieved by such courses.

These are not matters of immediate concern to me, because their significance is secondary to that of two other features of such programmes. The first is that no distinction is made in the planning and designing of such courses between different types of value; and the second is that the concern of the programme is with students' explanation of their views rather than justification.

There are various different kinds of value judgement, by which I do not mean that there are different judgements to be made (e.g., good or bad) or that there are different subjects to make judgements about (e.g., fishing, politics, books). I mean that whatever specific judgement one makes in relation to any topic or activity may in principle involve reference to a limited number of different kinds of value. We have to distinguish, at least, aesthetic values, moral values, intrinsic worth, preference, and prudence. Thus we can inquire into the aesthetic quality of something ("is this a beautiful building?"), the moral or ethical quality of a course of action ("is it right to spend money on erecting this building?"), the worthwhileness of something ("is reading poetry a worthwhile activity?"), people's preferences ("do you prefer your coffee black or white?"), and the prudence of a course of action ("is it wise to do this?").

It is no doubt possible to categorise values in a different way, and there may be other kinds of value, but these are some obvious major kinds. Any particular question about any particular subject matter, such as "should I go fishing tomorrow?" or "ought the government to tax smokers?", will either fall into one of these categories or be capable of being broken down into a number of subsidiary questions, each of which would fall into one category or another. It is arguable that some of these questions are not really distinctive in kind, and even that some of them, while they appear to make sense, do not in fact do so, at any rate not in the form in which they appear. (For example, some believe that the question "is this activity intrinsically worthwhile?" is more or less meaningless, unless it is interpreted in some other way such as "do I want to engage in this activity for its own sake?")[3]

But we generally talk as if these different kinds of question are distinguishable and meaningful, so for the time being I will assume that they are.

Being different in kind, each of these types of question has to be approached in a different kind of way. The considerations that have to be taken into account in attempting to answer an aesthetic question are quite different from those that have to be taken into account in dealing with a prudential question. In the former case, broadly speaking, to cope with the question, you need to know something about aesthetic theory and aesthetic concepts. In the latter case, you need to know about likely consequences of various actions and what your preferences are. Clearly, competence in talking coherently about moral matters does not necessarily imply competence in dealing with questions about aesthetic value or intrinsic worth. Nor is a person who is clear-headed about his preferences necessarily very good at sorting out a prudent course of action for himself or others. Furthermore, some of these types of value question require a great deal of sophisticated understanding, if they are to be handled adequately: a reasonable and convincing argument about the rights and wrongs of abortion is not something that everybody could manage, and it is not something that anybody could manage without considerable education in moral philosophy. A position could be adopted, of course, without any difficulty at all, but the ability to explain and defend that position in reasonable terms is not something that grows on trees. Finally, we should note that some of these types of question are not only more complex, but also more important than others. Moral questions, whatever one's particular moral stance, are by definition of paramount importance: they concern what people ought to do, regardless of preference, prudence, profit, and so forth. By contrast, questions about one's preferences are often of very little moment.

Since all of this is so, it would seem of considerable educational importance that we bring children to see that it is so, and that we enable them to cope adequately with the different kinds of question in an appropriate manner. For example, it would seem important to teach people that the question of whether abortion is morally defensible or not has got nothing to do with one's personal emotional preferences, and is not adequately addressed by appeal to some allegedly authoritative ruling from, say, the church.   The question has to be answered by an intensive conceptual inquiry into what constitutes a person, a foetus, and an abortion, combined with a thorough grasp of ethical theory and mastery of ethical concepts such as "right," "wrong," "good," "bad," "freedom of choice," "interests," and "suffering." It will be necessary therefore to enable people to engage in this kind of inquiry. But this is something that, on the face of it, values clarification is not concerned to do, partly because of its preoccupation with explanation rather than justification.

Values clarification is certainly concerned with the giving of reasons. It would be unfair and misleading to suggest that its proponents are concerned only to elicit opinions. But "giving reasons" is an ambiguous phrase that may mean either "explaining why one holds a position" or "justifying that position."[4] If I happen to think that abortion is wrong, I might explain my position in a number of ways. For instance, I may say that my church forbids it, that I get upset at the thought of it, that I knew a woman who had one and lived to regret it, that I come from a society that forbids it, or that my mother disapproves. But none of these explanations in itself determines whether there is good reason to say that it is wrong. To deal with that question I have to provide justification in terms of moral argument.

There is no necessary reason why people should not take the material prepared for values clarification courses and use it in such a way that they help students to recognise different kinds of value question for what they are, and to answer the more complex kinds of question, such as the moral and the aesthetic, in ways that involve an attempt to justify their position. I dare say some teachers do this. But some do not, and the theory behind values clarification does not expect them to. For values clarification is not designed to develop understanding of the appropriate ways in which to set about justifying moral judgements, aesthetic judgements, or judgements of intrinsic worth. It presents all value questions without distinction, so that the questions of what you look for in a friend, what you would do if you had a chance to steal some money with impunity, and what kind of music you like are treated in the same manner; and in each case the emphasis falls on explaining why you hold the view you do, rather than on attempting to demonstrate that it is a good, correct, or reasonable view. There may be possible benefits in this approach: at the very least it encourages people to exchange views and give some account of themselves. But it clearly runs the risk of suggesting that all value claims are essentially just a matter of "what turns you on," that they are all equally important, and that there is no particular need to justify any value claim. And it certainly does nothing to enable students to become more proficient at dealing with the business of weighing and assessing argument and seeking for the truth in complex areas such as morality and aesthetics.

Why, given these obvious shortcomings, did we ever adopt values clarification and why is it still with us today? Partly, I'm sorry to say, yet again, because of our persistent view of the human mind as a machine that has lots of parts, each of which performs a different task for us. Treating creativity, critical thinking, imagination, and values clarification as formal intellectual processes divorced from specific content, we imagine that people can handle any material critically or creatively, provided that they have been encouraged to exercise the faculty in question on something. Thus, if we practice clarifying some values, we seem to think, people will necessarily be able to cope with all value questions. But the more serious error in this particular case is the failure to show concern for justification of value judgements, and that is directly traceable to our peculiar and incoherent adherence to a vague idea of relativism.

III: Relativism

There are many different sorts of relativism or different senses of the word. There is in addition some danger of overlap and confusion with other terms such as "subjectivism" which may also be interpreted in a number of ways. To add to the difficulty, it is not my claim that we are wrongly addicted to a clear and specific form of relativism, but rather, that we have a wavering commitment to a not very clearly worked out notion of relativism. Furthermore, that commitment is often implicit in our actions rather than explicit in our theory. So, in what follows, I shall attempt merely to explicate certain truths about value judgements, which are not duly recognised, rather than to nail down concepts such as relativism, subjectivism, and objectivity. I shall ignore completely the more general relativist thesis that maintains that there is no such thing as objective knowledge of a real world, and that all knowledge claims are no more than the perceptions of particular individuals, except to remark here that, if this is so, the thesis itself cannot claim to reveal an objective fact about the world; it must, on its own terms, be construed as the idiosyncratic perception of a few that the rest of us can safely ignore.[5]

Objectivism in the moral sphere is generally taken to mean that certain broad judgements such as "no one should deliberately inflict pain on another simply to take pleasure in the suffering" are true, and remain true, whatever anyone happens to think or wants to do, and however people actually behave. It is important to stress that we are concerned with judgements at the level of ultimate principles, since few people would wish to maintain that more specific and particular judgements, such as "you ought not cheat on your income tax returns," are necessarily and always true. By extension, those who believe in the objectivity of value judgements of other kinds would argue, for instance, that some books just are superior to others, whatever particular readers may happen to think, or that some ways of life are intrinsically superior to others.

The obvious problem with objectivism is that, whereas we have agreed procedures for demonstrating the truth of other kinds of factual claim such as that London is the capital of England or that metals expand when heated, it is not clear that we do have any agreed procedures for establishing that we should not willfully inflict suffering, that Shakespeare is superior to Agatha Christie as a writer, or that the life of the philosopher is superior to the life of the thief. Some claim that the answer lies in intuition: one does not demonstrate the truth of these claims, one simply sees it, as most people see the physical world around them. If some do not see it, then they are morally blind, just as some are physically blind. But, whereas very few people are physically blind, and all those that have sight see more or less the same things, a great many people have very different moral perceptions. We therefore face the awkward question of whose intuition is to count.

Such problems have led some to espouse subjectivism, which in essence is the view that moral judgements are merely a matter of personal taste. "Causing suffering is wrong" is not a judgement that can be true or false, but an expression of one's preferences, as is the judgement that Shakespeare is a good writer or the life of the libertine a poor one. A very serious objection to this thesis is that it in no way accounts for our strong sense that that is not what we mean when we make such judgements, and that it does not account for the palpable difference between saying "causing suffering is wrong" and "coffee tastes better with sugar in it." Admittedly this observation does not refute subjectivism. It could be true, and our sentiments could be misleading us. But it does mean that for most people commitment to subjectivism in this sense would be inconsistent, for they do not sincerely believe that moral judgements are simply personal preferences. If they did, they wouldn't get steamed up about them in the way that they do.

Attempts to refine subjectivism shade into relativism. The relativist likewise maintains that there are no universal standards of good and bad or right and wrong. He cannot, however, logically maintain that what is right is whatever actually is thought to be right in a particular time and place; for to say that would be to enunciate an objective principle to the effect that one ought always to do what the social group in which one finds oneself demands. The immediate issue is not that one might wish to challenge this claim, but that it would be an objectivist claim, and therefore incompatible with the idea of relativism. He is therefore forced into maintaining that there is no such thing as right or wrong in the normal senses of those words. There is not even an obligation to abide by the majority preference. Rather, there are various values to be found in differing times and places, and these, though they come to be labelled right and wrong, are in fact no more than preferences.

One can see why people should be tempted to espouse relativism. First, it is clear that different societies have different values, and each sincerely believes that its values are correct. Secondly, within societies, values change over a period of time. Thirdly, there is the difficulty of establishing the truth of value claims.

The first point can be quickly set aside. In the first place it is not entirely evident that there are no moral principles that have always had assent. Certainly, value judgements about specific activities, such as burying the dead or getting married, vary. But is it really the case that any society has denied the value of respect for persons or justice? Is it not rather the case that they interpret these high level principles in different ways, as is appropriate to different circumstances? Did the Gestapo believe that inflicting suffering for its own sake was morally acceptable? I doubt it. They elaborated an involved, albeit nonsensical, thesis designed to establish that certain groups were non-people, so that what they did was, in their eyes, comparable to our treatment of animals. In the second place, even if there is evidence that values vary, that does not directly relate to the question of whether they should. Just as the fact that a society has lost the ability to multiply doesn't make it any the less true that $5 \times 7 = 35$, so the fact that some societies do not value kindness does not in itself establish that they should not. Empirical evidence about differences and changes in values, while it may be suggestive, is irrelevant in any direct way to the question of the truth of value judgements.

The real issue is that of demonstration or proof. A danger that we have to guard against here is that of being so dominated by the scientific paradigm that we assume some kind of empirical demonstration is needed. Indeed, I would hazard the suggestion that some people assume that value judgements cannot be matters of fact, simply because they are not empirically demonstrable. But there are many truths that are not empirically demonstrable, such as the truths of mathematics and truths of logic. Empirical proof is not only not available here, it would be quite wrong to look for it. You can establish empirically what people think is right and good, but not what is right and good. But is it true that there is no kind of demonstration available? Surely not. The fact is that any clearly conceived activity or department of life carries with it, by virtue of its being clearly conceived, certain criteria that not only define the activity but also necessarily define quality within the sphere; for if an activity is defined in terms of doing a, b, and c, then if the activity is to be well done, a, b, and c must be well done. It follows that the successful performance of a, b, and c constitute criteria for quality in the activity.

For example, the game of cricket is defined in terms of various aims, procedures, practices, and norms. To play cricket is to engage in a specific kind of activity according to certain rules. Just as one determines whether somebody can play cricket by whether he can engage in the activity according to the rules, so one determines that some people are better than others at cricket by reference to how successfully they compete. Without doubt, there will be marginal difficulties of judgement. Was Donald Bradman the greatest batsman of all time? Was Len Hutton better than Peter May? But most judgements will be quite straightforward and objective. For example, Peter May was a better cricketer than Robin Barrow. You wanted a value judgement that was a matter of objective fact and you have one.

What is true of cricket is true of any other definable activity. There are good lawyers and bad ones, good politicians and bad ones, good poets and bad ones, morally good people and morally bad ones. It is true that some areas are considerably more ill-defined than others, and that some activities involve criteria that are harder to recognise and perceive than others. But the principle remains the same. When it comes to some of the areas we are interested in, such as morality, literature, and art, we do indeed encounter both kinds of difficulty. Morality is not as clearly defined as cricket, and the question of whether an author has style is less directly ascertainable than whether a batsman scores runs. But it is absurd to pretend that we have no idea at all what morality, art, or literature involve. We have a very good idea, and we would have an even better one if we concentrated more on the historical development of these concepts, and gave more attention to studying them.

Throughout these pages I have had occasion to refer to the spectre of relativism. We ask children to explain what they would do in a certain moral situation, perhaps even to say why, but we don't ask them to justify it, nor do we readily teach them what they ought to do and why. We talk about gifted children, but shirk from identifying them by reference to the superior quality of work they produce, preferring to do so by a bizarre set of irrelevant tests and hypotheses about the kind of characteristics they are likely to have. We emphasise critical thought, but hesitate to demand immersion in substantive bodies of knowledge that would allow them to achieve high standards of thought. We talk of creativity and imagination but do not call for work of quality, and shrink from making judgements of quality about their responses on tests. And there are many other indications of our relativist leanings: our emphasis on process rather than substance, our reluctance to select material (except for political reasons such as the desire to combat sexism or racism), our reluctance to instruct, our reluctance to assess student responses, and our preference for brainstorming to quality discussion. Above all, in our reluctance to establish a curriculum centred on worthwhile subject matter.

Of course, as I have said, this insidious relativism is not explicit or coherent. The very same people who will not correct a child, may believe passionately in the objective value of caring. But it is there, and partly explains our preoccupation with form at the expense of substance. It is no accident that moral philosophers of this century have tended to reduce being moral to a matter of abiding by certain procedural and formal principles such as sincerity and consistency. They have done that because they are reluctant to espouse substantive values, even though it is clear that morality is not simply about consistency, but at least also about people's well-being and about virtue, from which simple observation many judgements can be drawn.[6] In the same way, the preoccupation with getting children to abide by certain formal rules of composition, or to go through certain formal procedures of reasoning, rather than to reason and write about certain things in accordance with certain substantive values, is at least partly attributable to our flirtation with relativism.

We have every reason to make judgements about the worth of certain subjects and materials and about moral behaviour. We have every reason to instruct students in these values. The superiority of Shakespeare, for example, is not the prejudice of an elite; it is a fact that can be established easily enough through an understanding of literature, and by showing that Shakespeare plays the game better than most.

Chapter 7

Curriculum Content

I: Intelligence

In the preceding chapters I have argued that the nature of certain key educational concepts is such that a curriculum based on lessons and programmes devoted directly to exercising and developing the abilities themselves, without careful regard to the subject matter on which they are exercised makes little sense. If we are serious about cultivating critical thought, imaginative thought, and creativity, and about educating the emotions, developing the capacity to cope adequately and autonomously with questions of value, ensuring that we neither squander natural endowment nor fail to develop giftedness in various areas, and preparing the ground for the deployment of intuition and insight, it is necessary to design a curriculum that is based on certain subject matters that have relative importance and that can be studied in a disciplined and organised way.

The argument for this conclusion may be repeated in summary form by reference to the concept of intelligence, since intelligence is another of the broad concepts that encapsulates something of the ideal to which we are striving. We hope that our educational system will produce intelligent individuals. Yet, while we say that, and while we make various assumptions and claims about intelligence, the extraordinary fact is that most of our research and practice relating to intelligence is conducted without any clear theory or definition of intelligence.[1] We have not explicated clearly and unequivocally what it means to be intelligent, and then proceeded to draw out logical implications for teaching and to conduct empirical inquiry in the light of that definition. We have adopted practices in the light of no single clear concept of intelligence, with the result that a critical examination of the topic uncovers a number of implicit but unrecognised, distinct, and not always compatible, assumptions about the concept itself, and a number of questionable claims relating to it.

As with giftedness, the underlying assumption, when faculty psychology was in the ascendant and work on intelligence testing took off at the turn of the century, was that intelligence was an innate quality. One was born with a certain potential degree of intelligence, as one was born with a certain potential stature. No one denied that circumstance and environment were necessary conditions of realising one's potential, and therefore played some part in determining whether, whatever one's innate potential, one grew up with a particular stature or intelligence. For clearly, whatever the genetic inheritance, a child that is starved and otherwise denied the benefits of a satisfactory environment is not likely to grow into a large and healthy adult; by the same token, it may be presumed, on any view of intelligence, that a child deprived of all mental stimulation will not grow up to be highly intelligent. Nonetheless, the basic assumption of faculty psychology was that intelligence itself was the product of innate genetic endowment.

Since that time, developments in research into intelligence testing have not substantially modified that presumption. There have been many who have argued explicitly and strongly against it, maintaining that factors such as the family, social, and educational background are crucial, and that to all intents and purposes it is the environment rather than natural endowment that determines intelligence.[2] But even as that argument rages, intelligence testing, and psychological views of intelligence generally, persist in treating it as something innate. Faced with overwhelming reason and evidence to reject the thesis that an individual is born with an innate general intelligence, a famous modification introduced the idea of intelligence being a combination of a general factor and a variety of more specific competencies. Subsequent to that, Guilford, for instance, has proposed a model of the intellect which has 150 distinct abilities.[3] But, however much the notion of intelligence is broken down in this way, the assumption remains that there are various mental functions, such as grasping relationships, abstracting, and problem solving, that an individual has a fixed innate ability to perform, to a greater or lesser degree. It is accepted that the environment may affect the manifestation of the potential, but the potential is presumed to be innately determined. Hence, we still use I.Q. tests widely without a qualm, in the belief that we are measuring the individual's innate ability.

The tests themselves have been criticised in a number of extremely important respects. I am not concerned here with what may be termed technical criticisms of particular tests, such as that they have low validity or reliability ratings or that the statistical method employed in analysing a test is flawed. I am referring to criticisms that strike at the very heart of the idea of intelligence testing.

In the first place, since such tests are generally based on vocabulary, recognition of objects, interpretation of situations (usually depicted in drawings), numeracy, and problem solving, they are necessarily culture and language bound to some extent. Secondly, the manner of interpreting the tests presupposes that intelligence is distributed across the population in accordance with the principle of normal distribution. That is to say, it is assumed that a minority of individuals are particularly intelligent, a minority particularly unintelligent, while the majority are grouped in the middle. Ironically, this assumption might be plausible if we were concerned with a normative conception of intelligence that was not predicated on a belief in genetic endowment. For, if intelligence is something that we develop in people, and if it is an honorific term, then we should not expect to find a society in which everyone was equally intelligent—for in such a case we would cease to regard intelligence as anything very special. But, if we are talking about an allegedly innate potential, there seems no good reason at all to assume that it is normally distributed. We are told that, as a matter of fact, height is normally distributed throughout the population. But so what? Visual capacity, to take another example, is not. Why should intelligence be? But the assumption that it is plays a large part in determining how to construct the tests, and hence indirectly in determining how intelligent an individual is.

Many years ago it was said that intelligence had to be defined as "what the intelligence tests test."[4] This remark of Boring's has perhaps proved unfortunate in that its slightly humorous air and frankness deflect serious criticism; it suggests somehow that "it's all right; we know the limits of what we're doing." But what it clearly reveals is that there is no connection established between intelligence tests and any other known conception of intelligence. When we ask children (or adults) to do a test which consists of such items as: provide a synonym for "car"; which is the odd one out in the list "apple, apricot, pear, tomato"? complete the following: "a bird flies; a fish _____;" define "pen;" complete the following series of numbers "1, 3, 7 _____;" what is wrong with this scene? (a picture of a couple sitting out in the rain is shown, or a rabbit chasing a dog)—all that we are entitled to say is that we are testing their ability to do these particular things.

They are clearly culturally bound (if you have never come across a rabbit, why should it strike you as odd that it chases a dog?) and they clearly relate to language acquisition and other learning. Establishing suitable items for different age groups is necessarily going to be influenced by cultural norms. The items are essentially trivial, and confined more or less to the level of informational knowledge. There is absolutely no reason, beyond the fact that the assumption has been made, to presume that some innate ability is being monitored. Above all, therefore, one must ask why, if intelligence is to be defined as what intelligence tests test, anyone should be interested in intelligence.

Treating "intelligence" in this way is indicative of most of the unfortunate tendencies in our thinking about mental concepts that I have drawn attention to. It reveals our fixation with the idea that abilities are largely innate, even though we seldom explicitly say as much, and very often inconsistently proceed to do things that imply that they are not. It reveals our underlying commitment to the idea that these abilities are generic. Even when we break the notion of intelligence down into sub-abilities, we proceed as if, for example, one's talent for "grasping relationships" was generic, rather than, as it obviously must be, a context-bound ability. I am very good at grasping relationships in some areas, and very bad at it in others. Nor could I be expected to grasp relationships in areas that I do not understand. It reveals our tendency to think in terms of skills: intelligence is seen solely in terms of performing certain operations, not in terms of understanding and quality of performance. It reveals our unyielding commitment to the scientific paradigm: surely part of the reason that we continue to take intelligence testing seriously is that we are more comfortable with procedures that seem to allow of direct observation and measurement, than we are with procedures that unashamedly rely on indirect appraisal and judgement. It exposes in dramatic relief our failure to see the necessity of adequate conceptualisation as a precursor to action of any sort. It also bears more general testimony to our reluctance to take the philosophic-artistic side of things as seriously as the scientific-materialist, for it is notable that intelligence testing does not make much allowance for the idea of intelligence in the arts.

If we set aside all these prejudices and presumptions and start where we should begin, with a consideration of the concept of intelligence, the whole picture will be seen to alter radically. Whether or not intelligence is affected by genetic endowment (and I have no doubt that it is to some extent), certain things are clear: intelligence is not the same thing as having a certain genetic endowment, which is to say that we do not mean by the remark "he is intelligent" that "he has a certain genetic endowment." People can prove themselves intelligent in some spheres and not in others. People can be taught and otherwise come to learn and understand things, such that they are enabled to think and act more intelligently than they would otherwise have done. The question of whether some individual is well suited to engaging in an activity or pursuing a particular course of study is not as well answered by a global estimate of his intelligence, however derived, as it is by considering whether he has particular knowledge, understanding, interest, and ability related to the activity in question. The admission to university graduate programmes, for instance, on the basis of such things as GRE scores, Miller's Analogy scores, cumulative grade point average, or class of undergraduate degree, while it makes some sense from an administrative point of view and may even be the only practicable procedure, is nonetheless clearly less appropriate than examining individuals in relation to the specific programmes they wish to enter would be.

Whatever the sources and causes of intelligence may be, the ascription of intelligence to a person is made on the strength of his talking or acting intelligently. Since we admire intelligence, we are not inclined to regard people as intelligent on the strength of their doing trivial things intelligently, although, since it is not a moral term, we may regard a master criminal as intelligent. What we expect to see in the thought and action of an intelligent person are conceptual finesse, logical reasoning, including the ability to recognise entailments and implications, attention to and the ability to weigh evidence, and the ability to distinguish logically distinct kinds of question and to treat each kind appropriately, all displayed in important areas of life. (By "conceptual finesse" is meant the possession of a rich store of carefully discriminated concepts, and the ability and inclination to analyse concepts.)[5] We do not specifically mean by "intelligent," "well-informed," "knowledgeable," or "having a good command of language." However, in the world in which we live, it is difficult to see how a person could proceed intelligently without being relatively well-informed and without a good command of language, since one could not reason logically or weigh evidence adequately in the absence of a well-developed language and a good stock of information for very long.

Therefore, if we intend to develop intelligence, we must determine what are the important areas, the significant information, and the distinctive areas of language that matter. It is quite true that one can exercise and develop people's ability to proceed intelligently, critically, imaginatively, and so forth in any area, from studying swing bands to running a basketball team. But since the ability to proceed intelligently in those activities will not in itself enable one to proceed intelligently in others, we have to determine what areas are most important, either because of their intrinsic value, or because of their relevance to a wider range of human interest.

II: Vocational and topic courses

One answer to the question "what is it most important for students to study in school?" is vocational courses. The reasoning behind this view is seductively straightforward: society needs various jobs to be done and individuals need to find gainful employment. Schooling is a preparation for a life that will last three to four times as long as schooling itself, and satisfactory employment will be a significant factor in a satisfactory life. What could be more important or useful than providing students with vocational courses in such things as automobile maintenance, accountancy, word-processing, or home economics?

The first objection to such courses is that usually they involve no more than training in specific skills. As such they do not contribute to developing the mind or educating the individual. They do not help to enhance the critical, imaginative, or creative ability of the individual. Secondly, there is strong evidence that they do not do much to help the individual find secure employment, since our forecasts as to what kind of manpower society will need have proven to be very inaccurate. Thirdly, and most serious of all, they curtail and limit the opportunities and freedom of choice of individuals: train a person to be an automotive mechanic and you effectively make him one, leaving him very little chance of doing something different with his life.

Technical and vocational courses could no doubt be taught in a way that made them to some degree educative (for instance, "automobile maintenance" could, and sometimes does, involve science education). Nor is it necessary to argue that they should be rooted out of our schools: word processing is a useful enough skill, which may lead to better employment prospects and may serve other purposes as well. Nonetheless, such courses are in themselves peripheral to education, and, unless they are treated in such a way and expanded to such an extent that calling them "word processing" and "accountancy" becomes a misnomer, they make a minimal contribution to the ideal. If they have a place in school it must be a marginal place in the overall curriculum. To the claim that they are useful and important, even if not educational, the reply is that they are of restricted usefulness, the use they have is bought at the price of limitation on the individual's freedom of choice, and there is no reason why such things should not be learned in the home or on the job. It is true that, as things are, some homes are poor and most employers do not operate apprenticeship schemes. But I am arguing about what we ought to aim for, what it makes sense that we should do, and I am suggesting that the expense of a public system of schooling, and the elaborate infrastructure for training teachers, is largely wasted, if it is geared towards domestic and industrial training. We need schools, and it is worth paying for them, to teach important things that could not easily be learned in other ways.

A recent book on liberal education was aptly titled *Beyond the Present and the Particular*, the argument being that a study of the liberal arts and the established disciplines of inquiry, while it may look esoteric, academic, impractical, and irrelevant to our real concerns, is to be welcomed, because it liberates the individual from the stultifying effects of preoccupation with the immediately present and the particular forms that ideas have taken in our society.[6] Such preoccupation is resolutely uncritical. It takes for granted that the things we do and the ideas we have here and now are all that is worthy of consideration. It does nothing to feed the imagination or encourage creativity. If we are to serve the ideal outlined in the first chapter, if we are to develop the qualities of intellect and imagination that have been discussed, if we are to enable individuals to develop their minds, and society to adapt to changing circumstances, and perhaps even improve itself in some ways, the very last thing we should do is ennoble the here and now by concentrating on fitting people to the demands of society as it is. The view that vocational schooling is relevant, useful, and practical can only be maintained by highjacking those terms, and pretending that they have a specific meaning which they do not in fact have. "Relevant" does not mean "relevant to the current needs of industry;" "useful" does not mean "useful for immediate economic satisfaction;" and "practical" does not mean "disassociated from intellectual understanding." All these terms require an object to complete their sense; there has to be relevance to some purpose, usefulness for some purpose, and practicality for some purpose. The question of whether a pursuit or course of study is relevant, useful, or practical therefore becomes a question of what purposes you have in mind. Vocational courses are largely irrelevant, useless, and impractical, given the purposes we have in mind.

There are a number of studies that indicate that industry itself is moving towards favouring a general education for potential employees, rather than a vocational one. But while there is therefore some empirical evidence that vocational courses are not particularly worthwhile on their own terms, it is more appropriate here to stress that the values of autonomy, understanding, tolerance, and intelligence demand something other than such courses.

Another currently popular way of answering the question of what is worth studying is to propose topic or issue-centred subjects. For example, many curricula now include subjects such as sex education, peace education, environmental education, and women's studies. It is not disputed that these are, or may be, important issues. Sexual relations are an important aspect of most of our lives, they are complex and not always easy to cope with, and some greater understanding of the area would no doubt be welcome to most of us. The question of the role and treatment of women is one that nobody could reasonably dismiss as unimportant or uninteresting. Peace, like motherhood, is something nobody would dare to be disparaging about. But there are three strong objections to designing the curriculum around issues such as these: they tend to remain at the informative level rather than to develop understanding; they tend towards indoctrination rather than education; and one cannot adequately study these topics except in the light of disciplined understanding. The first two objections are only contingent, but the likelihood that they will be features of such courses as actually taught is strongly increased if there is any truth in the third objection. I shall therefore comment on that first.

The question is how on earth one could expect to have a thorough, intelligent, critical, and imaginative study of sex, peace, the environment, or women, if one did not know a great deal about these subjects both historically and in contemporary terms, and if one were not competent at dealing with sociological, philosophical, and scientific issues. A discussion about sexual relations ought to involve awareness of the historical development of sexual concepts, changing attitudes to sexual practices, and competing values. It should involve understanding of the proper way in which to assess the plausibility of different value judgements. It should involve appreciation of our own tradition and those of other societies. It ought to involve careful scrutiny and assessment of empirical research into particular matters, such as the causes of various diseases or the effectiveness of methods of birth control. It ought to involve an exploration of concepts such as "love," "lust," "marriage," "obligation," and "fidelity." Similarly, the study of peace should start with an attempt to define peace, and go on to include consideration of why throughout history people have made war, what kinds of motivation and instigation they have had, and what kinds of justification they have proffered. In this case, one would be hard pushed to avoid getting into some fairly deep discussion about religion. One would also need to get involved with politics, nationalism, justice, and human nature. If one did not actually read, say, Euripides' *The Trojan Women*, Tolstoy's *War and Peace*, and Clausewitz' *On War*, one would at any rate need to engage in discussion of the points, arguments, beliefs, and attitudes that such books raise. If women are to be the focus of attention, then one would need to know about the role of women in various historical and social contexts, the belief systems that underlay those varying roles, the achievements of woman through history, the contemporary legal situation, as well as to become immersed in sociology, psychology, and philosophy in order to debate the various empirical, conceptual, and evaluative claims that lie at the heart of any contribution to women's studies.

As with any educational issue, since we are necessarily referring to taking people from a state of relative ignorance to relative understanding, there is a question of degree here. I must not be allowed to suggest that children cannot study peace, because they cannot discuss it with the erudition and intelligence of a Bertrand Russell. And, of course, an obvious rejoinder to my point in the previous paragraph would be that a well constructed course in sex education, peace studies, environmental studies, or women's studies, seeks to do as much of that sort of thing as is possible. But here we have to ask ourselves what makes more sense: to study history, literature, philosophy, science, sociology, and the like, in such a way as to get as thorough a grasp as possible of their content and nature, and then put that information and understanding to use in discussing particular topics, or to focus on a few topics and thereby hope to branch out into the discipline based understanding?

There are a number of considerations that surely force us into recognising that the former approach makes altogether more sense. First, if we push the argument to its limit, the topic-based approach becomes discipline based. That is to say, if you are really going to work on the business of analysing the concept of love, you are going to start doing philosophy for a number of lessons; if you are really going to study the role of women in history, you start a history course; if you are really going to read Euripides and Tolstoy, you begin to study literature. Secondly, there is a danger in learning to philosophize or to study history or literature exclusively through particular topics, in that one may find it difficult to preserve the necessary detachment. The agenda for an introductory course in philosophy, science, or history is predominantly focussed on initiating students into the nature of the types of inquiry; the agenda for a course in sex education or peace studies focusses more on resolving problems in those areas. Thirdly, it is easier to teach people the disciplines when emotions are not involved and nobody much minds what the conclusion is. Fourthly, one is not teaching history, philosophy, or science properly, if one concentrates exclusively on the issues of peace, sex, the environment, or women.

At this point we should turn to the other two objections. For very often the fact is that such topic-based courses are not taught as a way into various subject matters and disciplines, even if they could be.   Nor are they conceived as opportunities for a neutral exploration of the topic, drawing on information and disciplines that form the rest of the curriculum. They are introduced in order to get particular information and points of view across. Thus a great deal of sex education is unashamedly no more than the attempt to impress certain alleged facts on children, such as the facts of sexual reproduction and claims about the consequences of various sexual practices. When that is indeed all that is done, we have the following objections: this in no way deserves the name of sex *education*. It seems pointless to divorce this kind of information from its natural home in biology and science. And it is misleading to divorce this information from questions about love and human relationships generally (in a way that it is not misleading in biology. Biology does not focus on sex; it focusses on biology which includes sexual reproduction. Sex education ought to be about sexual relationships, if it is to take place at all). It is also unclear why imparting such information needs to be the responsibility of schools rather than parents or mass media.

Some sex education and, I venture to say, most peace and women's studies, does not remain on the purely factual level. It involves a heavy dose of values and attitudes, put across in a partisan spirit. That is to say, much of the "education" in these areas consists in trying to get children to adopt particular values and attitudes. When it reaches the point of brooking no serious dissent, as it often does, we are not dealing with education at all but with indoctrination. The truth is that what we should do in respect of sex, peace, and women, what views are credible or correct, are extremely complex questions. Nobody who thinks that he knows, and is intending to teach, without qualification, that homosexuality is wrong, that intercourse should only take place within marriage, that Reagan is a warmonger, that we should unilaterally disarm, that Greenpeace should be supported, that we should practice positive discrimination in favour of women, or that we should object to the use of the generic "he," should be allowed near a classroom. Not because these views are necessarily wrong, but because they are certainly not necessarily right.

And so we get back to the initial point: being incredibly complex areas, involving a great deal of information, a great number of disciplines, a large amount of open-mindedness and open-ended discussion, as well as a degree of maturity and experience, these are not topics that it is sensible or worthwhile to focus on as subjects in a school curriculum. If people do not have the requisite knowledge, understanding, and ability to handle them, then we have no choice but either to reduce them to low-level informational courses or find ourselves moving into indoctrination.

The conclusion is that, since the mental abilities we are concerned with are not generic skills, and since some subject matters are of greater intrinsic worth than others, deal with more useful information, and involve powerful types of inquiry that have widespread application, we require a curriculum based on such subjects. Courses, lessons, or programmes that profess to develop a skill or ability, or that emphasise the process of creativity, critical thinking, etc., are to be resisted because they develop the ability only in relation to the trivial material they deal with. Courses in genuine skills are not necessarily to be dismissed, but cannot provide the essence of an educational curriculum. Courses based on topics and issues cannot go far in the absence of the development of disciplined understanding, and run the considerable risk of turning into indoctrination.

III: The core curriculum

The subjects that should form the core of the curriculum for all students are: literature, history, the natural sciences, ethics, aesthetics, geography, philosophy, and mathematics. This largely follows from points that have already been made in previous chapters, but it may be elaborated and consolidated here. These subjects have in common that they are developed and distinguishable bodies of knowledge, each of which requires considerable study if it is to be adequately understood, each of which contains a great deal of information in the form of conclusions and claims that have already been generated, and each of which has enormous utility in respect of the number of important issues to which it is relevant.

Literature and history tell us about ourselves, as no other subject comes near to doing, essentially because they deal with us as the complex wholes that human beings are, in a way that the social and natural sciences emphatically do not. If you really want to understand an individual you need a well written biography, or the equivalent, that provides a detailed case study, and the accumulation of such biographical understanding of individuals enables one to more completely understand the human race. But the natural sciences do tell us about the physical world, including the physical aspects of the human body. Philosophy tells us about meaning and about a variety of crucial abstract concepts, while two of its branches, ethics and aesthetics, tell us respectively about morality and art. Mathematics tells us about number and space. Geography tells us about the natural world.

It is not simply that these are all self-evidently important things for every individual to know about, in a way that football and the French language are not. It is also that they percolate into most of the issues in life that we choose to and need to think about. Moral and aesthetic questions crop up all over the place; all sorts of problems presuppose scientific understanding for their resolution; mathematical ability is necessary for a hundred daily activities; few issues are not illuminated by understanding of human nature, whether general or behavioural, and few problems are not better understood in a historical context.

These subjects cover most of what we most urgently and most often need to know in order to make sense of our lives and to make decisions about our world. Some of them in addition involve a particular and unique kind of way of dealing with a unique but omnipresent kind of question. The natural sciences embody the scientific mode of inquiry, which is vital to many, but appropriate only to certain, questions. Ethics embodies a quite different kind of inquiry that is necessary to dealing with moral questions, as aesthetics does in respect of questions about art, and philosophy does in respect of questions about meaning generally. Mathematics is seldom taken to be anything other than *sui generis*. These unique forms of inquiry related to unique kinds of question all need to be understood, not just because each kind of question happens to be of some importance, but also because it is crucial that we do not confuse them. We cannot afford to have people attempting to solve moral problems as if they could be handled scientifically, or confusing them with aesthetic questions. Conversely, understanding of these modes of inquiry is a most powerful weapon, for they cover all the kinds of question of which we are aware. (It should, incidentally, be apparent, but it is worth stressing, that the reference is not to different questions, or questions about different kinds of thing, but to different kinds of question. Thus one may ask a question in psychology such as "does aversion therapy help people to give up smoking?", but it is a scientific question in kind, to be answered in the same manner as a question in chemistry about the effects of mixing two substances.)

One might hope that the above considerations alone would be enough to convince people that these subjects are worth studying to a degree that other in themselves perfectly estimable subjects are not. But in the context of the argument of this book there is more to be said: the nature of the concepts that we have considered is such that, if people are to be able to think critically about important issues, they will have to acquire understanding of these subjects, for they cannot think critically if they cannot differentiate between a moral problem and a scientific one, and if they cannot handle both appropriately. And they cannot think critically about peace, sex, women, and the environment, if they lack the knowledge these subjects provide. They cannot hope to be creative or imaginative about their private affairs, the situation in Northern Ireland, or the problems of acid rain, if they do not know about these things, and cannot maintain standards of quality in their reasoning. But to know about these things variously involves knowing about people, knowing some history, understanding ethics, knowing some science, knowing some geography, and, perhaps I may be permitted to add, being able to count. Their emotions will not be educated, their intuitions will be impoverished and unassessable, and their caring will be a hideous caricature of the real thing, consisting in gesticulations and grimaces, if they do not have the understanding referred to. Without minds developed in this way, people cannot, logically cannot, be intelligent, autonomous, or tolerant. For these concepts presuppose understanding important things as they are, and these subjects provide that understanding.

By "literature" I mean the study of literature, and not, for example, creative writing. Students should be brought to understand the nature of various literary traditions, such as fiction, poetry, *belles lettres*, and biography; they should come to understand the criteria for excellence in these fields, and above all they should read and discuss them. In this way they become familiar with this aspect of the arts, and they are empowered to understand some of the best of what has been said and thought about matters central to human interest. They will then be in a position to talk about themes such as love and death, peace and war, males and females, and much else besides, more critically, intelligently, creatively, and imaginatively than they would otherwise have been.

There are various empirical claims that lend some credence to the view that the study of literature enhances critical ability. For instance, it has been claimed that teachers of English tend to do better than teachers of science on tests of creativity and intelligence. However, it would be inappropriate for me to avail myself of this kind of evidence, in view of what has been said about the nature of such tests. It seems clear to me that such a finding might be expected in view of the fact that the tests are predominantly tests of vocabulary and rapid response without concern for calculation. But in any case this should not become an empirical issue. The point, put over-simply, is that, if you want people to think intelligently about issues that people have written about intelligently, it makes sense to get them to read what has been written. Either way, it is somewhat disheartening to note that there are various indications of the very slight amount of reading in which we engage. One in five adult Canadians is functionally illiterate, for example, and one in two never reads a book from one year's end to another.[7]

By the study of history I mean coming to an understanding of the fact of historical change, of the factors that may contribute to it, and the problems of historical inquiry. But I also refer to understanding of the historical development of particular concepts. By philosophy, I mean the business of conceptual analysis and logical reasoning. By the study of science I mean coming to an understanding of the development of science and the nature of scientific inquiry as it is currently understood, in addition to gaining knowledge of scientific truths.

What I mean by ethics should be clear from what has already been said; and geography and mathematics, while they are not always very well known, have the merit of being fairly readily understood to be what they are. I do, however, need to add a word about aesthetics. I am conscious of the fact that throughout the preceding pages I have concentrated on aesthetics as a type of understanding, and have avoided any mention of engaging in one or more aspects of the arts. Reference has always been to the study of art, rather than the practice. That imbalance requires comment, and so too does the lack of explicit reference to such curriculum favourites as drama, music, dance, and the plastic or visual arts. The main reason for the omission is a recognition that this is too large and complex an issue to be treated adequately within a different and broader context. There is something to be said for keeping silent on matters to which one cannot do justice. Nonetheless, I shall briefly indicate some of the points that pertain to this matter and that on another occasion might profitably be elaborated on, explained, and argued about. The first point is simply that, while the core curriculum outlined is focussed primarily on developing understanding (although, of course, the argument is that emotions, imagination, aesthetic sensibility, and so forth are thereby developed and enhanced), I in fact intend "aesthetics" to be understood to cover both the study and the practice of the arts. The reasons that I have for including practice in the arts in the core curriculum constitute the remaining points referred to. Whilst recognising the difficulties and their contentious nature, I accept (i) the view that understanding art is enhanced by experience of art and engagement in artistic production, (ii) the view that the ability to play music, to paint, to act, etc., improves the quality of the life of the individual, while the consequent existence of art enriches the quality of life generally, and (iii) the view that the development of artistic sensibility, which involves understanding but also requires experience, is itself desirable as a part of liberal education, for the capacity to order reality imaginatively in new, different, and illuminating art forms is part of what it means to be free. For these reasons, then, I would conclude that the core curriculum for all students should include engagement with one or more of the arts. (It is a further question as to how to determine which arts.)[8]

I should conclude by guarding against some of the persistent misconceived objections that this kind of view of curriculum is subject to. One is the attempt to discredit the notion by remarking on its familiarity. A particular form of this criticism stresses that it is fairly obviously familiar to the proponent of the view as well. This is a depressing objection because not only is it irrelevant to the wisdom of a proposal whether it is new or old, and whether its proponent has some particular motive for supporting it, not to mention that it is rather impolite to impute unworthy motives to someone on no evidence, it is also detrimental to the very quality of thinking we are supposed to be concerned about. Our concern should be with the quality of the reasoning given in support of a proposal. If an argument such as the one put forward in these pages is unsound or is not an argument at all, that will have to be demonstrated by reasoning. It is not demonstrated by drawing attention to the fact that the curriculum looks a lot like the curriculum of the traditional English grammar school.

It may also be correctly observed that some of my comments on the subjects of the core curriculum are similar to those of various other theorists, most particularly Paul Hirst.[9] That is hardly surprising, since I believe that Hirst asked one of the important questions for educationalists (what is the nature of knowledge?) and answered it in broadly the right kind of way. I am certainly glad to take this opportunity to express my indebtedness to some of his work. But again, the question of whether what I say is the same as what he says has no bearing on the question of whether what is said is plausible or true. And attention should be drawn to the fact that we are not saying exactly the same thing, albeit I am partly relying on an argument very similar to, and without question derived from, his. The lists of subjects we end up with are not identical. Rather more importantly, where he sees eight forms of knowledge as he calls them, I see only five. Most important of all, I do not offer such a specific account as Hirst does of his forms. I am not satisfied that he has made the case for saying that, by the three criteria he introduces to define a form of knowledge, there are the eight he specifies, nor that by those criteria we can pick out the five unique ways of dealing with unique kinds of question that I discuss. I am content with the less clear cut observation that these five distinct kinds of question, requiring a particular type of treatment, manifestly do exist. And whereas Hirst's argument was (correctly on this point, I think) that a developed mind must mean a mind that encompasses whatever logically distinct types of understanding there are, and that an educated person should have a developed mind, mine has not been. I do endorse that argument, but I have concentrated on showing that if people are to be critical, imaginative, creative, able to cope with value judgements, educated in respect of their emotions, and socially competent, they will need to study certain subjects.

The most serious objection, and certainly a very common one, to the curriculum I argue for is that we have tried it, we have it still to some extent, and it doesn't work. But this objection may turn out to be double edged, for in what sense are we entitled to conclude that it doesn't work? It is certainly true that we do not have a nation of critical, caring, creative people. It is certainly true therefore that, insofar as such a curriculum has been in place, it has not "taken" with all students. But who has actually got any evidence to the effect that where it has "taken" it has not proved effective? Nobody. And nobody could have, if the argument is sound, because according to the argument this *must* be a suitable kind of curriculum for the purposes in question. The case is not that the curriculum has been shown to be the wrong one, but that we have failed to teach it in a way that allows it to "take" with students.

Now this is an altogether different kind of point, and one that may be readily conceded. We cannot imagine that merely to implement or sustain such a curriculum will solve our problems. We need to teach it in ways that both engage students and do justice to the reasons we have for teaching it. Specifically, therefore, we have to teach science and history in a way that involves providing understanding of the nature of such activities and the problems they incur, and we have to teach critically, imaginatively, and creatively, while demanding responses and activity of a like order from students. But my concern has been to establish that we should recognise precisely this point, and not throw the baby (the curriculum) out with the bath water (our poor way of teaching it). We should be worrying about teaching for critical thinking, developing the imagination, and so on, but we must face up to the fact that we have to do these things in the context of a curriculum such as has been outlined, and not suppose that provided we are interested in this kind of thinking and activity it does not matter in what context we encourage them, or whether people gain any disciplined understanding.

I have not yet said anything directly about pedagogy, partly because it is not the main focus of this particular book, partly because, as I have argued throughout, how one should teach seems to me essentially answered by understanding the nature of what you are teaching and the reasons you have for teaching it, rather than by adopting particular generic teaching skills, and partly because my major concern has been to emphasise that, while how we teach certainly matters, we have made a terrible mistake in concentrating on methodology divorced from the question of educationally worthwhile content. But, in the final chapter, I shall have a little more to say about pedagogical matters.

Chapter 8

Pedagogical Points

I: Teacher education

I was once described as "a friend of the teacher," with reference to the fact that I have argued that teachers should be given more autonomy to determine what specific materials, texts, and topics they should use in the classroom, and how they should teach.[1] However, I have also argued that if teachers are to be encouraged to exercise such autonomy, they need to be educated properly themselves.[2]

My point has never been that as a matter of fact teachers are wiser and more to be trusted than school boards, administrators, or researchers. It is that the nature of education is such that a great deal of the research on which people base their curriculum and policy decisions is misconceived, and consequently misleading, and that what it is best to do in a classroom depends a great deal on particular situations and people, and cannot readily be encompassed in general rules. I do not dispute that there are some general rules and principles, and, as this book confirms, I believe that our educational aims and the broad structure of curriculum should be hammered out by a process of argument, and adopted universally. But once we have agreed that we ought to be teaching literature in a particular kind of way, the details, such as whether to read *Anne of Green Gables* or *The Wind in the Willows*, and whether to adopt instruction or discussion, are best left to individuals to decide in the light of what they know about themselves, their class of children, and other things going on in a particular school. I am sceptical, not only of the claim that we know a great deal that is specific about the rules of good teaching, other than what we can establish by reasoning, but also of the idea that there are many such rules to be known.

I must, therefore, risk losing my credibility as a friend of the teacher, and talk about some of the manifest shortcomings in our approach to teacher certification and education, and, by extension, in many of our teachers. In fact, if there is an argument for training teachers in various generic skills, imparting to them specific rules of procedure and technique, and allowing them little latitude for selecting their own material and designing their own courses, it would have to be the rather dismal one that this is a necessary fail-safe device: granted that the best teachers don't need and should not follow close and demanding prescriptions for teaching, the majority do, because they are not very good. Sad to say, I have heard this explicitly said on more than one occasion. Sadder still, it may be true.

I base what I have to say in this chapter on a consideration of the kinds of practice that educationalists and curriculum guidelines advocate, on the kind of teacher education we provide, and on the nature of our educational theorising. I am drawing deductions about the sorts of thing that go on in schools from what we say should go on, prepare teachers to do, and formally require of them in policy documents. I appreciate that there are some teachers who simply ignore all the guff, and get on with inspiring children with poetry or mathematics, fascinating them with learning and scholarship, riveting their attention to scientific and other forms of inquiry, and provoking and nurturing imaginative and critical treatment of worthwhile subject matter. But such empirical evidence as I have, drawn from experience in schools, teacher training institutions, and universities, does not make me particularly sanguine.

Much of our work in educational theory and research rests upon the idea that our problem is that we have not discovered enough, we do not yet understand enough, about education. As we find out more, as we are doing all the time, our ability to control and improve education will increase. I think that this is substantially incorrect. No doubt there are some useful things that we do not yet know and may find out in the future. But a great deal of what we find out is simply irrelevant to the business of educating, as opposed perhaps to the business of training, behaviour modification, or imparting information. Most of our problems arise not from ignorance about how to achieve what we want, but from our failure to properly conceptualise what we want. It is arguable that we are doing very well, if what we want are creative, imaginative, and critical people in the senses logically implied by the way we set about testing, talking about, and teaching these things. The fact that in quite different senses we don't seem to have a society characterised by intelligence, critical capacity, creativity, and imagination, suggests to me that we are doing the wrong things because we have not worked out what these qualities actually involve.

It is often said that education is a new discipline. But it is no such thing. It is neither new nor a discipline. As a subject matter for critical reflection and inquiry, somewhat akin to politics, it has a considerably longer history than any of the developed disciplines, such as science or history, let alone psychology or sociology. And it is not a discipline, either in the strict sense of a subject defined exclusively in terms of a nucleus of concepts, a specific kind of question, and an appropriate type of inquiry and testing, as the natural sciences are, or in the weaker sense of a subject matter treated predominantly from one particular perspective as, say, history is. It is an area of inquiry or a subject matter that needs to draw on the findings of many disciplines, because it gives rise to philosophical, scientific, sociological, psychological, and historical questions.

What is new is the conception of education as an applied science, an area in which the aims and integral conceptual questions have been sorted out, so that we are left with only technical questions, which we answer by drawing on the sciences (natural and social), very much as engineers draw on the natural sciences. But this new conception has nothing to recommend it, and can only be explained in terms of some deep-seated need for certainty based on observation, and fear of whatever cannot be so nailed down. For this view, far from emerging when there is clarity and agreement on concepts and aims, has emerged in defiance of what agreement there was, in cultures that are noteworthy for their openness and hence variety of opinion on such matters, and has turned such agreed aims as there were on their head by effectively redefining them to suit the scientific paradigm.

It could be argued that there has been a substantial measure of agreement on what education necessarily involves, and how to set about achieving it, throughout history, evidenced both by the continuity of certain broad practices and by the writings of people as diverse as Plato, Rousseau, and John Wilson. But to know that, people would need to study history and philosophy. Since by and large they don't, such reasonable agreement as there has been, such truths as have been established in the appropriate manner, have to be re-asserted, re-discovered, and re-established. We do not primarily need to discover more; we need to understand what has already been perceived. To put the point picturesquely: Plato did not fail to devise a programme in critical thinking of the sort we espouse today, or an intelligence test, or a schedule of teaching behaviours, because he did not know as much about human psychology, classroom dynamics, and learning as we do, although it is true that he didn't. He did not devise such things, because, having a pretty clear idea of what he was about, having formulated and argued for his aims, having given thought to the nature of knowledge and other crucial educational concepts, he could see that such stratagems were largely misconceived and irrelevant. The world has certainly changed dramatically in a number of significant ways (covering such diverse matters as values, scientific knowledge, and understanding of human behaviour) since Plato's time, so that one could not reasonably take his specific educational proposals and implement them wholesale. But the world has not changed so much that the idea of education, the nature of knowledge, or even the basic patterns of human behaviour, are essentially different. In terms of principles there is no necessary reason to assume his contribution more outmoded than that of some guru of twenty years ago, or, indeed, today.

Many teachers today, too many, have not had an education that provides them with a substantive body of worthwhile knowledge and understanding. That this is so may reasonably enough be attested by anyone who over the years has taught some thousands of pre-service and graduate teachers and found that a substantial majority of them have no grasp of philosophy, no critical appreciation of the nature of, and problems in, empirically based inquiry into human behaviour, no historical understanding of the world as a whole (as opposed to, say, some recollection of the Tudor kings, the American War of Independence, or the Settlement of Canada), and no familiarity with any such works as Homer's *Odyssey*, Chaucer, John Stuart Mill's *On Liberty*, Shakespeare's plays, Trollope's novels, or Gibbon's *Decline and Fall of the Roman Empire*. It is true that this observation is not based on certain commonly accepted means of gathering data such as questionnaire or structured interview, nor has care been taken to ensure a random sample and so forth. But why should it be? The information has been gathered in an entirely appropriate manner (by lengthy communication with individuals, by reading their essays, etc.), and the conclusion is based on a clear understanding of what it is that is being looked for and not found. It is in fact a model of empirical inquiry, being more concerned to be clear about what is being inquired into and to adopt a mode of searching that is appropriate to the nature of what is being sought, than to obfuscate the issue by emphasising technical and formal merit. So let us turn to some of the considerations that both show that this state of affairs is to be expected, and throw light on some of the things that we need to set right.

In some jurisdictions one does not even need a degree to teach, something like a two-year period of study leading to certification being regarded as sufficient. Many teachers have a B.Ed. degree, which, while it may take many particular forms, will always include a substantial part that is devoted to general education courses rather than a specific subject matter. Those that come into teaching with a first degree in some academic discipline generally have relatively poor degrees. The nature of many degree courses, particularly in North America, is such that it is possible to have a degree in a subject having taken a varied number of peripheral courses or without having undertaken a coherent study of the subject. For example, there are teachers of English who have never studied poetry at University, and others who have barely studied literature, having concentrated on such things as composition, journalism, and creative writing.

Now I do not wish to put myself in the invidious position of suggesting that a degree is proof of competence or scholarship. (Indeed my final remark in the previous paragraph sufficiently indicates that I do not think that.) I wish merely to draw attention to the fact that on the face of it, for one reason or another, many teachers are not particularly well grounded in the subject that they are going to teach. To some extent this is recognised and deplored, but it is felt that there is little we can do about it: teachers of French Immersion, for example, are extremely thin on the ground in British Columbia, for a variety of social and political reasons, and consequently we more or less have to employ people whose French is really not adequate. Science and maths teachers are in short supply in most of the western world, and it is difficult to tempt those who are well qualified away from lucrative positions in industry and business into teaching. The fact remains, whatever the practical difficulties in overcoming the problem, it is a problem, unless one does not accept that a competent understanding of one's subject matter is a necessary prerequisite for teaching it.

As to that, we must be cautious. It is not necessary to be a top flight academic to teach secondary students, as again we all know from our experience of good academics who can't teach and relatively poor ones who can. But it is necessary, it must be necessary, for a teacher to have a thorough understanding of the nature of the subject matter being taught. As a teacher of science I need to understand the nature of scientific inquiry, I need to have a clear grasp of what makes for good scientific research, and I need to understand the specific material that I teach. I do not have to be in the top flight academically, if that means to have proven myself a first-rate researcher or to have a complete grasp of the most up-to-date and sophisticated theory. I do not even have to be aware of all the latest scientific theory and findings. (The extent to which I do have to be up to date is largely determined by whether recent work involves dramatic reconceptualisation of theoretical perspective, and whether recent findings have pertinence to the school curriculum.) But I do have to understand science as it is currently conceived and to be thoroughly familiar with theory, experiments, and claims that form the basis of the curriculum.

Understanding what science is is necessary because that is fundamentally what we should be teaching in the secondary school. We also provide information, but information without an understanding of how we came to acquire it is not our goal. It is not educational in itself, it does not develop the mind, and it can be misleading and dangerous: if we do not understand why something is presumed to be so, we are not in a position to question whether it truly is so, nor to recognise when it is subsequently shown not to be so. To this end, the study of the history of science should be an integral part of the study of science for all students, inclusive of those who are going to teach it. For our perception of what science itself is has changed and developed over the centuries, and varies to this day in different societies. One of our objections, for instance, to the work of certain Soviet scholars, such as Lysenko, is that it is not truly scientific. A thorough understanding of the nature of science presupposes understanding not only what scientists do and how they proceed, but also why we have come to think that they should proceed in this way, and what were the deficiencies of earlier or rival conceptions of science. I do not see how a teacher could hope to teach science in a way that serves the purpose of providing this understanding, if he has not himself pursued a course of study that develops it.

In the same way, if one is teaching literature, then one needs not merely to have made a specialist study of the novels of Ernest Hemingway, or to have taken courses in composition and the like, but to have an understanding of the main genres of writing, to appreciate the defining characteristics of such genres, and consequently to have some sense of what makes for quality within each one. The fact that a concept such as poetry has changed a great deal through history, and today is extremely fluid, makes no difference to this principle. If we are teaching people about poetry, as opposed to about some particular author's work that may be classified by some as poetry, then we have to teach them about the various conceptions that there have been and are, drawing attention in each case to the criteria that define the concept and have to be considered in estimating quality. One therefore has to know about at least some of such things as Greek lyric poetry, medieval verse, heroic couplets, free verse—one has to know formally what they involve, and be equipped to talk about examples in such a way as to lead to discussion on how effects are achieved and where success is obtained. This has no necessary implications for directing students into conformity: one is not teaching them that they should write sonnets or in the manner of the metaphysical poets. One is helping them to understand these forms and the purposes that they may achieve. What they choose to do themselves is quite another question: what we are doing is teaching them about what can be done in this sphere.

Precisely what a teacher of literature, science, or mathematics should be familiar with is debatable, and best left to those familiar with the various subjects. But that there must be broad understanding of the field seems indisputable, for that is what it is to understand the nature of the subject and that is what we are trying to provide. We are not, at secondary school level, trying to produce poets, mathematicians, or scientists in the sense of academic leaders, still less poets of this or that school, mathematicians specialising in this or that, or scientists preoccupied with this or that. We are trying to develop the mind by giving it understanding of various distinct and important types of activity, and by giving it various kinds of information that can feed the imagination and provide data for critical understanding.

In the past, understanding one's subject matter has sometimes been seen as the paramount criterion for selecting teachers. Until very recently, the great private schools in Britain, and many of the grammar schools, had virtually no interest in educational theory as a qualification, and did not even require their teachers to be formally trained. They looked for individuals of a certain kind (referring to their moral character in the broad sense, or, less charitably, their personal and educational background), and a good qualification in the subject to be taught (sometimes adding sporting prowess as a desideratum). In America one hundred years ago, as Lee Shulman has recently brought to our attention, the emphasis in qualifying teachers in some States was almost exclusively on mastery of subject matter to be taught.[3] I do not say that we should return to this state of affairs, or that understanding of one's subject matter is the sole criterion of a good teacher, and I hope I have made it clear that I mean something specific by understanding one's own subject matter, and do not necessarily equate it with a good degree. But I do find it astonishing that Shulman, in the paper cited, should appear to be surprised and to think that he has come across a bold and forgotten idea: could anyone who had been thinking about education and had not been sidetracked into a specialist concern with research methodology, who had not become a victim of our obsession with the idea of a science of teaching and teaching as a generic skill, have ever failed to realise the importance of such understanding?   And is it not, anyway, absolutely clear that this understanding is a necessary condition of the good teacher?

Part of the disparagement of teacher training and the study of education in the past derived from a conviction that good teachers are born not made, whereas today our extensive teacher education programmes, running sometimes to as many as five years and much preoccupied with the study of education in one form or another, bear witness to the fact that we firmly believe they are made not born. The truth may lie somewhere in the middle, particularly if the terminology is modified and made more precise.

"Born" does not seem a helpful word, since, if taken literally, it drags us back into unnecessary and difficult to resolve argument about innate endowments. But what does seem clear, and what need not be disputed even by those strongly committed to teacher education, is that some individuals seem better equipped to teach than others by dint of their personalities (regardless of the origin of their personal characteristics). Qualities such as enthusiasm for a subject matter and interest in communicating that enthusiasm, sense of humour, tolerance, patience, and vitality, would seem to be desirable in a teacher, because they contribute to judicious stimulation; but they are not amenable to much development within a teacher education programme in a way that other basic attributes that are truly skills, such as voice projection, may be.

"Made" is a poor word to use as well. But good teachers do not and cannot emerge purely on the strength of personality. They have to acquire the understanding referred to above, at least, and, given their role as overseers of the general development of individuals, intellectual, moral, imaginative, artistic, and emotional, they also require a far broader understanding. So, in a word, if not made, good teachers do have to be "educated".

Personality and education, then, are two important criteria for determining the quality of a teacher.   Yet there is little that a teacher education programme can do in respect of the first, and only a limited amount it can do in respect of the second, if the individual's own prior schooling has not served to educate him. However, notwithstanding the importance of these two factors, which in all probability will owe little to a programme of teacher education, there is an important place for such a programme conceived of in terms of the study of education. The question is what form it should take. The problem is that some of the misconceptions we have been concerned with in this book are in evidence here too, and lead us to an inappropriate kind of teacher education. Our preoccupation with skills, generic abilities, and the scientific paradigm, combined with our scant respect for historical and philosophic-artistic understanding, lead to a conception of teacher preparation which is training rather than education, and inappropriately so. (It may be worth remarking that, until about forty years ago, the favoured phrase was "teacher training," now it is "teacher education." The paradox is that by and large what we do is still training.)

The preparation of teachers is widely seen as a matter of introducing them to a variety of models, strategies, techniques, and behaviours of teaching, rather than initiating them into a thorough exploration of the idea of education and its logical implications. The same fundamental assumptions operate here, not surprisingly, as run through our attitudes and practices in the teaching of children. Teaching itself is seen as a generic skill or set of skills such that, assuming one can teach at all, one can teach anything, since what matters is not the ability to communicate a particular kind of understanding, but the ability to communicate. It is seen as something that one perfects by the exercise of particular skills.

Teaching has been called an art, and some writers today still seek to elaborate it in terms of metaphors from the arts. But a persistent and powerful, if not dominant, trend is to see it in scientific terms. The essential difference is between seeing it as an activity that crucially depends upon insight, judgement, and particularity, and as an activity that depends upon general rules, measurement, and observable behaviours. Before we go any further let us acknowledge that in fact it involves both; we are considering appropriate emphases.

Teaching is not a skill, even though it is often referred to as such. Nor is it a set of skills. That is to say, the business of teaching cannot plausibly be reduced to a number of discrete physical performances that can be perfected by practising them in and of themselves. Skills, in this sense, are involved. For example, writing legibly on a blackboard, voice projection, a particular look of feigned pained horror, and flicking chalk, are all skills, and some of them are important. But teaching, as we have already seen, involves certain character attributes and understanding of subject matter, which are not skills, or, if you prefer, are skills in a quite different sense such that one cannot perfect them by practice alone. In the one case you have to have them (or do whatever is necessary to change your personality), and in the other you have to study and learn. But there are also other aspects of teaching that are not skills, such as exercising judgement, making decisions, and perceiving situations accurately. One does not practice these things; one needs to understand what one is trying to achieve, what will lead to what consequences, what people are like, and what various signs may mean. Experience no doubt plays a part, for one needs to apply theoretical knowledge, and one may increase understanding through experience. But what is clear is that most of the vital elements in teaching, while experience and practice play a part, are acquired by a process of thinking and understanding. One cannot teach somebody to exercise judgement except by way of teaching them to recognise criteria for making judgements in particular contexts, and encouraging them to do so.

Nor are most of the elements in good teaching generic abilities or qualities. One does not have or lack judgement across the board, one does not have the ability to explain, one does not have interpersonal skill (if that is a skill or set of skills at all, which I doubt). What one has is the ability to exercise judgement in certain cases, the ability to explain some things, and the ability to relate to some people in some situations. We may concede that some teachers may have these abilities well-honed in a wide variety of areas, perhaps all the important ones. So the idea of someone who effectively communicates all the time, or who can explain anything, is not a nonsense. We may concede also that just as teaching involves some skills, so some of these qualities which are not themselves skills may nonetheless incorporate them. For example, although the ability to communicate is not exclusively a matter of skills, good communication may involve some skills such as eye contact. And *bona fide* skills, by virtue of what they are, do have application across the board: the skill of reading (in the sense of what is sometimes termed "decoding"), which is a part of the ability to study, is applicable in any context. But the fact remains that a person who is good at explaining the nature of science is not necessarily going to be good at explaining politics, a person who is capable of exercising judgement in philosophical discussion is not necessarily capable of exercising it in discussing domestic matters, a person who gets on well with his football cronies is not necessarily going to get on with his mother-in-law. And this is not due solely, or necessarily at all, to such factors as lack of interest or emotional blockages. It is necessarily true, because, in order to explain politics you have to understand politics, in order to exercise judgement in discussing domestic matters you have to understand them, in order to communicate with your mother-in-law you have to be willing to do so and have certain understanding. The idea of developing in teachers the ability to listen, explain, relate, interest, and so on, therefore does not make sense, unless we mean the ability to do these things in various specific contexts. We do not want courses in teacher-student interaction, so much as in how to interact when teaching French, when counselling, or when coaching baseball, and a large part of the difference between them comes from the differing nature of the activities.

When it comes to teaching strategies and techniques of a more specifically pedagogical or instructional type, the same principles apply. Some skills are involved, and they, by definition, can be referred to and practised in themselves, since they can be put to use in any context. For example, one may refer to the business of recapitulating material from a previous lesson, writing legibly, or employing a specific range of questioning techniques as skills. Even in some of these cases, the ability may be affected slightly by the context (for example, I cannot formulate any question in physics, if I don't know physics), but nonetheless we may allow that it is possible to inform students of different kinds of question and train them to pose them. But the point is that such skills are but a small part of teaching; illegible handwriting won't help, but it may not prevent someone from being a good teacher, and good handwriting certainly won't make a good teacher.

Furthermore there is the question of whether the sorts of skill advocated are all desirable. Writing legibly as opposed to illegibly is, but is writing necessary at all? Is it the case that it is always desirable to recapitulate or ask a variety of questions? The research says that it is. But the research arises from, and is conducted in the spirit of, an approach to education that involves all the misconceptions and errors we are concerned to expose. For example, the claim that use of varied questioning techniques is effective is based upon the kind of research that focusses only on the directly observable, and takes little or no account of what it is to be successfully educated or to teach physics well. We may have established that this technique leads to better performance on a certain kind of test. But we have not seriously examined the question of whether performance on that kind of test is educationally worthwhile.[4]

My view would be that very few of the precepts of instruction that are validated by empirical research are in fact necessary conditions of good teaching in any situation. But, whether that is so or not, it is certainly the case that most of them have not been demonstrated to be so in the light of the educational ideal and the consequent conception of good teaching with which we are concerned.

Another approach to pedagogy is to present student teachers with various models of teaching or to draw conclusions from research into broad styles. I bracket these two together because both involve presenting teaching in terms of one or more sets of behaviours. One might therefore call them the package-deal approach. Research that seeks to arbitrate between, say, traditional and progressive styles of teaching is open to the familiar objections: it is conducted without an explicit conception of what constitutes educational success, it is confined to observable phenomena (and simply ignores factors such as humour, enthusiasm, command of subject matter), and in addition it unaccountably presumes that one has to adopt one style or another. This is true also of models of teaching.[5] But one does not have to choose between being a progressive or traditionalist, a Socratic interlocutor or a Piagetian developmentalist. One can form a style of one's own that crosses boundaries, and one can switch from style to style.

What is certain is that how one should proceed as a teacher is substantially a function of what one is trying to achieve. This means that one needs to know both what one's ideal is and about the nature of what one is teaching. Of course one also needs also to know what there is to be known about motivation, learning, and child psychology. But, since that is hardly disputed, what needs emphasising is the paramount importance of the thing that we are not doing: initiating teachers into the business of sustained and rigorous reasoning about the nature of the enterprise in which they are engaged.

The conclusion to be drawn is that the preparation of teachers should be based on considering how to teach particular groups of children particular things. We do not want courses in giftedness teaching, classroom interactions, or pedagogical principles, so much as courses in, for example, how to teach history to sixteen-year-olds. One's strategy for teaching such a course must be based upon an understanding of the nature of history and an understanding of one's educational aims.

II: The rivers of India—process and content

A distinguished professor of education recently delivered a public lecture in which he maintained, in terms representative of much of today's rhetoric, that education was a process. Speaking for myself, I confess that I am still not entirely clear what this phrase is supposed to mean. But the gist of this gentleman's thinking was tolerably clear: teaching is a matter of interrelating and communicating with people. The object of the exercise is to set various mental processes, such as critical thinking, imagination, and creativity going, so that they may develop and improve through practice.

Nothing at all was said about what types or manner of interrelationship and communication were required, or about what should be communicated, or in respect of what we should interrelate. No mention was made of what should be thought about critically, what kinds of thing we should be imaginative about, or in what spheres we should seek to be creative.

This was not because the professor wished to set aside such questions for another day, but because he conceived these processes as being, in each case, uniform in their realisation, and perfectible through exercise in any context. He was not guilty of the palpable idiocy of believing that one can communicate without communicating anything, or be imaginative without being imaginative about anything. But his position did entail that the question of what people are to be critical about, to communicate, and so forth, is unimportant. Content is regarded as immaterial (rather than non-existent), and process is all. A member of the audience raised this very point, asking "But what about the matters on which people are to exercise these abilities? What about teaching students something? For example, what about the rivers of India? Surely one needs to know something, in order to interrelate, communicate, be critical, and so on? If that is true, don't we have to take seriously the question of what they should know? Don't we have to ask whether it is important to know about the rivers of India?" The professor thought not.

But, as I have attempted to argue throughout this book, we do. Given, what nobody explicitly denies, though many, like the professor, inconsistently put themselves in the position of seeming to deny it, that one has to think about something, if one is thinking at all, and given that, despite our flirtation with relativism when it suits us, some things are more useful, important, and valuable than others, we have to consider what things we want people to be able to think about. Furthermore, because the form or nature of thinking, the criteria whereby we determine whether it is good, critical, creative, intelligent, or imaginative thinking, vary from context to context, we logically cannot ensure a good quality of thinking all round, except by judiciously selecting various contents that cover the major important types of thought and provide information pertinent to thinking about particular issues. Knowing about the rivers of India may not turn out to be particularly important, but the question remains and must be faced: is this information that is relevant to thinking sensibly about something important?

It is not denied that thinking critically involves some activity, that may loosely if misleadingly be called a process, of thought, nor that encouraging people to practise thinking critically is necessary for improving their capacity to do so, nor even that practising thinking critically about relatively trivial matters may have some indirect long-term beneficial consequences for the capacity to think critically generally. (To take one plausible example, such practice may excite and reinforce the inclination to be critical.) But what is being asserted is that preoccupation with the activity or process divorced from the question of content is necessarily inadequate: the nature of the process changes in that it takes on a particular form in different contexts; the process, however formally acceptable it may be, is pointless if there is a lack of relevant information or data on which to work; and some things are more worth thinking about than others.[6]

A lot of our educational research, a lot of our teacher education, and a lot of our school practice is incoherent, because it proceeds without giving due attention to the question of content. Research into general concepts such as progressive styles of teaching or teacher warmth, and into more specific instructional techniques, is rarely conducted with reference to the differing nature and purposes of teaching various subjects. Consequently, we have claims about the value of seminars or questioning techniques which are not related to any particular idea of what we are trying to achieve in various different situations. That cannot make sense, since whether something is a desirable means must necessarily be connected to the question of what it is supposed to be a means to. Similarly, claims about creativity or intelligence don't have any plausibility if they are not context-bound. Training teachers to communicate, teach for critical thinking, or adopt certain strategies makes no sense, if consideration is not given to the varying nature of subject matter and aims. And a school curriculum based on the idea of nurturing various abilities, without regard to context, cannot guarantee progress in the areas in which we want it.

In stressing the importance of content, I am not aligning myself with those writers who seek to establish some specific list of books and topics with which everyone should be conversant.[7] There may be some books and topics that one would hope any educated person would be familiar with and informed about. But it would be difficult to get widespread agreement on more than a short list. In any case, far more important is to get agreement on the *types* of book and the *types* of issue that people should be able to handle. Therefore, I do not seek to establish that the school curriculum should involve study of at least 100 specific books, and ten or twelve particular issues. I do not say people should know about the rivers of India. But I do suggest that there are certain disciplines and subjects which between them introduce students to information and types of reasoning that are important for dealing with a wide range of important questions. You do not have to teach everybody about the rivers of India, but you do have to give everybody some understanding of geography and some geographical information. Some information, whatever it is, is necessary to develop the understanding. And the understanding is necessary because geographical issues and problems loom large in a variety of important issues, such as the characteristics of peoples, the economy of societies, the political decisions of nations, and ecological concerns. The disciplines I have cited (philosophy, science, aesthetics, ethics, mathematics) are clearly a necessary part of any school curriculum. The subjects (literature, history, geography) may be more tentative, but I find it difficult to conceive of equally important alternatives.

Such a curriculum is necessary for attaining towards the ideal outlined in the first chapter. People who cannot distinguish between scientific questions and moral questions, who do not understand how to set about resolving aesthetic disagreements, who do not have historical awareness and therefore do not appreciate the way in which particular concepts have developed, the way in which particular events have come about, and something of the way in which human beings tend to behave, both uniformly and idiosyncratically, who do not have the kind of detailed and imaginative understanding of human beings that literature cumulatively provides, and who in other respects lack the knowledge and kinds of understanding this curriculum provides, cannot be expected to display the qualities we purport to be concerned with. They cannot think critically in these significant areas. But more than that, they cannot be imaginative or creative in respect of matters that draw upon these areas, for those concepts entail understanding. More generally, whatever their respective I.Q.s may be, whatever bizarre method of determining someone as gifted is used, such people cannot be expected to prove either intelligent or gifted. For they will not be able to proceed intelligently or in a gifted manner in significant aspects of life.

Emphasis on content does not preclude the need for teaching it in an appropriate kind of way. Doubt about the value of research into teaching and pedagogy is not synonymous with thinking that how one proceeds does not matter. The main points here are: (i) that much actual research into teaching strategies is unconvincing, because it has been conducted without reference to a clear concept of success, and with inadequate conceptualization of some of the concepts involved.[8] And (ii) that much of what we should do is most appropriately and most easily discerned by a process of reasoning about what we are trying to achieve and the nature of the subject we are teaching. Of course any such reasoning must also take account of what we know about students' ability to understand, but it is arguable that experience of teaching and knowledge of particular students is more important here than generalisations about student development, learning, and understanding culled from psychology.

Let me here refer to one particular example: the essay. You will not find in a manual of teaching any sustained consideration of the value of writing essays as a teaching technique. Nor as a matter of fact is a great deal of time spent in schools requiring people to write essays, with the foreseeable result that not many first-year university students do it very well. Yet the essay can be shown to be a most important element in teaching, if only we give serious thought to what it involves and what we want to achieve. If we do that, we see a straightforward logical connection, for getting people to write essays well is one and the same thing as getting them to exhibit some of the qualities we are concerned with, in a way that, by contrast, multiple choice exams, brainstorming, problem solving, critical thinking exercises, and creativity tests are not.

I do not mean by an "essay" any specimen of writing. A poem is not an essay. A piece of creative writing, as it is usually conceived, is not an essay. A short story is not an essay. But nor is a summary of research findings, a description of an event or a process, or an outline of a point of view. The word "essay" derives from the French word "essayer" meaning "to try." An essay, in one sense, therefore comes to mean "an attempt or trial," and the kind of essay I am referring to draws on this idea of testing or putting something up for trial. An essay is an analytic or interpretative kind of writing. It involves taking some idea or issue and examining, weighing up, putting it to the test. When it is well done it has the merits associated with these activities: it is rigorous, clear, fair, well-informed, and so on. In requiring people to write essays we are therefore requiring them to think in a sustained way about something, to organise their thoughts coherently and effectively, and to display critical acumen, imagination, and creativity—the very concepts we are concerned with.

Nonetheless, the essay (at least of the type referred to) is no longer emphasised and celebrated by educators. Presumably, this is partly because the dominant misconceptions of the key educational concepts that we all value in name inhibit us from recognising that an essay calls for the very qualities we want, whereas multiple choice exams do not. But it is also partly because the dominance of the scientific paradigm leads us to believe that the essay cannot be assessed in an objective way. However, the only sense in which this is true is that essays cannot be quantitatively measured and that assessment requires well-educated markers. It is not true that the quality of an essay is a mere matter of opinion. The quality of an essay depends upon criteria of excellence that will vary from subject to subject, but are nonetheless in each case specifiable and identifiable. To give a precise numerical value to an essay may be difficult, but that doesn't stop it being a matter of fact that some essays are better than others. A teacher may reasonably rank order his students' history essays, but in order to do so objectively he will need to understand the nature of history and be well versed in the particular subject matter under discussion. The undeniable evidence that different teachers' assessments of essays do not always coincide and that individual teachers sometimes assess the same essay differently on different occasions, though important in itself, is not relevant to this argument. In the first place, one of the reasons for this is that teachers do not share a clearly worked out understanding of the criteria of quality they are looking for. In the second place, to adopt a form of assessment simply because it avoids such problems is absurd if it does not serve the educational purposes we are committed to. If "objectivity," in the peculiar sense of "directly and uncontentiously observable and quantifiable," were really our concern, we could make the marking of essays "objective" tomorrow. All we would have to do is focus on features such as the length, the spelling, and the punctuation. But there are other things that should matter a great deal to us as educators, and these are qualities that by their nature have to be assessed by the judgement of the well-educated mind.

This brings us back to the broad question of the nature of our times. For, of course, despite the ubiquity of standardised tests, multiple choice exams, and such like, some essays are written in our schools and many at our universities. But the commonest type of essay is not the reflective, argumentative, truth pursuing, reasoning type that is quintessentially educative, but the "research" essay, wherein the emphasis falls on the gathering of information, the process whereby it is acquired, and the formal protocol of presentation. What is striking is the widespread preoccupation with form rather than substance, and that I think is characteristic of our times. In all sorts of way, in all sorts of department of life, we see this relentless preoccupation with the appearance of things divorced from the reality behind them. I should say straightaway that I am not trying to set up substance against form. On the contrary, just as with process and content, I am arguing that form and substance are necessarily related and cannot be isolated from one another. But so much of what we do proceeds as if they could be, and emphasizes the form of things, without regard to the substance or the material that is being formed.

A very obvious example of our emphasis on the formal is provided by the way in which we focus on people's formal qualifications, when making appointments. No doubt we do other things too, but the fact remains that you more or less have to have a Ph.D. to become a professor in North America, and you have to have a degree in administration to become an administrator. What the doctoral thesis is, is quite literally of secondary importance, for that question only comes into play when candidates without the degree have been weeded out. Whether a particular degree in administration is worth having is scarcely an issue. You have to have one. One can see reasons for this, most notably reasons of convenience, but the point remains that, increasingly, formal qualifications are necessary conditions of employment, even though everyone knows that they are just that, and that many without the formal qualifications could do a better job than those with them.

The essay, as I have said, exists in name. But it often is only in name, because people are taught the formal characteristics of an essay and assessed in terms of them, rather than the substantive qualities. Essays, students are taught, should have a certain number of paragraphs, should start with a statement of the position to be argued, and meet various other generic criteria of the good essay. For example, a university professor teaching a third-year class on Shakespeare's historical plays recently informed his students that their essays would be exclusively assessed in terms of their writing as opposed to the content. Eight specific qualities were then referred to:

1. Punctuation must be correct.
2. Spelling must be correct.
3. In referring to speeches made by characters in the plays, the present tense must be used. (E.g. "King Henry speaks of . . ." rather than "King Henry spoke of . . ." in Act III, scene 2.)
4. The words "toward" and "towards" must not be used.
5. Subject and verb must agree.
6. The word "quotation" must be used rather than the word "quote."
7. Writing must be concise (e.g., avoid such phrases as "Because of the fact that . . .").

8. Wordiness should be avoided (E.g., avoid "felt no grief or emotion.").

This may be an extreme example. But it is a true one, and the nature of it does not seem to me atypical.[9] I should make it clear that, while only the first of the tutor's demands seems to me clearly essential, because punctuation is to some large extent a means of making sense, I am not out of sympathy with any of his requirements: correct spelling aids communication and implies concern for accuracy. "Quote" is an ugly word. Subject and verb should certainly agree (though it is not clear here whether we are talking about appearance or substance). Writing should avoid repetition, pleonasm, etc. (though the difference between concision and avoiding wordiness is not clear). But whatever one thinks, it is clear that this is almost all about the appearance of the thing: it is form in the sense of style. Failure to abide by most of these rules does not necessarily make an essay a bad one in terms of its critical and creative qualities, and adherence to them certainly does not make it a good one. The objection is twofold: first, it is far from clear that they are all good rules, even as points of style. (Why should an essay necessarily have a certain number of paragraphs? Should one always be as concise as possible? Doesn't it rather depend on what you're trying to achieve?) Secondly, and much more importantly, these things may make for a good-looking essay, but they won't make a good one. A good one will be dependent on the quality of what you say substantively, and on what you say being couched in an appropriate and telling form. And that can only come about from having something to say about the play, and understanding how to say that effectively, rather than having some general rules on how to present an essay.

It may be said, of course, that the phenomenon of third-year university students having their essays on Chaucer assessed purely in terms of avoidance of split infinitives and the like, with an explicit refusal to take any account of what is said about Chaucer's poetry (again an actual example), is really an instance of my other point that universities are having to do work that should have been done in secondary school. There is some truth in this: there are some basic rules and features of good writing that could and should be taught at an early stage.[10] However, it is more to the point here to stress that our educational goal should be to develop and perfect formally and stylistically well wrought *substantive reasoning*. It is the substantive reasoning, not the style, that matters, in so far as the two can be separated, and, in any case, the style only becomes significant and assessable when fused with a particular substance.

A rather different example is provided by another true story concerning the assessment of a university professor for tenure. Ten publications of the professor in question were submitted for review to a colleague from the same discipline in another university. The reviewer listed the categories in terms of which he assessed the work: critical acumen, emotion, rhetoric, originality, etc. He did not explain what he meant by these terms, nor provide examples of where he found them displayed in the papers. What he did do was present his conclusions in the form of a chart with the papers numbered one to ten down the left hand side and the categories listed across the top. Then he put a score out of ten for each category against each paper in turn. Thus Paper 3 scored 6 on rhetoric, 2 on critical acumen, and 4 on emotion. What he thought he was doing I cannot say for certain. But it seems that he thought that the use of figures and charts somehow made the judgement more objective, more scientific. He had quantified. But, whatever he thought he was doing, it is evident that his review has become pure form. No doubt he had his substantive reasons for his judgements, but they are not there. All the effort has gone into presenting conclusions in a certain manner, none at all into finding a suitable manner of explaining and justifying the conclusions.

Again, that is a peculiarly bizarre example, but I think readers will know from their own experience that this kind of preoccupation with form without regard to substance is not uncommon. It is inherent in our behaviouristic approach to human activity generally. When we ask whether certain people care, what we actually do is ask whether they perform certain tasks and rituals—we ask whether they appear to care. But smiling, shaking hands, and so on, though they may have their value and significance, are not to be confused with actually caring. It is inherent in our morality, sometimes explicitly, though supposedly humorously, stressed when we talk of the eleventh commandment "Thou shalt not be found out." But at a serious level, many people are not concerned with what people do, so much as with what they appear to do. (I am reminded of Professor Higgins' remark to the effect that "The French don't care what they say actually, as long as they pronounce it properly.") It is inherent in politics and advertising, where all that matters is the image.

In education, a most significant point is that form dominates our activities in research and teaching. We have preconceived ideas about the form of a thesis, such as that it must contain a literature search and adopt a certain style of footnoting. But why? Such prescriptions are trivial in themselves, unless they effect the substance, and whether they do depends on the particular nature of a thesis. Researchers, when they engage in critical debate about their work, generally concentrate on formal arguments and characteristics. They want good reliability ratings, or argue in the abstract for a certain type of research design. They do not ask "is this mode of research appropriate to the nature of what I am inquiring into?" They do not examine the coherence of the manner of establishing reliability in relation to the kind of inquiry in progress. Teachers are encouraged to adopt certain formal procedures: what matters, they are taught, is that they should engage in eye contact, write out lesson plans, recapitulate material to students, and so on. But in itself none of this necessarily matters. What matters is doing things of one sort rather than another and in one way rather than another, *because it is appropriate in a particular case to do so.*

III: Conclusion

It is difficult to know where to begin in concluding this book. One of the fundamental messages has been stated by others so often and so well that one feels a little embarrassed about re-iterating it. "The centre of true scholarship is what the wisest men have written about the most important questions," writes George Grant, echoing Matthew Arnold and voicing the sentiments of thinkers from Plato to the present day, and expressing what might properly be regarded as a mere truism, were it not for the fact that our age seems unable even to recognise that it is true. We no longer have the patience or the ability to study what the wisest have said about the most important questions. Instead we come near to denying that there are any particularly important questions or that anybody can be wiser than anybody else. How should it be otherwise? How could a generation brought up on procedures rather than ideas know anything of wisdom? Naturally "modern academic writing is strewn with impertinent précis written by those who think they can say in few words what wiser men than they have said in more." Indeed "there is every reason to be suspicious of the trappings of scholarship these days." And that is to refer to the supposedly well-educated in our society.[11]

In this attempt to explore some of the logical sources of our confusion, an overriding, umbrella-like, theme of the distinction between the manner in which we do things and the nature and quality of what we do has emerged. The major misconceptions in our educational thought and practice that were outlined in the first chapter, and illuminated and explored subsequently, all, in their different ways, betray this preoccupation with form and appearance at the expense of substance. The materialistic outlook is the very apotheosis of such an attitude. The dominance of the scientific paradigm confirms our preoccupation with things that can be directly observed. The lack of historical, cultural, and philosophic-artistic awareness reveals our disinclination to probe into the behind the scenes element, the explanation of things in a context, as opposed to the perception of things as they now seem. The relativism is a straightforward assertion that how things appear is how they are. The talk of skills, generic qualities, and processes is merely a very extreme instance of the abandonment of any recognition that the form that things take is meaningful only in terms of the substantive element that is being formed. What we do in schools is largely irrelevant to our professed aims, because we misconceive these aims and because we fail to tackle the substantive issues.

We urgently need better educated teachers. That is to say teachers who are well versed in the subjects specified. We need teachers who have had a liberal education, because that is the foundation of sound human understanding and interaction, and of appreciating the significance of teaching particular subjects. It enables one to make sense of educational theory and research, to communicate with students, as well as to understand how it is appropriate to proceed in the classroom. To teach science, one has to know the science, but one also has to know what makes science distinctive, which implies knowing about other things, including what education is about.

Once we have such teachers we shall be in a position to re-introduce an effective liberal education for children in our schools. The challenge is a serious one. It is also a very old one. For, in essence we are dealing today with that same tension between sophistry and philosophy that consumed Plato's energies. To Plato, the sophist was one who claimed to be able to teach the art of persuasion, the ability to speak winningly and convincingly, the capacity to please and to gentle one's audience, making the weaker argument appear stronger, even, to use Aristophanes' phrase, making the worse cause appear the better. The philosopher by contrast is motivated not by a desire to dominate or win, nor to appear clever or be popular, but by a passionate desire for truth. So much so that his proudest boast may have to be that he recognises how little he knows. The distinctive mark of the philosopher is his determination to understand the concepts he works with properly. It is that conceptual rigour that is so sadly lacking in educational discourse today. The message then and the message now is simple: until philosophy becomes an integral and directing force in our educational thinking, until we become motivated more by a genuine desire for understanding and wisdom than by a desire for accolades and for practical success, we shall continue to make the sorts of error referred to above, and we shall continue to fail generations of individuals in respect of education, with dire consequences for the state as a whole. More generally and more eloquently:

> "Until philosophers are kings in their cities, or the kings and princes of this world have the spirit and power of philosophy, and political greatness and wisdom meet in one, and those commoner natures who pursue either to the exclusion of the other are compelled to stand aside, cities will never have rest from their evils—no, nor the human race as I believe, and then only will this our ideal state have a possibility of life and behold the light of day." (Plato, *The Republic*, Book 5, 473.d. Trans. Benjamin Jowett)

Notes

Foreword

1. Erich Fromm, *The Fear of Freedom* (Routledge, London, 1942).

Chapter 1

1. Of course, an expert in photography may be so partly because he has scientific understanding, and an expert in Rembrandt may be so partly because of his aesthetic understanding. The distinction is between those who, while being very well informed in some subject matter, lack understanding of various ways of thinking, and those who, while they may not have any particular specialist information, nonetheless do possess the latter.

2. Again, I am not suggesting that the two are mutually exclusive. In practice, individuals hone their historical abilities by studying a specific subject, such as the Tudor kings and queens, and, as a result, also become knowledgeable in that area. The distinction is between an emphasis on getting people to know about particular historical subject matter and getting people to develop a keen sense of the norms of historical inquiry.

3. On dogmatism, see further R. Barrow, *Injustice, Inequality and Ethics* (Wheatsheaf, Sussex, 1982).

4. For more detailed consideration of the concepts of education, indoctrination, training, and socialisation, see R. Barrow, *The Philosophy of Schooling* (Wheatsheaf, Brighton, 1981).

5. For a recent defence of liberal education, see Charles Bailey, *Beyond the Present and the Particular* (Routledge & Kegan Paul, London, 1984).

6. I have already entered the debate in *Injustice, Inequality and Ethics* (op. cit.). See also Peter Singer, *Animal Liberation* (Jonathan Cape, London, 1976), and Tom Regan and Peter Singer (eds.), *Animal Rights and Human Obligation* (Prentice Hall, New Jersey, 1976).

7. It is perhaps worth noting that some of the old myths are re-appearing with a vestige of scientific respectability. Plato's conviction that love was the product of an innate disposition on the part of the soul to search for and recognise its other half—"the desire and pursuit of the whole"—bears a striking similarity to recent claims that the fundamental basis of the feeling of love is a chemical attraction between individuals' pheromones. Though I confess that I believe that there is evidence that environment and cultural conditioning also play a part, and the old romantic in me hasn't entirely given up on the idea of some more mystical element being at work as well.

8. See, in particular, John Searle's succinct and compelling argument to the effect that computers are irredeemably syntactical, while the mind is semantical, in *Minds, Brains, and Science* (Harvard University Press, Cambridge, Mass., 1984). Kieran Egan has suggested to me that one could imagine a computer that was not qualitatively different from a mind. But that is incorrect and misses the fundamental point, which is, as Searle puts it, that "the nature of the refutation [of the thesis that the brain is just a digital computer and the mind a computer programme] has nothing whatever to do with any particular stage of computer technology. It has to do . . . with what a digital computer is." Presumably what Egan means is that he could imagine something with mind that in some other respects was like a computer. So he might. But it wouldn't be a computer. In other words, according to the argument, a computer programme that was a mind is as logically inconceivable as a squared circle. See also J. Z. Young, *Philosophy and the Brain* (Oxford University Press, Oxford, 1986.)

9. See, e.g., Theodore Roszak, *The Cult of the Imagination: the folk lore of computers and the true art of thinking* (Pantheon Books, New York, 1986).

10. Some may question whether what I say here is consistent with what I say below about skills (Ch. 4: 3). I think that it is. I am not maintaining here that reasoning skills are generic and that they may be acquired through the study of classics. I am suggesting that certain dispositions, certain understandings, aesthetic sensibility, and a specific cultural awareness might be developed, in addition to facility in rational thought relating to

these matters. See Gilbert Highet, *The Classical Tradition* (Oxford University Press, Oxford, 1964).

11. See, for example, Nidditch's exploration of the argument that, since we live in the Age of Science rather than in an age of Christian neo-classicism, "the curriculum of the secondary school should be constituted by science studies," in "Philosophy of Science and the place of science in the curriculum," in G. Langford and D. J. O'Connor (eds.) *New Essays in the Philosophy of Education* (Routledge & Kegan Paul, London, 1973). See also my discussion of that paper in *Common Sense and the Curriculum* (Allen and Unwin, London, 1976).

12. See, for example, A. W. Halpin, *Theory and Research in Administration* (Macmillan, New York, 1967), or the misleadingly entitled *The Philosophy of Leadership* (Blackwell, Oxford, 1983), by Christopher Hodgkinson.

13. E.g., "Studies show that between 1964 and 1982 philosophy students scored at least 5 percentage points above average in admission tests to U. S. professional and graduate schools." From "Philosophy weighs hi-tech ethics," *Financial Post*, Aug. 24, 1987.

14. As Weizenbaum writes, in the context of teaching at M.I.T.: "I am constantly confronted by students, some of whom have already rejected all ways but the scientific to come to know the world, and who seek only a deeper more dogmatic indoctrination in that faith (although the word is no longer in their vocabulary). Other students . . . sense the presence of a dilemma in an education . . . that implicitly claims to give a privileged access-path to fact, but that cannot tell them how to decide what is to count as a fact." W. H. Weizenbaum, *Computer Power and Human Reason: from judgement to calculation* (Freeman and Co., San Francisco, 1976).

15. See, in particular, Ch. 4 below.

16. For further discussion of conceptualisation, see R. Barrow and G. Milburn, *A Critical Dictionary of Educational Concepts* (Wheatsheaf, Sussex, 1986), under "concept" and "analysis." But, see also, below, Ch. 3.1.

17. Cf. J. S. Mill's discussion of pleasure in Ch. 2 of *Utilitarianism*, ed. M. Warnock, (Fontana, London, 1962).

18. On the important issue of confusing the trappings and the nature of empirical research, and related issues concerning scientism, see, in addition to below, K. Egan, *Education and Psychology* (Methuen, London, 1984) and

Robin Barrow, *Giving Teaching back to Teachers* (Wheatsheaf, Sussex, 1984).

Chapter 2

1. Certain people, such as Howard Gardner, *Frames of Mind* (Basic Books, New York, 1983) and Jerry Fodor, *The Modularity of Mind* (Harvard University Press, Cambridge, Mass., 1983), are interested in re-introducing a variant of faculty psychology. Thus, to quote the *Oxford Companion to the Mind* (1987, ed. R. L. Gregory): "There has recently been some return to the old notion of 'faculties', as the brain is now seen to be organised with many 'modules' of cells in small regions, each responsible for a particular ability . . . *though of course many other parts of the brain must also be involved.*" (My italics). Nonetheless, while divisions in terms of the vocabulary of faculty psychology "are still made in textbooks . . . the notion that they are strictly distinct and localised individually in different regions of the brain has been very largely abandoned."

2. Northrop Frye, *The Great Code* (Academic Press, Toronto, 1981).

3. To be precise, I should say "they must necessarily become less dogmatic and parochial, if such knowledge is active."

4. See, for example, William Hare, *Open Mindedness and Education*, (McGill - Queen's University Press, Montreal, 1979).

5. Two of the more sophisticated recent contributors to the debate are, Richard Rorty, *Philosophy and the Mirror of Nature* (Princeton University Press, New Jersey, 1979) and Alasdair MacIntyre, *Whose Justice? Which Rationality?* (Duckworth, London, 1988). But I am concerned about conceptions of relativity considerably less esoteric—the sorts of issue well discussed in Renford Bambrough, *Moral Scepticism and Moral Knowledge* (Routledge & Kegan Paul, London, 1979), or N. L. Gifford, *When in Rome* (State University of New York, Albany, 1983).

6. E.g., N. Postman and C. Weingartner, *Teaching as a Subversive Activity* (Delacorte Press, New York, 1969). See also M. F. D. Young (ed.), *Knowledge and Control* (Collier Macmillan, London, 1971). For another perspective see A. Flew, *Sociology, Equality and Education* (Macmillan, London, 1976).

Chapter 3

1. The word "gifted" itself is not particularly new, of course. But its use as the educational term of commendation *par excellence*, replacing, e.g., "clever," "intelligent," "talented," and "able" is new. Cf. "personal skills," "communication skills," "learning experience," "learning environment," "empathy," "lateral thinking," "mainstreaming," "aptitude treatment interactions," "brainstorming," and "paradigm" as examples of fashionable periphrases for familiar notions.

2. B. S. Miller and M. Price (eds.), *The Gifted Child, the Family and the Community* (Walker and Co., New York, 1981).

3. See Collins *Dictionary and Thesaurus in One Volume*, 1987.

4. On the use of metaphor in educational discourse, see, in particular, Israel Scheffler, *The Language of Education* (Thomas, Illinois, 1962), and G. Milburn in *Canadian Journal of Education*, 9, 361-75, (1984), and *Theory and Research in Social Education*, 13, (3), 1985.

5. On what it does mean, see Elizabeth Telfer, *Happiness* (Macmillan, London, 1980), and Robin Barrow, *Happiness* (Martin Robertson, Oxford, 1980).

6. There are in fact very few who explicitly maintain it. David Pratt comes close with his claim that we could produce "measures for 99 percent of the objectives identified in school programs" (*Curriculum Design and Development*, Harcourt, Brace, Jovanovich, New York, 1980). More common is the habit of acting as if it were the case, without actually stating it as one's belief. One is thus spared the awkward task of making the belief seem plausible.

7. See B. Bloom, *Taxonomy of Educational Objectives, Handbook I: The cognitive domain* (David Mckay, New York, 1956).

8. See R. Barrow, *Happiness* , op. cit.

9. For research on teacher warmth see M. J. Dunkin and B. J. Biddle, *The Study of Teaching* (University Press of America, New York, 1974), Ch. 5. For a detailed critique of such research, see R. Barrow, *Giving Teaching back to Teachers* (Wheatsheaf, Brighton, 1984), Ch. 6.

10. This list is based on J. L. Carroll and L. R. Laming, "Giftedness and Creativity: Recent Attempts at a Definition: a literature review," *Gifted Child Quarterly*, 1974, 18.

11. Alternatively, he is using "definition" in the old and rare sense of "setting of bounds; limitation."

12. K. W. McCluskey and K. D. Walker, *The Doubtful Gift: strategies for educating gifted children in the regular classroom* (Ronald P. Frye, Kingston, 1987).

13. N. Hobbs, "Who are the Gifted?" in B. S. Miller and M. Price (eds.), *The Gifted Child, the Family and the Community* (Walker and Co., New York, 1981).

14. W. Abraham, "Recognising the Gifted Child," in Miller and Price, op. cit.

15. B. S. Miller, "Gifted Children and their Families," in Miller and Price, op. cit.

16. Paul A. Witty, "Education Programs for the Gifted," *School and Society*, 1959, 87.

17. *Education of the Gifted and Talented*, Report to the U. S. Congress by the U. S. Commissioner of Education (Washington, D. C.: U. S. Government Printing Office, 1972).

18. See below, Ch. 5.

19. Ann Weiner, "Our Gifted and Talented: What are their needs and what can we do?" in Miller and Price, op. cit.

20. J. R. Whitmore, *Giftedness, Conflict and Underachievement* (Allyn and Bacon, Boston, 1980).

21. The fact that we do not have adequate conceptions of these things naturally continues to plague us and complicate the matter here. It may be the case that there is some innate and fixed ability that is measurable by some test, and, if intelligence or giftedness are defined in terms of performance on the test, then "intelligence" and "giftedness" in that sense would, by definition, be unaffected by environment. But, as we shall see, there is no good reason to accept either that performance on the tests is

what we mean by intelligence and giftedness, or that test performance is unaffected by environmental factors.

22. Somewhere at the heart of this lies the ambiguity of the term "potential." Sometimes it is taken to refer to what a person will achieve, sometimes what he could achieve in optimum conditions, sometimes what he will achieve barring unlikely accidents. Appeal to the idea of potential obscures rather than solves the problem. If the potential in question is supposed to be a potential for being gifted, then giftedness itself cannot be an innate endowment. It may be claimed that giftedness is embryonically present in certain individuals and needs a particular set of environmental conditions to allow it to flourish and find a developed form. But to treat giftedness as analogous with the seed of a flower in this way begs the question of whether it is true. And how could we begin to justify the analogy without having a clear conception of giftedness in full flower? If, on the other hand, the suggestion is that giftedness means having a potential (i.e., giftedness is a potential) then one must ask what it is a potential for. "Giftedness" cannot be defined as "having a potential for giftedness" any more than a "cow" can meaningfully be defined as "a cow with four legs." (To put it formally: the definiens or definition cannot include the definiendum or term to be defined.)

23. S. P. Marland, *Education of the Gifted and Talented* (U. S. Government Printing Office, Washington, D. C., 1972). Referred to by Guy R. LeFrancois, *Psychology for Teaching* (Wadsworth, Belmont, Cal., 1988).

24. Of the many important contributions to this debate about nature/nurture (usually in respect of intelligence), I would cite Liam Hudson, *Contrary Imaginations* (Methuen, London, 1966), Brian Simon, *Intelligence, Psychology and Education* (Lawrence and Wishart, London, 1971), D. Fontana, *Psychology for Teachers* (Macmillan, London, 1981), and John Kleinig, *Philosophical Issues in Education* (Croom Helm, London, 1982).

25. J. S. Renzulli, "What makes giftedness: re-examining a definition," *Phi Delta Kappan*, 1978, 60 (3).

26. R. S. Peters, *Ethics and Education* (Allen and Unwin., London, 1966).

27. Reference should obviously be made to Gilbert Ryle, *The Concept of Mind*, (Hutchinson), where the broad line of argument utilised here is famously employed.

28. See J. C. Williams, *Education of the Gifted and Talented* (Washington, D. C., 1974).

29. McCluskey and Walker, op. cit.

30. C. J. Maker, *Training Teachers for the Gifted and Talented: a comparison of models* (Council for Exceptional Children, Virginia 1975), lists the first three course titles referred to.

31. J. S. Renzulli, op. cit.

32. These items are taken from Willard Abraham's checklist provided in "Recognising the Gifted Child," in Miller and Price, op. cit.

Chapter 4

1. D. Pratt, *Curriculum: Design and Development* (Harcourt, Brace, Jovanovich, New York, 1980).

2. A. Osborn, *Applied Imagination* (Scribner, New York, 1957), and S. J. Parnes, *Creative Behavior Workbook* (Scribner, New York, 1967).

3. Example quoted by Guy R. LeFrancois, op. cit.

4. W. J. Gordon, *Synectics: The Development of Creative Capacity* (Harper and Row, New York, 1961), and A. Y. Baldwin, "Webbing: A technique for developing instructional activities for the gifted," *Roeper Review,* 1979.

5. S. J. Parnes "Do you really understand brainstorming?" in S. J. Parnes and H. P. Harding (eds.), *A Sourcebook for Creative Thinking* (Scribner, New York, 1962), H. H. Anderson (ed.), *Creativity and its Cultivation* (Harper and Row, New York, 1959), and J. W. Haegele, *Creativity and Innovation* (Rheinhold, New York, 1962).

6. D. Child, *Psychology and Teaching* (Holt, Rinehart and Winston, London, 1973).

7. Kieran Egan describes this sentence as "extraordinary," but does not elaborate. Is this an instance of his well-known irony? If not, what does he find extraordinary: that we may accept these things sometimes, that we accept them at all, or that we don't accept them all the time?

8. Tasos Kazepides believes that we should be using the word "activity" rather than "process." I think he is correct, but, since educationalists tend to use the latter word, I have too.

9. As does Harvey Siegel, I think, in his *Educating Reason* (Routledge, London, 1988). He suggests an analogy between critical thinking and cycling. But (i) Why should we accept such an unlikely analogy? (ii) Many bikes are pretty much alike in essentials. Whether, e.g., physics and philosophy are is what is at issue. (iii) Is it actually true that the cyclist can ride any bike? Has Siegel tried a penny-farthing? The main point here is that those who criticise the idea of critical thinking as being generic are primarily concerned to argue that if you want to be a critical thinker in respect of, say, science, you have to understand science. This is a point that Siegel does not in fact deny. See also J. McPeck, *Critical Thinking* (Martin Robertson, 1981).

10. In order to make my point, I have phrased this paragraph strongly. It is of course true that in practice my knowledge of the language generally and, perhaps, my knowledge of certain related activities such as gymnastics, might enable me to contribute critically to a discussion of ballet. But the fact remains that in so far as the talk is centred on concepts and experiences peculiar to ballet my knowledge of language, gymnastics, and logic alone will not allow me to participate meaningfully.

11. On this topic, see further, P. H. Hirst, *Knowledge and the Curriculum* (Routledge & Kegan Paul, 1974), P. H. Phenix, *Realms of Meaning* (McGraw Hill, New York, 1964), M. Degenhardt, *Education and the Value of Knowledge* (Allen and Unwin, London, 1982), and Robin Barrow, *Common Sense and the Curriculum* (Allen and Unwin, London, 1976).

12. E. de Bono, *Lateral Thinking: a textbook of creativity* (Ward Lock Educational, London, 1970).

13. See, for example, G. Warnock, *The Object of Morality* (Methuen, London, 1976), R. S. Peters, *Authority, Responsibility and Education* (Allen and Unwin, London, 1973), Phillipa Foot, *Virtues and Vices* (Blackwell, Oxford, 1978), Robin Barrow, *Injustice, Inequality, and Ethics* (Wheatsheaf, Sussex, 1982), and W. D. Hudson, *Modern Moral Philosophy* (Macmillan, London, 1970), in respect of moral objectivity. In respect of criteria for aesthetic judgements, see, e.g., J Hospers, *Meaning and Truth in the Arts* (University of North Carolina, 1946), B. R. Tilghman, *But is it Art?* (Blackwell, Oxford, 1984), and R. Scruton, *The Aesthetic Understanding* (Methuen, London, 1983).

Chapter 5

1. Plato, *The Republic* (trs. Desmond Lee) (Penguin, Harmondsworth, 1974). Egan thinks that I should be more cautious about Plato's views (and a great deal else besides). But I am satisfied that what I say in the text is reasonable. See my *Plato, Utilitarianism and Education* (Routledge, London, 1975).

2. R. S. Peters, *Reason and Compassion* (Routledge & Kegan Paul, London, 1973).

3. Furthermore (see n. 1), Egan wants to blame this on Plato, as is conventionally done. I would rather blame it on people who have misread and misunderstood Plato.

4. On the concept of imagination, see further, K. Egan and D. Nadaner (eds.), *Imagination and Education* (Teachers College Press, New York, 1988), M Warnock, *Imagination*, (Faber, London, 1976), and J. M. Shorter, in D. F. Gustafson (ed.), *Essays in Philosophical Psychology* (Macmillan, London, 1964).

5. On the concept of emotion, see further R. W. Hepburn, in R.F. Dearden *et al.* (eds.), *Education and the Development of Reason* (Routledge & Kegan Paul, London, 1972), and Erroll Bedford, in D. Gustafson, op. cit.

6. On happiness, see Barrow, *Happiness*, op. cit., and Telfer, *Happiness*, op. cit.

7. For an intriguing study of the role of fiction in maintaining a stiff upper lip, see J. Richards, *Happiest Days* (Manchester University Press, Manchester, 1988).

8. On love, see Robert Brown, *Analyzing Love* (Cambridge University Press, Cambridge, 1987), and Roger Scruton, *Sexual Desire* (Weidenfeld and Nicolson, London, 1986).

9. G. Ryle, *The Concept of Mind* (Hutchinson, London, 1949).

10. R. Barrow, "Some observations on the concept of imagination," in K. Egan and D. Nadaner (eds.), *Imagination and Education* (Teachers College Press, New York, 1988).

11. When I say "it makes no sense," I mean, of course, that it makes no sense literally. No doubt we will continue to use such phrases, and

figuratively they have meaning. The problem is that we confuse a plausible figurative sense with an impossible literal one.

12. McCluskey and Walker, op, cit.

13. See, for example, J. P. White, in R. F. Dearden *et al.*, *Education and the Development of Reason*, op. cit., R. Barrow and R. G. Woods, *An Introduction to Philosophy of Education* (Routledge, London, 1988), R. K. Elliott, "Versions of Creativity," in *Journal of Philosophy of Education*, Vol. 5, No. 2, 1971, and M. Degenhardt, in I. Lloyd (ed.) *Philosophy and the Teacher* (Routledge & Kegan Paul, London, 1976).

14. J. S. Bruner "The conditions of creativity," in H. E. Gruber, G. Terrell, and M. Wertheimer (eds.), *Contemporary Approaches to Creative Thinking* (Atherton Press, New York, 1962).

15. E. P. Torrance, "Developing creative thinking through school experience," in S. J. Parnes and H. P. Harding (eds.), op. cit.

16. The view outlined here is substantially that which was put forward in more detail in Ch. 10 of my *Moral Philosophy for Education* (Allen and Unwin, London, 1975).

17. As pointed out above, this does not necessarily imply articulating rules. But a Cicero is a great speaker inasmuch as his rhetoric embodies certain rules.

18. For a more detailed description and criticism of this example, see R. Barrow, *Giving Teaching back to Teachers*, op. cit.

19. H. Lytton, *Creativity and Education* (Routledge & Kegan Paul, London, 1971).

Chapter 6

1. Cf. Webster's New World Dictionary: "Skill, 1. a great ability or proficiency; expertness that comes from training, practice, etc." See also contributions by Robin Barrow, Richard Smith, and Morwena Griffiths to a discussion on the concept of skill in *Journal of Philosophy of Education*, Vol. 21, No. 2, 1987. On caring, see Nel Noddings, *Caring* (University of California Press, 1984).

2. For an exposition of values clarification, see, e.g., S. B. Simon, L. W. Howe, and M. Kirschenbaum, *Values Clarification* (Hart, New York, 1972),

L. E. Raths, M. Harmin, and S. B. Simon, *Values and Teaching* (Merrill, Columbus, Ohio, 1966), and J. Meyer, B. Burnham, and J. Cholvat, *Values Education* (Wilfred Laurier University, Waterloo, 1975). For critical evaluation, see D. B.Cochrane, C. M. Hamm, and A. C. Kazepides, *The Domain of Moral Education* (Paulist Press, New York, 1979), and A. C. Kazepides in *Journal of Educational Thought*, Vol. 11.

3. See I. M. Gregory and R. G. Woods, "Valuable in itself," *Educational Philosophy and Theory*, Vol. 3.

4. In fact "explaining" is itself ambiguous. The point is that one can give different kinds of reason or explanation for holding an opinion and only one kind will serve as justification.

5. Does anybody really maintain such a thesis? Some contributers to, e.g., M. F. Young (ed.), *Knowledge and Control* (Collier Macmillan, London, 1971) certainly seem to and have been taken to do so. And some, such as Antony Flew, *Sociology, Equality and Education* (Macmillan, London, 1976) have taken the position seriously enough to mount an incisive attack on it.

6. Of the many strong arguments to the effect that morality is partly to be defined in terms of a specific kind of content, see G. Warnock, *The Object of Morality*, op. cit.

Chapter 7

1. A point that has been made a number of times in a number of ways, but succinctly by John Kleinig, *Philosophical Issues in Education* (St. Martin's Press, New York, 1982).

2. Recent argument surrounding the work of H. J. Eysenck in the U. K., e.g., *Race, Intelligence and Education* (Temple Smith, London, 1971) and A. R. Jensen in the U. S., e.g., *Environment, Heredity and Intelligence* (Harvard Reprint Series No. 2, 1969), may obscure some of the earlier seminal works on the subject such as Brian Simon, *Intelligence Testing and the Comprehensive School* (1953), reprinted, with additional material, as *Intelligence, Psychology and Education* (Lawrence and Wishart, London, 1971).

3. J. P. Guilford, "Cognitive psychology's ambiguities: some suggested remedies." *Psychological Review*, 1982, 89.

4. E. G. Boring, "Intelligence as the tests test it," *New Republic*, 1923, 35 (June 6th).

5. For a more detailed explication of conceptual finesse, see R. Barrow, "Conceptual Finesse," in *Paideusis*, Vol. 1. No. 1, Fall 1987.

6. C. Bailey, *Beyond the Present and the Particular* (Routledge & Kegan Paul, London, 1984).

7. Figures derived from *The Book of Numbers* (Pelham Books, London, 1979).

8. The above comments on art are made at the very proper insistance of my colleague Stuart Richmond that I do something to rectify an otherwise glaring omission.

9. See in particular Paul H. Hirst, *Knowledge and the Curriculum* (Routledge and Kegan Paul, 1974).

Chapter 8

1. *Times Educational Supplement*, 22.2.85.

2. *Giving Teaching back to Teachers*, op. cit.

3. Lee Shulman, "Those who understand: Knowledge growth in teaching," *Educational Researcher*, Feb. 1986.

4. For a detailed consideration of the nature of much empirical research in education and its logical deficiencies, see, R. Barrow, *Giving Teaching back to Teachers* (Wheatsheaf, Sussex, 1984). For a theoretical study of the problems inherent in the scientific paradigm that dominates psychological research, see, Kieran Egan, *Education and Psychology* (Teachers College Press, New York, 1983).

5. See, e.g., B. R. Joyce and M. Weil, *Models of Teaching* (Prentice Hall, New Jersey, 1979).

6. See ch. 4 note 8.

7. E.g., E. D. Hirsch, *Cultural Literacy* (Houghton Mifflin, Boston, 1987). I find Hirsch's criticisms and concerns about our current educational predicament a great deal more convincing than his solutions. Similarly, A. Bloom, *The Closing of the American Mind* (Simon and Schuster, New York, 1987), goes rapidly down hill after the first part.

8. Sometimes the inadequacy is due to failure to analyse a concept clearly. Sometimes it is due to the wrong kind of definition being provided. Sometimes it takes the specific form of inappropriately using behavioural definitions of concepts that are not definable in that way. Sometimes it takes the form of ignoring factors that can't be so defined.

9. Sorry, but self-interest prevents me from identifying either this pedant or the distinguished professor with the fried brain referred to at the beginning of this section.

10. But one should not make it a rule never to an infinitive split. As Partridge, *Usage and Abusage* (Penguin, Harmondsworth, 1964) wisely says, "Avoid the split infinitive wherever possible; but if it is the clearest and most natural construction, use it boldly. The angels are on our side." The angels are presumably H. W. Fowler and C. T. Onions.

11. Quotations from George Grant, *Technology and Empire* (Anansi, Toronto, 1969).

Index

Other titles of interest from The Althouse Press:

TAKING EDUCATION SERIOUSLY
John Wilson and Barbara Cowell

CONTROVERSIES IN TEACHING
William Hare

GIVING TEACHING BACK TO TEACHERS:
A CRITICAL INTRODUCTION TO CURRICULUM THEORY
Robin Barrow

A SCHOOLMAN'S ODYSSEY
Harold Disbrowe

PHILOSOPHY OF SCHOOLING
Robin Barrow

TEACHING AS STORY TELLING: AN ALTERNATIVE APPROACH
TO TEACHING & CURRICULUM IN THE ELEMENTARY SCHOOL
Kieran Egan

THE MAKING OF CURRICULUM
Ivor Goodson

RESEARCHING LIVED EXPERIENCE: HUMAN SCIENCE
FOR AN ACTION SENSITIVE PEDAGOGY
Max van Manen

STAFF DEVELOPMENT FOR SCHOOL IMPROVEMENT:
A FOCUS ON THE TEACHER
Marvin F. Wideen and Ian Andrews (Eds.)

INJUSTICE, INEQUALITY AND ETHICS
Robin Barrow

Further details from:
THE ALTHOUSE PRESS
Faculty of Education
The University of Western Ontario
1137 Western Road
LONDON, Ontario, Canada
N6G 1G7

Tel: 519-661-2096
Fax: 519-661-3833